D0121826

HAUTE CUISINE *for your* HEART'S DELIGHT

HAUTE CUISINE *for your* HEART'S DELIGHT

A *Low-Cholesterol Cookbook for Gourmets*

BY CAROL CUTLER

Clarkson N. Potter, Inc./Publisher NEW YORK
DISTRIBUTED BY CROWN PUBLISHERS, INC.

Printed in the United States of America

Library of Congress Catalog Card Number: 72–80841
ISBN: 0–517–500485

Published simultaneously in Canada by General Publishing Company Limited.

Inquiries should be addressed to Clarkson N. Potter, Inc., 419 Park Avenue South, New York, N.Y. 10016.

First Edition

Designed by Ruth Smerechniak

Second Printing, March, 1973

Contents

to BJ

the reason for it all

Foreword

For many years, the image of the nutritionist was that of the plump little cherub who holds the cornucopia in the corner of baroque painters. He (more often, actually, she, a comfortable-looking graduate of the chemistry or home economics department of a land-grant college) told us to eat more of the "protective" foods—more whole-grain or enriched bread or cereals, more meat, fish, and eggs, more fruits and vegetables, more butter or enriched margarine, and above all more milk. The nutritionist was welcomed at all state fairs like a benevolent uncle or aunt, asked to judge which of the fat and dimpled babies should be crowned as an example to its contemporaries. Farm organizations greeted him (or her), state legislatures enthusiastically voted additional funds for nutrition departments, and everyone from the American Meat Institute to the National Dairy Council to the United States Department of Agriculture was united in one great paean to the four (or five, or seven) Food Groups.

Alas, the honeymoon is now over. The specter of Banquo is a more welcome guest at the national feast than the present-day nutritionist. Farm-produce organizations denounce him. The Department of Agriculture tries to ignore him and industry as well as consumers try to pretend that, if they close their eyes long enough, he will go away. Furthermore, the image of the nutritionist has changed. Instead of the pleasant, middle-aged, midwestern lady trying to get everyone to eat more of practically everything, he tends to be a man trained in medical or public health disciplines, concerned with such depressing areas of knowledge as the causes of mortality, the incidence and prevalence of serious diseases, and the mechanism of development of obesity or arteriosclerosis.

And, indeed, the viewpoint of nutrition for the United States (at least for that great majority of our population that has enough—and more than enough—to eat) has changed dramatically. The pioneer studies of Ancel Keys, just after World War II, showed that periods of food deprivation in Europe were accompanied by a drastic decrease in mortality from diseases of the heart and blood vessels. He ascribed the improvement, primarily, to a decrease in the overall fat content of the diet. Since these early studies, a quarter of a century and hundreds of millions of dollars' worth of research later, we now have a much better idea of the "risk factors" in the development of heart disease. Undetected and uncorrected high blood pressure is perhaps number one. There aren't that many pathological conditions that can be detected by a casual yearly "checkup" by your doctor, but the detection and control of hypertension has been shown to cause a drastic decrease in mortality and morbidity (chiefly from strokes and coronaries). Prevention of hypertension is not at hand, but there are strong indications that cutting down on the amount of salt in your diet (you can substitute other seasonings) is a beneficial measure.

High blood cholesterol is number two and close to number one. Other factors in your life remaining the same, as your cholesterol level climbs from 150 mg per 100 ml of plasma (the average value for thin, fit populations living a life with considerable physical activity) to 250 mg per 100 ml of plasma (the average value for present-day Americans), the chances that you will have a coronary will triple. A high cholesterol level is in turn related to a diet too high in calories, too high in fat, and particularly too high in "saturated" fats and cholesterol. (Saturated fats are primarily the "hard" fats: meat fat, butter, hydrogenated vegetable fats, and coconut fat. Cholesterol is a waxlike fat present in all animal tissues in certain amounts, one that becomes dangerous if it piles up in your blood vessels.) Polyunsaturated fats (found in corn oil, soybean oil, cottonseed oil, safflower oil, or fish liver oils) tend to lower blood cholesterol, whereas monounsaturated oils (such as olive oil) have little effect (except as a source of calories). Don't let anyone tell you that the "cholesterol theory" is no longer held. A high cholesterol is but one of the factors in the development of diseases of the heart and the blood vessels, but it is an important one. And we now have well-established equations that predict the average rise in blood cholesterol if you consume additional saturated fats and cholesterol—or its decrease if you switch to less total fat and to more polyunsaturated fats among these fats.

Other important "risk" factors are overweight (particularly if your blood pressure or your cholesterol is high) and lack of activity. We have evidence, indeed, that a diet high in fat, tolerated without an excessive rise in cholesterol by a manual worker who puts in ten to twelve hours of hard physical labor daily (like a Finnish lumberjack or an Alpine farmer), is conducive to high cholesterol levels in an urban dweller or suburban commuter—even if he or she manages a couple of games of golf or tennis a week! The automobile, the labor-saving gadgets, and the automatic tools have thus made it necessary to worry about our cholesterol a great deal more than our grandfathers, would have—just as they have made it necessary to worry much more about overweight. And we have to worry: since 1950 our total national expenditures for medicine (prescription drugs, hospital costs, doctors' fees) have grown from twelve billion dollars a year to a figure in excess of seventy-five billion a year, surely a gigantic increase, even taking into account the growth of the population and the depreciation of the dollar. And yet during this period there has been no increase whatsoever (actually, lately, a tendency to a decrease) in the life expectancy of American men at age twenty. And the "Average Remaining Lifetime" at age twenty of women has hardly increased at all. Our men have slipped from twelfth to about fortieth in "ARL" at age twenty, and our women are now about twenty-third. As you look at the causes of this downslide, the reason becomes obvious: the explosive development of cardiovascular diseases has more than made up for all the decreases in death from other causes and has nullified both our increase in medical knowledge and in medical services.

Carol Cutler, as a humane, responsible person with a sense of the gravity of the problem but a fitting sense also both of the realities of the pleasures of good eating and of the necessities of daily life, has addressed herself in this book to what the Romans called the Golden Mean and the Chinese the Middle Way. She knows that we have retained from our Puritan heritage a fondness for the accents of Jeremiah and Isaiah but that, in the twentieth century, we are very unlikely to act on any message of asceticism or renunciation unless it is made easy and pleasant. She has therefore attempted to marry in one cookbook the cornucopian lady of old and the frowning doctor of today by producing a cookbook that, at the same time, makes full use of the richness of our food supply and our culinary traditions, and yet is sparing of calories, cholesterol, and saturated fats. That she has succeeded so well is a signal achievement, not only in public health but in gastronomy as well (or should it be first in gastronomy and in public health as well?). Anyway, to all whose blood cholesterol has risen since adolescence and is nearing or beyond the excessively high cholesterol level that we, in America, now call "average," this book should be both a lifesaver and a delight.

JEAN MAYER,
Professor of Nutrition, Harvard University

HAUTE CUISINE *for your* HEART'S DELIGHT

Introduction

When I first began to plan this book, I had a tentative title in mind. It was "The How-to-Keep-Your-Husband-Alive-Without-Boring-Him-to-Death Cookbook." That title was, of course, much too long, and it got dropped en route. I rather regretted giving it up, though, because it tells what this book is all about and what it hopes to do.

It should be made clear at the outset that what follows is a collection of recipes for gourmets, not hospital patients. Feeding the unfortunate victim of a heart attack is a task for doctors and dieticians, not for a French-trained chef. We are concerned here with preventing heart disease—to the extent that a low-cholesterol diet can do so—by serving interesting and attractive foods. My theory is that if food tastes good, no one will object because it is also healthful.

The key words in lowering one's cholesterol level are *regular* and *daily*. The smart thing is not to wait for trouble but to try to ward it off by day-in and day-out sensible eating. Of course, "sensible eating" sounds terribly dull (because so much of it is), but it needn't be. I honestly think that if you carefully follow the recipes worked out for this book, members of your family won't even be aware that they are getting low-cholesterol food; they'll be having too good a time at the table.

In the modern world, 100 percent control of your diet is difficult. When traveling, dining with friends, and eating in restaurants it is hard to avoid high-cholesterol food. What I propose is that you maintain strict control over what you eat at home every day. Then, on the occasion when a quivering soufflé is placed before you—enjoy it. But the soufflé must be the exception, not the rule. By following a careful diet most of the time, you have, so to speak, cholesterol credit in the bank. So you can cash in that credit when you dine out from time to time.

For one to stick with a low-cholesterol diet at home the cooking must offer more than boring grilled and boiled dishes. The fact that butter, egg yolks, cream, and animal fats are taken out of the cooking repertoire does not automatically mean that the kitchen's symphony has to be full of flat notes. An herb-flavored fish, for example, can be enveloped in a *papillote;* eggplant can be given the marvelous flavor of Provence; and egg whites can be transformed into a lovely caramel-flavored dessert (*Palais de Glace*) that arrives with its own crown of glistening jelly. Low-cholesterol dining can be anything but grim; it can be *haute cuisine.*

My introduction to low-cholesterol cooking took place more than twenty years ago. My brother-in-law, a heart specialist, was one of the early men in his field to argue that there was a direct connection between coronary artery disease and the amount of fatty foods in the diet. In those days, most people—including many doctors—scoffed at "the cholesterol theory." They don't anymore. The best medical opinion has now come around to insisting that fatty foods be eliminated from our diet, as much as possible.

When I first tried low-cholesterol cooking, the results were far from exciting. Later, however, I lived for twelve years in France, gaining exposure to the glories of French cooking and having the chance to study at the best cooking schools there, the Cordon Bleu and the École des Trois Gourmandes.

It turned out to be easy to reproduce classic French dishes at home —when using ingredients like egg yolks, cream, butter, bacon, pork fat, and so on that their recipes called for. The challenge came in trying to re-create these dishes without their supporting cast of artery-poppers. Through trial and error and the advice of cooking experts and friendly chefs, I worked out this collection of recipes. Most of the recipes have been changed from their classic form by removing forbidden products and substituting healthful ingredients that give similar flavors. In other cases, the contents did not have to be changed; the trick was in doing the recipe in a different way.

I don't want to boast, but I have made every dish in this book with good results. They have been served to knowledgeable members of the family, friends, and even finicky French gourmets. The last mentioned, if they had known they were eating low-cholesterol meals, would have found fault with the preparation. They didn't know, and they didn't complain. In fact, many of them praised the lightness of the cuisine.

There are more advantages to this kind of cooking than just lowering cholesterol intake. Among the welcome side effects: weight control is easier because rich and fatty foods do not appear on the table; and it is an economical way of eating, since vegetables, fish, and poultry are used much more and are among the less expensive items that go into the shopping basket. In fact, vegetables, fish, and poultry are staples in the low-cholesterol diet. What meats are bought are not prime cuts, well marbled with fat, but leaner, cheaper cuts. Dinner parties become easier to give, since much cooking is done in advance. Why? To save time for the hostess and so that food can be chilled in order to skim off all fat. There is still another bonus: many classic dishes, like *Coq au Vin,* taste better reheated.

Since this book is for the person who has no real heart problem and wants to keep things that way, the style of eating it recommends is less rigid than that for a patient on a remedial diet. For that reason, a few recipes for fried foods are included; they rate low in cholesterol, but high in calories. An occasional treat (within limits) is allowed, so one chicken liver recipe is included. It is good enough to take the place of a far richer and more dangerous dish.

All recipes are rated for cholesterol on a scale from 1 to 4:

(1) No Cholesterol
(2) Very Low Cholesterol
(3) Low Cholesterol
(4) Fairly Low Cholesterol

This is a very narrow range, and almost every recipe can be used freely. Each recipe is also rated for calories per portion. These counts are for the basic recipe and do not include optional ingredients.

Who should follow a low-cholesterol diet? Everyone should, I think, and I'm not alone in so thinking. Most medical advice points in that direction. Heart disease has reached epidemic proportions in the United States, accounting for more than six hundred thousand fatalities a year. The most vulnerable group is the American male between the ages of forty and forty-five. It suffers more than a third of the deaths. In their younger years, women are less prone to heart attacks, but by about fifty-five the incidence in both sexes becomes about the same.

Naturally, many factors play a role in bringing on heart attacks—family history, smoking, stress, high blood pressure, being overweight, diabetes, and lack of exercise. But, in addition, the one factor that appears in most heart cases is a high level of cholesterol and fatty substances in the blood. Doctors blame the excessively high cholesterol level in blood on the American diet. University researchers, federal government commissions, the National Institutes of Health, the American Heart Association—all have condemned the diet that appears on most American tables.

These medical experts are not concerned just with middle-aged men, but with everyone, including children; because the cholesterol that coats the inner walls of arteries builds up gradually, slowly narrowing and roughening the channels through which blood flows. If excess cholesterol builds up enough to interfere with the flow of blood in the coronary artery, a heart attack occurs. The objective of a diet low in cholesterol is to prevent this fatty buildup. Not long ago good news came from the University of Chicago. Researchers were able to show that diet-induced artery disease can be reversed. How? By switching to a more prudent diet. So, in most cases, it is not too late to start counting cholesterol.

The statistics and facts may seem grim, but the way to avoid being a statistic can be fun and good eating. Just have some *Haute Cuisine for Your Heart's Delight.*

CAROL CUTLER

Basic Guidelines and Shopping Hints for the Low-Cholesterol Diet

LISTED BELOW ARE CATEGORIES OF FOOD THAT ARE GENERALLY BOUGHT in shops and supermarkets. They are divided between those foods that are recommended for a low-cholesterol diet and those that should be avoided.

MEATS

YES	NO
All Lean Meat	Heavily Marbled and Fatty Meats
Beef	Spare Ribs
Lamb	Mutton
Pork	Frankfurters
Ham	Sausages
Veal	Bacon
	Luncheon Meats
	Organ Meats

POULTRY and FISH

YES	NO
Chicken	Duck
Turkey	Goose
Fish	Shrimp

FRUITS, VEGETABLES, NUTS

YES	NO
Most Fruits and Vegetables	Avocados
Olives in moderation	Cashew Nuts
Most Nuts	Coconut
Peanut Butter	Macadamia Nuts
	Chocolate

DAIRY PRODUCTS

YES	NO
Skimmed Milk	Whole Milk and Whole-Milk Products
Buttermilk	Chocolate Milk
Low-Fat Yoghurt	Cream
Evaporated Skimmed Milk	Whole-Milk Yoghurt
Low-Fat Cottage Cheese	Nondairy Cream Substitutes
Partially Skimmed Milk Cheeses	Whole-Milk Cheeses
Egg White	Butter
	Egg Yolk
	Ice Cream

FATS and OILS

YES	NO
Polyunsaturated Margarine and Liquid Oils of Corn, Cottonseed, Safflower, Soybean, Sesame Seed, Sunflower, and Salad Dressing or Mayonnaise Made of Any of the Above Polyunsaturated Oils (Peanut and Olive Oil may be used sparingly)	Butter
	Lard
	Salt Pork Fat
	Meat Fat
	Completely Hydrogenated Margarines and Vegetable Shortenings
	Products Containing Coconut Oil

MISCELLANEOUS

YES	NO
Gelatin Desserts	Most Frozen Dinners
Pretzels	Commercial Baked Goods
	Potato Chips

For the most part, recipes in this book do not specify exact amounts of salt and pepper to be used except above the usual ½ teaspoon. Salt-restricted diets may be involved for the reader, and the amount used of both salt and pepper is largely a matter of taste.

Shopping Hints

To be sure you are buying exactly what you want, careful label reading is a must. All food items are required by law to list ingredients in descending order of amount contained in the product. Check to see that polyunsaturated fats are at the top of the list, and ingredients like coconut oil are at the bottom, or not at all. A law being fought at the moment would require specific listing of kinds of fats used in the products. With such a law on the books, "Vegetable Oils" would no longer be a catchall for products containing both polysaturated and polyunsaturated oils. Usually coconut oil is used in these products and it is not allowed in low-cholesterol diets.

In a number of recipes that follow, low-fat Parmesan cheese is listed as an optional ingredient. In some cities it is difficult to find this low-fat cheese. In such cases the cheese can be eliminated completely, or use grated sapsago cheese, which is a Swiss cheese made of skimmed milk and herbs. Actually, once grated, a very small quantity of regular Parmesan goes a long way. The actual amount consumed would be negligible.

Most imitation cheeses are very high in saturated fats. Fischer Cheese Company has developed two imitation Cheddar-type cheeses that are made with corn oil: Cheezola and Count Down (99 percent fat-free cheese spread). These cheeses are available directly from the company. Their address is P.O. Box 12, Wapakoneta, Ohio, 45895.

Saint-Otho is a delicious Swiss cheese that is 95 percent fat free. It has true cheese flavor and texture, unlike most imitation cheeses, and is good eaten plain or toasted on crackers. It is sold to shops in a large wheel from which pieces are cut for the customer. It is distributed by Otto Roth & Co., 14 Empire Boulevard, Moonachie, N.J. 07074.

Mayonnaise is used throughout the book because it is perfectly acceptable for low-cholesterol diets. In making mayonnaise, one egg yolk is forced to absorb almost a cup of polyunsaturated oil, which really means you are getting more of the beneficial oil than egg yolk. In addition, mayonnaise is generally used sparingly, so the actual amount of yolk consumed is negligible. Tillie Lewis makes an artificial mayonnaise with no yolk at all, which can be used for very strict diets. It is available in health-food shops and large supermarkets.

Salad Dressings. Too many prepared salad dressings are made with a combination of oils that includes the polysaturated as well as the polyunsaturated. In addition, most bottled dressings have a thick, heavy, and unpleasantly metallic flavor. Making your own dressing is not only safer, but cheaper and more fun since flavors can be changed at whim. For basic proportions see the recipes for Dressings on page 243. One product that can be used to great advantage is dried herb seasoning, like those put out by Good Seasons. But don't follow the directions, or you will have a powerful dressing that will destroy any fresh salad taste. I like to use ½ to 1 teaspoon of it when mixing a cup of dressing; it is just enough to add some snap to the dressing without screaming herbs and spices.

Cakes and Cake Mixes. Read the label to be certain that no fats are added. Avoid chocolate mixes. Angelfood cakes are very low in fat and are a recommended dessert.

Bread and Crackers. Regular bread contains a very small amount of fat, but some types contain none at all including French bread, English muffins, and tortillas. Most prepared sweet rolls and pastries contain a considerable amount of saturated fats. Most crackers contain no fat.

Desserts. Packaged puddings and pie fillings are generally acceptable. A small amount of hydrogenated oil is used in some as a stabilizer, but the quantity is insignificant.

Eggs. BioNature Products Company of Minneapolis has recently put on the market an imitation egg made entirely of natural products. Called BioNature, the product contains no artificial coloring or flavoring. Its vitamin A content is the same as that of a whole egg, while the caloric count is half that of a fresh egg. BioNature is distributed nationally and is available in health food shops or the health food sections of grocery stores and supermarkets. Another egg product, Eggstra, is made by Tillie Lewis. It contains whole eggs that have been stretched with other nonfat ingredients to reduce its cholesterol content by 80 percent.

Fats and Oils. Liquid oils of safflower, cottonseed, corn, and soybean are available at all groceries. Read the label carefully on all margarine labels and look for those that list the first ingredient as "liquid oil." There are some brands of 100 percent corn oil, which is perfect.

Milk. Fresh skimmed milk is available from most supermarkets.

The cupboard should always be stocked with skimmed milk powder and cans of evaporated skimmed milk.

Soups. Most companies make a beef or chicken broth or bouillon that has less than 1 percent fat. Soups that are called "Cream of" usually have no cream in them at all and are handy to have for flavoring dishes in addition to using as soups. Canned chicken and beef broth, bouillon or consommé can be used in recipes calling for chicken or beef stock. If the canned product is not available, substitute 1 bouillon cube (chicken or beef) dissolved in 1 cup of boiling water.

Celery. Just to set the record straight, because the different terms used in various cookbooks are confusing, when a "stalk" of celery is called for in the following recipes, it means just one piece, sometimes called a rib. An entire head or clump of celery is referred to as a "bunch."

Parsley. When a sprig of parsley is called for it refers to one branch of the leaves with the stem; when only leaves are required the recipe will list "parsley leaves," or just "chopped parsley."

Garlic. Despite what some books claim about the flavor properties of garlic peel, I've never found it to be true. All garlic used in these recipes is to be peeled.

Menus

The following suggested menus are comprised of recipes found in this book as well as a few basic items normally found in the kitchen.

BREAKFAST

Half Grapefruit
Mock Blintzes

~

Fresh Orange Juice
Toasted Low-Fat Cheese Sandwich (see Shopping Hints)

~

Fruit Juice
Cereal and Skimmed Milk
Toast or Crackers and Jam

~

Sliced Fruit in Season
Buttermilk Pancakes made with egg white only

BRUNCH

Sliced Fresh Grapefruit and Oranges
Spanakopitta (Greek Spinach Pie)
Carottes Braisées (Braised Carrots)
Poires au Vin Rouge (Pears Poached in Red Wine)

~

Salade de Champignons (Mushroom Salad)
Potato Pancakes
Apple Sauce
Grilled Tomatoes
Peach Crisp

LUNCH

Pink Lady Soup
Gratin d'Endives au Jambon (Gratin of Endives and Ham)
Tossed Boston Salad with Herbed French Dressing I
Prunes in Port Wine

~

Poivrons Grillés (Grilled Green Peppers with Dressing)
Salmon Cakes
Mixed Salad of Endive and Grapefruit Sections,
Herbed French Dressing I
Fresh Fruit and Meringues

~

Broiled Grapefruit
Tarte à l'Oignon (Onion Tart)
Grilled Tomatoes
Pêches en Pichet (Peaches in White Wine)

~

Crème de Carottes (Carrot Soup)
Croustade de Champignons (Mushrooms on Pastry Shells)
Tossed Salad of Romaine and Chicory,
Herbed French Dressing II
Orange Sherbet

Gazpacho
Morue à la Boulangère (Smoked Cod with Potatoes and Onions)
Mixed Green Salad, Herbed French Dressing II
Fresh Fruit and Sesame Seed Cookies

Caponata à la Dickie
Morue Marinée (Marinated Smoked Cod)
Pommes de Terre à la Vapeur (Steamed Potatoes)
Tossed Salad of Romaine and Chicory,
Herbed French Dressing II
Apple Crisp

DINNER

Crème de Cresson (Watercress Soup)
Suprêmes de Volaille aux Duxelles (Chicken Breasts with Mushroom Stuffing)
Rice
Salad of Boston Lettuce, Herbed French Dressing I
Citron en Neige (Lemon Snow)

Gribi c Smetanoi (Mushrooms in Creamy Sour Sauce)
Volailles en Escabèche (Chicken in Lemon Aspic)
Concombres aux Herbes (Cucumbers with Herbs)
Pêches à la Midi (Baked Peaches)

Champignons Farcis et Tomates Grillées (Stuffed Mushrooms and Grilled Tomatoes)
Filets de Poisson en Papillotes (Fish Filets Steamed in Foil Envelopes)
Haricots Verts aux Amandes (String Beans with Almonds) as a separate course
Bananes Flambées (Bananas in Flaming Sauce)

Crème de Champignons (Cream of Mushroom Soup)
Carbonnades à la Flamande (Beef and Onions Braised in Beer)
Nouilles (Boiled Noodles)
Mixed Green Salad, Mayonnaise Dressing
Strawberry Granita

~

Fonds d'Artichauts Renaissance (Artichoke Hearts with Mushroom Stuffing)
Darnes de Saumon Braisées au Vin Blanc (Salmon Steaks Braised in White Wine)
Pommes Savonettes (Oven-braised Potato Slices)
Glazed Strawberry Pie

~

Turbot Salad à la Bouboulina
Poulet Grillé à la Diable (Grilled Chicken with Mustard Coating)
Concombres au Riz (Cucumber Shells Baked with Rice)
Pear Sherbet

SUPPER

Soupe à l'Oignon (Onion Soup)
Pâté de Veau et Jambon (Ham and Veal Pâté) served with small pickles
Choux de Bruxelles aux Marrons (Brussels Sprouts and Chestnuts) served as a separate course
Compôte d'Orange (Sliced Orange Compote)

~

Saumon à la Norvège (Fresh Salmon Cured with Dill), Mustard-Dill Sauce
Tarte à la Tomate (Tomato Tart)
Artichauts à la Clamart (Artichokes and Peas)
Apricot Whip

~

Smoked Haddock Soup
Jambon Persillé (Mold of Ham and Parslied Aspic)
Endive Salad with Herbed French Dressing I
Fruit Kebabs

~

Maquereaux au Vin Blanc (Poached Mackerel in White Wine)
Mozzarella in Carròzza (Fried Cheese Sandwiches), Anchovy Sauce
Shepherd's Market Onion Rings
Cold Soufflé with Fruit Jelly, Hot Sauce

Crème de Champignons (Cream of Mushroom Soup)
Chinese Chicken Salad
Courgettes Frites à la Arménienne (Fried Zucchini, Armenian Style)
Stuffed Bananas

Tomates Farcies de Luigi (Luigi's Stuffed Tomatoes)
Boudin Blanc (Chicken and Veal Sausage)
Flemish Potato Casserole
Fraises Cardinale (Strawberries with Raspberry Sauce)

SOUPS

HOMEMADE SOUPS ARE NO LONGER A RARITY ON THE AMERICAN DINNER table. The electric blender has played a major role in the revival of soup making, a once-popular home specialty that had fallen victim to the can opener.

This selection of recipes contains different kinds of soups, hot, cold, and two that aren't even cooked. All have body and richness without the usual addition of cream and egg yolk. These recipes are meant to be embellished upon. Change them to take full advantage of our abundant supply of fresh vegetables.

A well-prepared bowl of soup at the beginning of a meal usually signals good things to follow. It is an easy way to establish your culinary reputation early in the evening.

CRÈME DE CAROTTES

Carrot Soup

CHOLESTEROL RATING 1
CALORIES PER SERVING 175

This unusual soup is a delight to the eye. The color is a pale yellow-orange, heightened with the final fillip of bright carrot shreds on top. The taste is more pleasurable still.

8 servings

- *½ cup polyunsaturated oil*
- *1 small onion, thinly sliced*
- *2 medium potatoes, peeled and diced*
- *1 celery stalk, sliced*
- *1 pound carrots, peeled and sliced*
- *2 quarts hot water*
- *4 chicken bouillon cubes*
- *2 parsley sprigs*
- *1 teaspoon salt*
- *½ teaspoon pepper*
- *pinch saffron*
- *1 tablespoon potato flour, if necessary*
- *1 tablespoon Worcestershire sauce*
- *1 carrot for garnish (optional)*

In a large heavy pot heat the oil and add the onions, potatoes, celery, and carrots. Cover and simmer slowly for about 15 minutes, or until the celery and onions have wilted, but do not allow them to color. Then add the water, chicken bouillon cubes, parsley, salt, pepper, and the pinch of saffron which is more for color than taste. Bring to boil, cover, and simmer ½ hour. Remove parsley sprigs, cool a little, and then purée in an electric blender. Return to pot. Soup should be rather thick because of the potatoes, but if you find it a little thin, blend the 1 tablespoon potato flour with water and dribble in a little at a time until you have a nice, heavy consistency. Correct seasoning, add 1 tablespoon Worcestershire sauce, and heat. For a pretty presentation shred the extra carrot, blanch in fast-boiling salted water, drain, then sprinkle a bit over each cup of soup.

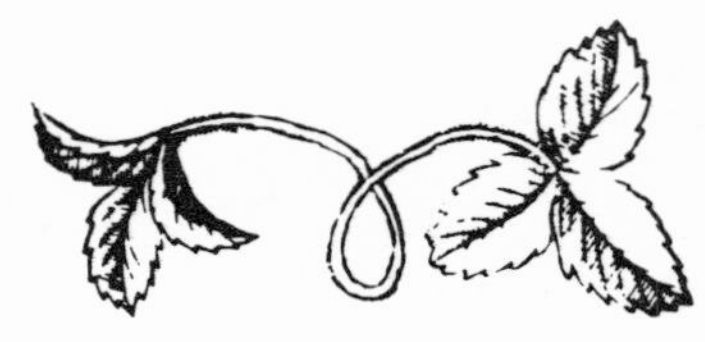

CRÈME DE CHAMPIGNONS

Mushroom Soup

CHOLESTEROL RATING 1
CALORIES PER SERVING 122

I'm a firm believer in using canned soups, but mostly to incorporate in other dishes. To begin a meal with a light and beautiful homemade soup is a genuine pleasure that justifies the small amount of time and effort required. This fresh mushroom soup is a perfect example of how soup can be a special taste adventure. Such delicacy just cannot come out of a can. The fact that a small amount of cream is not added, French style, at the end means that the soup remains still lighter and finer. Two shopping notes: mushrooms must be very fresh, meaning white, firm, and tightly closed; and the canned evaporated milk is essential to give body to the soup.

8 servings

1 pound fresh mushrooms
2 tablespoons polyunsaturated oil
1 medium onion, chopped
2 cups water
1 chicken bouillon cube
2 tablespoons polyunsaturated oil
2 tablespoons flour
1½ cups evaporated skimmed milk
salt and pepper

Wash and trim the mushrooms; slice ¾ of them (the other ¼ pound is reserved for the garnish). Heat 2 tablespoons of the oil in a heavy pot, add the sliced mushrooms and chopped onion. Mix well, cover, and simmer gently for 10 minutes, or until the mushrooms render their juices and the onions are soft. Add the water and chicken bouillon cube, cover and bring to a boil; simmer 15 minutes more. During this simmering period add the reserved whole mushrooms and let them poach for 2 to 3 minutes, remove with a skimmer, and when cool slice thinly and reserve for the garnish.

When the vegetables have finished cooking, pass through a food mill or put in a blender, but do not purée too fine. Rinse out the soup pot, dry, and add the remaining 2 tablespoons of oil. When hot, stir in the flour and whisk until smooth, then slowly add the evaporated skimmed milk, whisking all the time. Season with salt and pepper, and simmer slowly for 5 minutes. Stir in the mushroom purée and mix well. The soup should have a fairly thin consistency. If not, thin out with a bit more skimmed milk. Taste for salt and pepper, then ladle into individual soup bowls and garnish with a few slices of the poached mushrooms.

SOUPE À L'OIGNON

Onion Soup

CHOLESTEROL RATING 1
CALORIES PER SERVING WITHOUT TOAST 187
WITH TOAST 241

Onion soup is the most French thing there is, or so most Americans think. In reality, though, it is not very good in France. Not usually served at mealtime, the soup is generally considered a revivifying jolt at the end of a long evening when palates are a bit less discriminating. Les Halles, the sadly departed central market of Paris, was the traditional last stop for *une gratinée,* as onion soup is called, after a night on the town. The market is gone, but the restaurants hang on, still serving the same thin-flavored soup with just a few lonely strands of onions floating about. Mostly it is the thick gratinated cheese-on-toast that one notices.

Onion soup can be a perfectly delicious and warming broth. All it takes is enough strong flavor and a decent quantity of onions. And then, plain toast is the perfect topping for it.

6 servings

⅓ cup polyunsaturated oil
6 medium-sized onions, finely sliced
½ teaspoon any prepared French mustard
salt and pepper
1 teaspoon potato starch
1 teaspoon meat extract (BV)
1 cup dry white wine
2½ cups beef stock
6 slices toasted French bread

Heat oil in a heavy pot. Add the sliced onions, mustard, salt and pepper. Cook the onions over a very slow fire until they turn a dark brown and have reduced greatly in bulk. This should take about 30 minutes. The long, slow cooking is very important to give the onions a mild sweet flavor. Add the potato starch and meat extract and mix well. Continue stirring while slowly pouring in the wine and stock. Slowly bring to a boil and simmer for 15 minutes. Pour into a soup tureen or into the traditional earthenware soup bowls with a slice of toast on top.

CRÈME DE CRESSON

Watercress Soup

CHOLESTEROL RATING 1
CALORIES PER SERVING 146

Soup can be an elegant beginning to a meal, and this cool-looking pale green version proves it. The use of buttermilk is novel and brings a tangy note to the taste, especially when served cold. After watercress soup, your guests will never again want thick, creamy vichyssoise.

10 servings

2 bunches watercress (about 4 cups of lightly packed watercress)
¼ cup polyunsaturated oil
2 medium onions, chopped
1 tablespoon salt
2 tablespoons flour
4 cups chicken broth
½ teaspoon pepper
½ teaspoon salt (optional)
1 teaspoon tarragon
1 teaspoon dillweed
1 quart buttermilk
2 tablespoons lemon juice
1 teaspoon Worcestershire sauce
½ teaspoon curry

Wash and clean the watercress, reserving some of the nicest leaves for use as a garnish. Heat the oil in a large heavy pot, and add the onions. Cover and cook slowly until translucent. Add the watercress, sprinkle on 1 tablespoon salt, and stir well until thoroughly mixed with the onions. Cover and cook slowly for 10 minutes, or until cress wilts. Sprinkle on the flour and mix well again, cover, and cook for 2 minutes. Add the chicken broth, pepper, and the extra ½ teaspoon of salt if the broth is not salty enough. Cover and simmer for 30 minutes. For the last 5 minutes of cooking add the tarragon and dill. Let cool slightly, then ladle part of the cress and broth into the blender and pour in one cup of buttermilk, the lemon juice, and Worcestershire sauce; blend until smooth. Pour this portion into a large bowl and repeat the blending process until all of the soup stock and buttermilk have been used. Return the soup to the pot and taste for seasoning; correct if necessary. Add the curry and heat through for 5 minutes. The soup can be served hot, but is best if chilled thoroughly. A pretty garnish can be made by simply blanching the reserved watercress leaves and dropping a few onto each bowl of soup.

GAZPACHO

CHOLESTEROL RATING 1
CALORIES PER SERVING 95

There are two versions of gazpacho, the great Spanish cold soup. One is cooked and involves many steps, the other is uncooked and done all at once. I prefer this simpler uncooked method because it has more zest and tang and a fresher flavor. It is traditional to pass an assortment of garnishes with gazpacho so that each guest can select what he wants and mix it into the soup. These garnishes are usually tiny pieces of chopped tomato, cucumber, green pepper, chives, and crisp toasted croutons, equally tiny.

8 to 10 servings

4 cups fresh and ripe tomatoes, about 8 large tomatoes
1½ cups green peppers
1½ cups peeled cucumbers
1 or 2 garlic cloves, chopped
2 cups beef bouillon
½ cup lemon juice
¼ cup polyunsaturated oil
salt and pepper

Cut all vegetables into chunks. Pour one cup of bouillon into an electric blender, add ½ of the vegetables and all the garlic then work to a thick purée. Pour this purée into a deep bowl. Repeat process with the other cup of bouillon, lemon juice, oil, and other ½ of vegetables. Pour into bowl with other purée. Stir in salt and pepper. Let mixture stand for at least 3 hours so flavors will blend well.

Lacking a blender, put vegetables through a hand grinder or food mill using finest blade, then add liquids. Let the mixture stand for 3 hours, put through fine strainer.

Check seasonings again, remembering that once chilled the pungency of the flavors is slightly reduced. Serve quite cold, preferably accompanied by the garnishes.

PINK LADY

Tomato-Yoghurt Soup

CHOLESTEROL RATING 1
CALORIES PER SERVING WITHOUT CROUTONS 82

One doesn't often think of yoghurt in connection with France but the French, in fact, enjoy it very much. Many restaurants will include small pots of yoghurt on the abundant cheese tray. Perhaps this is partly due to Algerian influence. Whatever the source, the French know how to turn a simple product into something quite special. This tomato and yoghurt soup is one refreshing, low-caloried example, especially since the final addition of heavy cream is omitted here. The soup is served cold and has an attractive pale pink color.

When locally grown tomatoes are available, they should be used. Otherwise, I find a good brand of canned Italian plum tomatoes has more flavor than the hothouse-grown variety.

6 servings

2½ pounds fresh tomatoes or
1 2-pound 4-ounce can Italian plum tomatoes
juice of 1 lemon
1 garlic clove, sliced thin
¼ teaspoon celery salt
¼ teaspoon curry
salt and pepper
16 ounces low-fat plain yoghurt
croutons or paprika to garnish

If using fresh tomatoes, plunge in hot water and peel, then cut into chunks. If using canned tomatoes, drain, and remove the bay leaf that is generally in the can. In a blender put the lemon juice, sliced garlic clove, celery salt, curry, a little salt and pepper, yoghurt, and tomatoes. Blend until smooth. Taste for seasoning and adjust if necessary. Chill well. Serve with small croutons on top or a sprinkle of paprika.

SMOKED HADDOCK SOUP

CHOLESTEROL RATING 2
CALORIES PER SERVING 103

Despite the often unjustified slurs on English cuisine, English cooks do know how to handle fish. It is a staple in home cooking, and of all the ways that English women bring fish to the table, chowder is one of the favorites. The smoky flavor of this one makes it particularly satisfying on a cold night. A small bowl of it can lead off a meal, or a nonpuréed version can be cooked with extra onions and potatoes, and served as a hearty main dish for supper.

10 servings

2 medium onions
3 stalks celery
1 medium potato, peeled and quartered
1½ pounds smoked haddock
2 to 3 cups skimmed milk
1 teaspoon Worcestershire sauce
salt and pepper

Chop the onions and celery stalks and place in the soup pot with enough water to cover. Put on lid and simmer gently for about 10 minutes until the vegetables are softened. Add the peeled and quartered potato and continue cooking until the vegetables are almost done, about 15 minutes. If the haddock is large, cut it into 2 or 3 pieces and add to the vegetables. Continue cooking until vegetables and fish are completely cooked, about 20 more minutes. Take out the haddock to cool, then remove the tough skin and all bones.

Put 1 cup of the milk into a blender, add ½ the quantity of cooked vegetables and fish and blend until smooth. Repeat with the other ½ of the ingredients. Return the puréed soup to the pot and add the Worcestershire sauce, salt and pepper to taste (be careful with the salt), and thin with more milk if desired. Cook for about 5 minutes more.

ENTRÉES

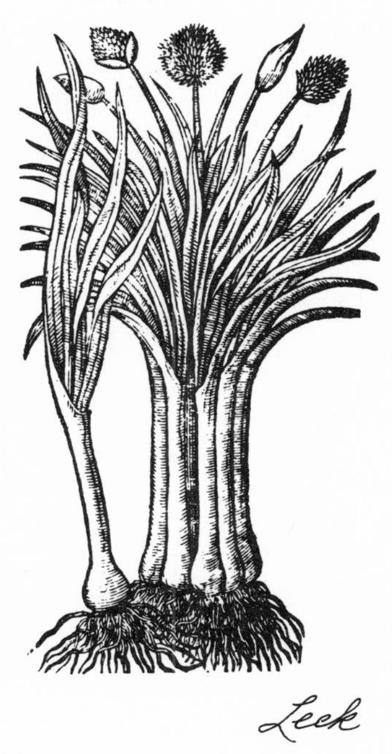

THIS CHAPTER AND THE ONE FOLLOWING ARE INTRODUCED TOGETHER because many of their recipes can be used as a first course at dinner or as a main course at brunch, lunch, or supper. A slice of *Tarte à la Tomate* (Tomato Tart) can be a smashing start to a stylish dinner. On the other hand, Stuffed Artichoke Hearts, which is suggested as a first course at dinner, will be no less appreciated as a luncheon main dish. Any of the suggested Supper Menus could also be used for Brunch, although you might want to change the first course to a lighter one, or just fresh juice or fresh fruit. By drawing from both chapters, a great many varied menus can be devised.

There are recipes elsewhere in the book that can also be brought into service here. From the chapter on fish, one can borrow Marinated

Cod or Smoked Haddock Salad; from Poultry, *Mousse de Foies de Volaille* (Chicken Liver Mousse). One, among many vegetable possibilities, is *Artichauts à la Barigoule* (Artichoke Hearts, Provence Style).

In these two chapters are included dishes that come from Greece, France, Italy, Germany, and China, offering a truly international flavor to low-cholesterol cooking.

Wine to serve with entrée and luncheon dishes can be almost as international. Light, fruity white wines from the Moselle region in Germany would be an excellent choice with Stuffed Mushrooms, Cucumbers in Creamy Sauce, or *Mozzarella in Carròzza,* which could also take a chilled Beaujolais. Rosé wines are particularly nice at lunch time and would be perfect with almost every recipe in the two chapters. Many people have a prejudice against rosé wines, considering them a compromise between red and white. The French don't think so. They drink rosé, especially their fine Tavel, regularly.

Wine should not be served with any dish that has a vinegar sauce, since the acid in it distorts the taste of the wine. That is why the French prefer to serve salad as a separate course and drink nothing with it. For this reason I would not advise serving wine with the *Caponata, Chou-fleur à la grecque* or the Broiled Grapefruit, which has a lot of acid in the fruit itself.

FONDS D'ARTICHAUTS RENAISSANCE

Artichoke Bottoms with Mushroom Stuffing

CHOLESTEROL RATING 1
CALORIES PER SERVING 218

The best of many flavors are locked in this elegant little first-course dish. The cooked artichoke bottom is filled with *duxelles* (minced mushrooms and onions), sprinkled with cheese, and baked. It comes to the table toasty hot, sitting high and pretty, and tasting as good as it looks. Don't be tempted to serve anything with this dish; it would dilute the effect. Why Renaissance? It's the name of a small street in Paris where this particular version was first put together.

6 servings

6 cooked artichoke bottoms according to instructions on page 150
2 tablespoons polyunsaturated oil
half a duxelles *recipe (page 39)*
2 tablespoons grated low-fat cheese (optional)
approximately ½ cup water

Rub the outside of the artichoke bottoms with the oil and fill with approximately ½ cup of *duxelles,* making a slightly pointed mound of the filling. Sprinkle lightly with the grated cheese, if used, and place on a baking dish. Pour in enough water to reach about the ¼-inch level in the dish. Bake in a 350° oven for 10 to 15 minutes. Lift carefully from the baking dish and serve on individual plates.

STUFFED ARTICHOKE BOTTOM VARIATIONS

Cooked artichoke bottoms filled with any number of tasty fillings can make an inventive luncheon main course or a special first course at dinner. Cook one artichoke bottom for each serving according to the instructions on page 150, and take out all the fuzzy choke. Then stuff with, among other possibilities:

Chicken Salad

Tuna Fish or Salmon Salad

Julienne Strips of lean boiled ham mixed with fresh string beans or asparagus tips and tossed with Herbed French Dressing II, page 243.

Cooked Diced Carrots and Peas or String Beans mixed with Mayonnaise Dressing, page 242.

Coulis de Tomates (Provençal Tomato Sauce), page 236, and baked according to the preceding directions for *Fonds d'Artichauts Renaissance.*

Filled with Low-fat Cheese (see Products, page 88) and baked according to preceding directions for *Fonds d'Artichauts Renaissance.*

CHOU-FLEUR À LA GRECQUE

Cauliflower, Greek Style

CHOLESTEROL RATING 1
CALORIES PER SERVING 150

This low-calorie dish should be offered more often than it is, if only for its refreshing flavor. When serving it as a first course I like to offer a variety of vegetables all cooked *à la grecque* in the same basic stock. Other possibilities include mushrooms, leeks, tiny onions, artichoke hearts, eggplant cubes (none of which need to be blanched as cauliflower does). If using more than one vegetable, start with the mildest in flavor, mushrooms for example. When the vegetables are gone, the cooking stock can be kept for a week or more in a tightly covered container in the refrigerator. The stock is also very good sprinkled on sliced tomatoes, or added to salad dressings.

6 servings

- *1 large head firm white cauliflower*
- *½ cup dry white wine*
- *4 tablespoons polyunsaturated oil*
- *2 to 3 shallots, chopped finely*
- *1 small garlic clove, crushed (2 if your taste is for more)*
- *1 large herb bouquet (6 parsley sprigs tied around 2 bay leaves)*
- *juice of 1 lemon*
- *1 teaspoon fennel seeds*
- *1 teaspoon basil*
- *1 teaspoon coriander*
- *½ teaspoon celery seeds*
- *2 cups beef stock*
- *½ teaspoon each salt and pepper*

Break the cauliflower into flowerets and blanch for 1 minute in rapidly boiling water. Then drain and run cold water over it immediately. This is to keep the cauliflower looking white.

Put remaining ingredients in a flat pan, cover, and simmer 15 to 20 minutes. Taste and correct seasoning. Add cauliflowerets and more beef stock or white wine (or both) to the pan until cauliflower is ¾ covered. Replace cover on pan and cook slowly until tender, about 15 to 20 minutes. Turn off heat and let the vegetable cool in the liquid. Remove it to a serving bowl together with a good deal of the stock; chill well before serving. Chopped parsley may be sprinkled on top before this dish is brought to the table.

CONCOMBRES CRÉMEUX

Cucumbers in Creamy Sauce

CHOLESTEROL RATING 1
CALORIES PER SERVING 80

Concombres à la crème is a popular hors d'oeuvre in France, especially in early summer when the young cucumbers are at their sweetest. I always felt that the thick rich cream that French restaurants add to the cucumbers tends to mask the delicate freshness of the vegetable. This preparation avoids that problem and heightens the natural goodness of the cucumbers as well.

The cucumbers are not cooked in this recipe, but the bitter water is drawn out by a preliminary salting. During the salting period, they become quite soft and a better vehicle for a coating of sauce. Finally, pale green cucumber slices are enveloped in a light white sauce with flecks of green dill sprinkled throughout and served on a bed of lettuce—as cool and pretty a way to start a summer meal as one can hope for.

6 servings

3 cucumbers
3 tablespoons coarse salt
3 tablespoons mayonnaise
¾ cup plain low-fat yoghurt
¼ teaspoon sugar
½ teaspoon lemon juice
pepper
1 teaspoon dillweed

Peel the cucumbers and cut in quarters lengthwise. With a flexible knife cut out and remove the seeds and center pulp. Slice the solid white flesh that remains crosswise and as thin as possible. Ideally the slices should be about 1/16 inch thick. If you have a very sharp vegetable slicer it would serve nicely.

Put the cucumbers in a bowl and sprinkle on the coarse salt, toss well, and put aside for at least 2 hours; 3 is even better. Mix the cucumbers from time to time. During this period you will notice water collecting in the bowl as the cucumbers give up their bitter juices and turn limp in the process.

Dump the cucumbers in a sieve and place under cold running water. Keep turning the slices over so that the salt is washed off all of them. They should be under running water for at least 3 minutes. With your hands push out as much of the water as possible while the slices are still in the sieve. Then taking handfuls at a time, squeeze out even more water. Finally dry them in a towel, forcing out any remaining water.

The slices should be very soft by this time. Put them in a bowl, spoon in the mayonnaise and mix well. Add the yoghurt, sugar, lemon juice, and pepper and mix it all together quite thoroughly. Finally add the dillweed, give one final turn. Taste for pepper and lemon juice. Correct if necessary.

To serve, line small bowls with crisp lettuce leaves and spoon the creamy cucumbers in a heap in the center. A small parsley sprig (not chopped) on top is pretty.

BROILED GRAPEFRUIT

CHOLESTEROL RATING 1
CALORIES PER SERVING 85

There are many advantages to this easy entrée dish: most of the preparation is done ahead of time; it is lower in calories than the version sometimes seen with honey on top, and it's a last-minute lifesaver when there are unexpected guests for dinner.

8 servings

6 grapefruit
1 teaspoon salt
1 teaspoon freshly grated nutmeg
1 to 1½ cups tawny port or Madeira

Cut 6 grapefruit in half and remove their sections into a small bowl. Cut out the remaining membranes from 8 of the halves, first squeezing out the juice from all the other shells so you can have the treat of fresh grapefruit juice at breakfast the next morning. Sprinkle salt and the freshly grated nutmeg over the grapefruit sections. Pour in enough port or Madeira to almost cover the sections. Mix gently, taking care not to break the sections, and let marinate for at least 1 hour, stirring occasionally.

When ready to serve, gently pile the grapefruit into the 8 shells, sprinkle on a little more nutmeg and pour on the marinade.

Place under broiler—a good 5 to 6 inches away from the flame—and let them heat through thoroughly and until the rind has a dark brown color. If necessary, move a little closer to flame for 1 minute to brown. (Obviously you can expand or reduce this basic recipe to make as many servings as you need, but always making certain you have enough extra grapefruit to fill the shells amply.)

CAPONATA À LA DICKIE

Cold Eggplant Appetizer

CHOLESTEROL RATING 2
CALORIES PER SERVING 320

Most Italian cookbooks give recipes for *Caponata,* a cold eggplant appetizer, and they are all pretty much alike. This version is different and far easier to make than the classic one that calls for frying lots of different chopped vegetables. Dickie's version is much like the lady herself, deliciously inventive. And I'm sure she won't mind if you add a few extra things of your own. It is almost a case of the more the merrier, but don't overdo it or you will have something resembling chop suey rather than *Caponata.* This version still remains thoroughly Italian.

With two kinds of beans included, the recipe makes a very substantial first course. On a hot summer day, it is an appealing main course for either lunch or dinner. It pleases anytime.

12 servings as first course
10 servings as main course

1 large eggplant, 1½ to 2 pounds
¾ cup polyunsaturated oil
1 cup pine nuts
1 cup canned chick peas, drained
1 cup canned red kidney beans, drained
½ cup chopped sweet gherkins or pickles
4 teaspoons capers
¼ cup chopped pimento
1 tablespoon minced candied or preserved ginger (not crystallized)
⅓ cup wine vinegar
1 tablespoon sugar
2 tablespoons tomato paste
6 anchovy filets
½ cup chopped olives (optional)

Cut the unpeeled eggplant into ½-inch cubes. Heat ½ cup of the oil in a heavy skillet and, when hot, add about ⅓ of the cubed eggplant. Keep the heat high and fry the eggplant pieces quickly, turning almost constantly with a spatula. When these eggplant pieces are browned all over, remove them with a skimmer into a large bowl and continue frying the rest of the eggplant, adding more oil if necessary. When all the eggplant is fried, remove to a side dish. Reduce the heat, adding a little oil if necessary, and add the pine nuts. Fry the nuts slowly until they turn a nice golden color. Add the toasted nuts to the bowl with the eggplant, again using the skimmer to leave behind as much oil as possible. If you notice an accumulation of oil in the bowl, pour off as much of it as possible.

Add to the eggplant and nuts the chick peas, kidney beans, gherkins, capers, pimento, and ginger. Toss all ingredients until thoroughly mixed. Meanwhile, in a small pot heat the vinegar, sugar, tomato paste, and anchovy filets. Bring almost to a boil and pour over the mixed *caponata* and toss again quickly. At this point add the olives if desired. Cover and let the hot sauce permeate the entire mixture. The anchovy filets will have melted in the heat, adding a tangy flavor that doesn't shout "anchovy."

Refrigerate for at least a day, but bring back to room temperature before serving.

Serve from a large bowl, or arrange individual portions on lettuce leaves.

POIVRONS GRILLÉS

Broiled Green Peppers with Dressing

CHOLESTEROL RATING 1
CALORIES PER SERVING 215

It is amazing what proper handling of the simplest vegetables can produce. Green peppers are generally thought of as something to be stuffed or added to a salad. A much more important role is given to them, however, throughout Central Europe and in Italy and France, especially in Provence. All of these cuisines have various recipes for preparing green peppers as an hors d'oeuvre, and one of the best is Provençal.

The recipe calls for green peppers only, but a more attractive display is made when red peppers are available to be mixed in. *Poivrons grillés* can be served as a first course alone or with anchovy filets accompanying them, in genuine French style.

6 servings

4 green peppers
2 tablespoons polyunsaturated oil
4 garlic cloves
1 cup Herbed French Dressing I (page 243)

Cut the peppers in half lengthwise and remove the stems, seeds, and white membranes. Put the peppers in a baking dish and rub the oil on, inside and outside. Let them stand in the dish, cut side down. Peel and split the garlic cloves in half and tuck one piece under each pepper half. The aroma of the garlic will flavor the peppers while they stand for about one hour.

Meanwhile, prepare the Herbed French Dressing and preheat the broiler with the rack set about 8 inches away from the flame.

Drain the oil from the peppers and the baking dish. If allowed to remain, the oil will splatter during the broiling and can cause flames on the hot grill. Broil the peppers for about 7 to 8 minutes, or until the skin blisters and turns brown in places. The peppers will not brown evenly. Turn once or twice during the broiling. Remove from the oven and discard the garlic.

Working fast, cut the pepper into strips about ¼ inch wide and put them into a bowl. Immediately pour 1 cup of the Herbed French Dressing over them, toss to coat each strip with the dressing, cover, and let stand for about 2 hours. It is most important to pour the dressing on the peppers while they are still hot and can better absorb the herb flavor. Mix from time to time. Serve at room temperature, not chilled.

SALADE DE CHAMPIGNONS

Mushroom Salad

CHOLESTEROL RATING 1
CALORIES PER SERVING 190

I've never understood why Americans don't make more imaginative use of mushrooms, which are in good supply almost the whole year. With only 125 calories in a whole pound, one would think that more advantage would be taken of them in this weight-conscious era.

This mushroom salad has never failed to please guests. It's a light and crisp beginning to a meal. To keep that crispness, though, the mushrooms must be superfresh and cannot be prepared too long before serving. The longer the dressing is on the mushrooms the more it draws out the moisture and makes them limp, which is not the texture you want. The salad can stand an hour—at most—in the refrigerator if need be. Another thing to keep in mind: the dish takes no more than 6 or 7 minutes to do, from slicing to the final sprinkling of parsley, so it's perfectly possible to prepare it while guests finish cocktails.

6 servings

1 pound very fresh white mushrooms
juice of 2 lemons
⅓ cup polyunsaturated oil
salt and pepper
⅓ cup Herbed French Dressing II (page 243)
¼ cup chopped parsley

Cut the mushrooms in thin slices and put them in a deep bowl. Immediately sprinkle on the lemon juice to prevent discoloration, then toss with two spoons so that the lemon juice will reach all the mushrooms. Pour the oil over the mushrooms and toss again. Sprinkle on the salt, pepper, and salad dressing and toss once more. Just before serving, sprinkle on the chopped parsley and mix well.

MARINATED MUSHROOMS AND ARTICHOKE HEARTS

CHOLESTEROL RATING 1
CALORIES PER SERVING 115

Here is another fresh mushroom dish, one that is spicy and can be prepared ahead of time.

6 servings

4 ounces frozen artichoke hearts
1 pound fresh mushrooms
¼ cup polyunsaturated oil
½ cup cider or wine vinegar
1 cup water
½ teaspoon dried basil
juice ½ lemon
1 teaspoon salt
½ teaspoon pepper
½ teaspoon dried thyme
½ teaspoon dried oregano
1 garlic clove, cut in half
2 bay leaves
2 tablespoons chopped parsley

Cook the artichoke hearts until they are tender. Drain. Rinse the mushrooms (which must be very fresh) and slice in half lengthwise. Put the oil, vinegar, water, basil, lemon juice, salt and pepper into a jar and shake vigorously to blend well. Put the artichoke hearts and mushrooms in a large bowl, pour the marinade over them and toss lightly. Tie the thyme, oregano, garlic, and bay leaves all together in cheesecloth and bury this herb bouquet in the middle of the vegetables. Cover the bowl and let it stand at room temperature for 1 hour, stirring occasionally, and moving the bouquet around a little. Place in refrigerator until chilled, about 2 hours. Remove herb bouquet. It should be served chilled, but not really cold, otherwise the subtle vegetable flavors will not emerge above the herbs.

If you prepare the dish a day in advance, remove it from the refrigerator about 1 hour before serving. This entrée is equally good but less festive with just mushrooms. The marinade may be refrigerated and reused; it keeps well tightly covered. A bit of it added to salad dressings gives a piquant flavor.

CHAMPIGNONS FARCIS AUX DUXELLES

Mushrooms Stuffed with Duxelles

CHOLESTEROL RATING 1
CALORIES PER SERVING 260

This stuffing is a variation of the French *duxelles,* a sautéed mixture of minced mushrooms and onions. Though the dish is not difficult to make, the mincing of the mushrooms is tedious, so be prepared. Unfortunately, there is no good way to get around chopping them by hand; any kind of grinder or food mill squeezes and crushes the mushrooms into pieces, making for a mushy product. Two things are essential: a very sharp knife and absolutely fresh mushrooms. The fresher they are, the firmer, and that makes the chopping easier. The best way to chop the mushrooms is on a large wooden block, holding a long, triangular-bladed knife at both ends and chopping up and down. The more you do it the better, since the mushrooms must really be fine, fine, fine.

If you have the patience to make the stuffing you will be rewarded with much praise, because this is a delectable way to begin a meal. I serve 3 to 4 mushrooms per person, depending on size, with grilled tomatoes as a nicely orchestrated accompaniment. The mushrooms can be served along with a roast, but they are so good I think they deserve star billing. The stuffing keeps well in the refrigerator and freezes perfectly (though sometimes you may want to add a few bread crumbs to the defrosted mixture). Throughout the book you will find many recipes calling for *duxelles,* so make plenty while you're at it.

6 to 8 servings

1½ pounds very fresh mushrooms
½ cup polyunsaturated oil
1 cup very finely chopped onions
¾ cup Madeira
salt and pepper
½ teaspoon nutmeg, freshly grated
1 teaspoon meat extract (BV)
½ cup fine bread crumbs
3 tablespoons undiluted cream of mushroom soup
½ cup finely minced parsley
⅓ cup grated low-fat Parmesan cheese
¼ cup polyunsaturated oil

Rinse the mushrooms carefully. Remove the stems from the 24 largest and most uniform mushrooms, reserve the caps for filling later. The stems from these 24 plus all the rest of the mushrooms are to be chopped as fine as possible.

While chopping the mushrooms, heat ½ cup oil in a heavy skillet, add chopped onions, and fry slowly until they are soft, but not colored at all. As soon as the mushrooms are chopped, put them into the pan with the onions, turn up heat to medium and fry quickly while stirring. The mushrooms will render some of their juice. Fry this down, then pour in the Madeira and turn the flame up a little higher to boil the wine quickly. Meanwhile add salt, pepper, and nutmeg (use plenty of nutmeg, the flavor should be almost noticeable). Reduce the flame to low and add the meat extract. When it has completely melted, add the bread crumbs and mix well. Add the cream of mushroom soup (undiluted) and cook for 1 minute. Taste carefully and correct seasoning.

Cool for 10 minutes, and add chopped parsley. Using a teaspoon, fill the reserved mushroom caps with the mixture, rounding out the tops uniformly. Put grated low-fat Parmesan cheese in a small saucer and dip each cap into it, nicely coating the stuffing. Place on oiled baking dish. (Up to this point, the dish can be prepared ahead of time.) Sprinkle a little oil over each mushroom and place in 350° oven for 10 to 15 minutes, depending on the size of the mushrooms. If they do not brown nicely on top, place under broiler for 1 minute. (One pound of mushrooms and these seasonings make 3 cups of *duxelles.)*

GRIBI C SMETANOI

Mushrooms in Creamy Sour Sauce

CHOLESTEROL RATING 1
CALORIES PER SERVING 178

Gribi c smetanoi is a Russian dish that unfortunately isn't found too often in the Soviet Union anymore. Mushrooms are not cultivated commercially there, so wild ones are picked and offered for sale at scattered farmers' markets. These pungent, yet delicate mushrooms are combined with a snappy homemade sour cream that spoils you for any other kind. Luckily, this low-cholesterol version comes very close.

This dish is especially successful as a first course for a dinner party, but is equally good served over toast as a luncheon main course.

8 servings

½ cup polyunsaturated margarine
1½ cups onions, finely chopped
1 pound firm, white mushrooms
2 tablespoons flour
1 cup skimmed milk
1½ cups plain low-fat yoghurt
1½ tablespoons lemon juice
2 teaspoons salt
pepper
¼ cup grated low-fat Parmesan cheese

Heat the margarine in a heavy pot, add the chopped onions, cover, and simmer slowly until they are transparent (about 10 minutes). Meanwhile, slice the mushrooms thin and add to the onions (do not slice the mushrooms in advance or they will discolor). Turn up the heat a little and mix the onions and mushrooms together thoroughly. Cover the pot and cook until the mushrooms seem to have given off most of their juice (about 3 to 4 minutes). Reduce the heat and sprinkle on the flour. Mix thoroughly and quickly, scraping the bottom of the pot so the flour does not stick. Then remove the pot from the heat and add the milk slowly, stirring constantly. Return the pot to medium heat and add yoghurt, lemon juice, salt and pepper. Do not undersalt, you will need about 2 teaspoons. Cover the pot and cook 2 to 3 minutes. This much can be done the day before and refrigerated.

Spoon the mushroom-sauce mixture into individual 1-cup baking dishes, sprinkle on the Parmesan cheese and bake in a 350° oven

10 to 15 minutes, or until it bubbles and is lightly browned on top. Serve at once with a teaspoon.

The individual serving dishes make the nicest presentation, but the recipe does equally well if put in a 9-inch pie plate and baked; in this case you may want to pass it under the broiler a few seconds to give it a darker top.

CROUSTADES DE CHAMPIGNONS

Mushrooms on Pastry Shells

CHOLESTEROL RATING 2
CALORIES PER SERVING 500

On the limited land retrieved from the sea, the industrious Dutch have developed a large and important hothouse vegetable industry. It helps keep much of northern Europe happy with fresh vegetables in the winter. The Dutch themselves are particularly fond of their fresh mushrooms. However, they regard them as a delicacy to be served as a separate course at the beginning of the meal. Usually the sautéed mushrooms come on toast, but I find that the toast gets soggy, which is not particularly appealing. I much prefer using fried pastries which remain flaky and crackling.

The one key to the success of this dish is to cook the mushrooms at the very last minute. If fried ahead they will become mushy. They are meant to be undercooked so they retain some of their crispness. But this presents no problem whatsoever. The onions can be fried ahead and put aside. The mushrooms can be washed, dried, sliced, and kept in a plastic bag in the refrigerator for a few hours. At the end no more than 5 minutes of final cooking time is needed. Your guests will excuse you those few minutes once they have tasted the *croustades.*

6 servings

6 croustades prepared ahead (page 245)
⅓ cup polyunsaturated oil
3 medium onions, thinly sliced
1 pound fresh, white mushrooms
juice of ½ lemon
salt and pepper
4 ounces lean boiled ham, cut in julienne strips
½ cup sherry
2 tablespoons polyunsaturated margarine
¼ teaspoon freshly grated nutmeg

In a large heavy frying pan, heat the oil slowly and add the thinly sliced onions. Cover and cook over low heat until the onions are quite soft and transparent; stir occasionally. This should take at least 20 minutes.

Place *croustades* in a single layer on a cookie sheet and reheat in 325° oven while cooking the mushrooms. Slice mushrooms thin. Turn up the heat under the sautéed onions and add the mushrooms. Quickly mix mushrooms and onions, cover and fry for 3 to 4 minutes so the mushrooms will give off their juices. During this cooking, add the lemon juice, salt and pepper. Remove cover and add the boiled ham strips, sherry, margarine, and nutmeg. Mix well, cover and bring to one good boil. Spoon at once onto reheated *croustades.*

This same basic recipe can be altered slightly to make it a more substantial dish to be served as a main course for lunch. This can be done by increasing the quantity of boiled ham to 9 or 10 ounces and adding ⅓ cup chopped parsley to the cooked mushrooms after removing the pan from the fire.

TOMATES FARCIES DE LUIGI

Luigi's Stuffed Tomatoes

CHOLESTEROL RATING 1
CALORIES PER SERVING 610

There is something about the bright sun of Italy that makes shiny red tomatoes seem most refreshing and appealing. Italians have a way with tomatoes and serve them in myriad guises from cocktail time right up to dessert.

Like most men, a friend named Luigi likes to improvise, and his stuffed tomatoes may contain any assortment of cold vegetables that happens to be handy. (This is something to keep in mind when looking at the bits and pieces taking up refrigerator space.) But basically, this is how Luigi goes about stuffing tomatoes. I like to make extras to have cold the next day.

6 servings

2 tablespoons polyunsaturated oil
1 cup long grain rice
2 cups water
1 teaspoon salt
¼ cup polyunsaturated oil
2 garlic cloves, finely chopped
½ cup pine nuts
½ teaspoon ground pepper
½ teaspoon rosemary
½ teaspoon oregano
½ teaspoon basil
6 large ripe tomatoes
½ cup polyunsaturated oil
½ onion, finely chopped
1 tablespoon tomato paste
1 tablespoon lemon juice
1 teaspoon Worcestershire sauce
¼ cup white wine
salt and pepper
3 tablespoons chopped parsley

Heat 2 tablespoons of oil in a small heavy pot, add the rice, and stir while it sautés briskly until the grains turn starchy white. Immediately add the water and salt. Once the water comes to the boiling point, cover the pot, reduce the flame, and simmer slowly for 20 minutes, or until all the water has been absorbed. Scoop cooked rice into a mixing bowl.

Meanwhile, heat ¼ cup oil in a small pan and add the garlic and pine nuts; sauté until they turn a light gold color. Add this to the cooked rice, along with the ground pepper, rosemary, oregano, and basil. Mix well and taste for seasoning. It should be a fairly spicy mixture, since further cooking will mellow the flavors somewhat.

Turn tomatoes upside down and cut off a slice from the bottom. (This is contrary to what is usually done, but the top, or pip end, of the tomato is wider and stronger than the very round bottom end; so by turning it upside down, you have a more solid base for stuffing and baking. There is less risk of the pip-end base softening or breaking.) Scoop out the pulp from the tomatoes and place it in a blender, or pass through a food mill. Fill tomatoes amply with the rice stuffing and arrange on a baking dish.

Heat ½ cup of oil in a small pan, add the chopped onion, puréed tomato pulp, tomato paste, lemon juice, Worcestershire sauce, white wine, salt and pepper. Cover and simmer for 10 minutes. Pour this sauce over the tomatoes and bake in a 350° oven for 20 to 30 minutes, or until the tomato cases are baked but still firm. Baste several times during the baking. When serving, spoon some of the sauce over each tomato and sprinkle with chopped parsley.

LES FARCES DE BORMES

Vegetables Stuffed with Olive Purée

CHOLESTEROL RATING 2
CALORIES PER SERVING 358

This is an original dish that I concocted with a maid in the south of France. We were vacationing in a friend's home in the town of Bormes-les-Mimosas, which is as pretty a place as its name implies. The maid-cook was a native of Provence and enjoyed making tapènade, the strong olive purée discussed on page 248. A sudden arrival of extra friends for lunch sent us to the refrigerator to stretch things a bit. There was some tapènade. I cooked up some rice in a hurry, added a few other things, and used this as a filling for tomatoes. They were christened *Farces,* a play on words between stuffing and comedy.

Since then these *farces* have become a staple in my house, but in many guises. For dinner they make a delightful first course when served in either hollowed out tomato halves, large mushroom caps, hollowed out chunks of cucumber cut 1½ to 2 inches thick or halves of hard-boiled eggs, from which the yolks have been removed, naturally. You can also make a combination platter. In a real emergency, the filling can even be put on a bed of lettuce and decorated with something bright, like carrot sticks, pimento, or red pepper strips.

4 cups of filling for 6 first-course servings

2 cups cooked long grain rice
1 cup tapènade (page 248)
¼ cup chopped parsley
½ cup mayonnaise
salt and pepper
raw vegetables for stuffing
parsley sprigs for decoration

Mix the rice with the tapènade, chopped parsley, mayonnaise, salt and pepper. Use a fork and toss lightly. Do not mash, but mix quite thoroughly. Spoon into the prepared raw vegetables and top with a sprig of parsley.

BRUNCH, LUNCHEON, and SUPPER DISHES

TARTE A L'OIGNON

Onion Tart

CHOLESTEROL RATING 1
CALORIES PER SERVING 320

I have never liked the classic French version of Onion Tart. It comes out as just a variation on a *quiche,* that rich concoction of eggs, cream, and cheese, and the onions are almost incidental to the custard. In Alsace, however, where much of the cooking has Germanic overtones, the onion tart is another matter. There the onion dominates and only enough custard is used to hold the whole thing together.

In this recipe, the cholesterol-rich custard is replaced by a thick purée of cream of mushroom soup, skimmed-milk cottage cheese, and egg whites. This basic binder can be used for other vegetable tarts, too. It's fun to experiment with leeks, mushrooms, broccoli, asparagus, or cauliflower.

Don't be afraid of the quantity of onions. The long slow cooking reduces the onions' bulk to one quarter and also turns the strong flavor into a sweet one. The tart looks its best when fresh out of the oven and nicely puffed up, but it can be reheated with no loss of flavor.

This is an excellent main course at lunch. In smaller portions (8 to 10 servings) it also makes an unusual first course for dinner.

8 servings

1½ pounds onions, thinly sliced
¼ cup polyunsaturated oil
1 garlic clove, crushed
1 bay leaf
2 tablespoons flour
1 teaspoon meat extract (BV)
1 teaspoon salt
½ teaspoon pepper
2 tablespoons polyunsaturated oil
2 egg whites
1 cup condensed cream of mushroom soup, undiluted
½ cup dry skimmed-milk cottage cheese
¼ teaspoon freshly grated nutmeg
1 9-inch unbaked pie shell (see page 216)
2 tablespoons grated low-fat cheese, or Parmesan

Slice the onions thin. Slowly heat the ¼ cup of oil in a heavy pot. Add the onions and mix throughly until the onions are well coated with the oil. Cover and simmer over very low heat for about 15 minutes, stirring often. Add the crushed garlic and bay leaf. Continue cooking for another 30 minutes, still covered and still stirring often. Remove the bay leaf, sprinkle on the flour, and mix well. Add meat extract, salt and pepper; mix thoroughly. Cover and simmer for another 5 minutes. Cool slightly.

Meanwhile, put into the blender the 2 tablespoons oil, egg whites, mushroom soup, cottage cheese, and nutmeg; blend until you have a smooth purée. Spoon ½ of the purée into the cooked onions and mix thoroughly. Repeat with the other ½ of the purée. Taste for salt, pepper, and nutmeg; correct if necessary. Spread the mixture evenly into the pie shell and sprinkle on the grated cheese. Place in 375° oven for 35 to 45 minutes, or until nicely browned on top and slightly puffed. Serve hot, but not superhot.

SPANAKOPITTA

Greek Spinach Pie

CHOLESTEROL RATING 1
CALORIES PER SERVING 475

This recipe has been worked out with both fresh and frozen spinach, and frankly, once you add all the onion, scallions, dill, and mint, the difference in flavor is minimal. Fresh spinach is a wonderful vegetable, good enough to serve in its pure, unadulterated form.

Since this version of the classic *Spanakopitta* uses low-fat cheese and no egg yolk, more oil is needed in it. Also, a novel way has been found to make a low-fat binding for the spinach. The fried onions with all the oil and the cottage cheese are puréed in a blender, resulting in a custardlike base to which the chopped spinach is added.

For the top crust, you can use regular pastry crust, rolled very thin; or if available to you, the thin Greek phyllo dough looks very attractive and authentic on the top. Some packaged versions of phyllo dough contain no egg at all, others have a little. But even if you can only find the kind with egg, it hardly matters since so little of the dough is used.

This is an excellent main course for luncheon or late supper, or in smaller portions as a first course for a special dinner party.

8 servings

3 packages frozen whole-leaf spinach
1 pound onions
¾ cup polyunsaturated oil
½ cup chopped parsley
1 bunch scallions (including a little of the green part)
1 tablespoon dillweed
½ teaspoon nutmeg (freshly grated)
⅓ cup grated low-fat Parmesan cheese
1 teaspoon chopped mint, fresh or dried
salt and pepper to taste
½ pound dry skimmed-milk cottage cheese
2 egg whites
pastry for double crust pie or pastry for single crust (see page 216) plus 2 sheets phyllo pastry dough
¼ cup polyunsaturated oil

Put frozen spinach in a colander to thaw and drain (this can be done overnight). Coarsely chop 1 pound onions (they do not have to be chopped fine since they will be puréed later) and fry in ¾ cup oil. Simmer in a covered pan until translucent. Don't be concerned if you seem to have a lot of oil; it is necessary since it is the only fat used in the pie. Meanwhile squeeze the spinach by handfuls to remove all the water and chop coarsely; put in a large bowl. Add the chopped parsley, thinly sliced scallions, dill, nutmeg, Parmesan, mint, salt and pepper, and mix thoroughly.

Put ½ the quantity of the cooked onions and oil with ½ the quantity of the cottage cheese in a blender and purée. Pour this over the spinach mixture and repeat with the remaining onions and cheese. Add this also to the spinach mixture and blend thoroughly. Beat the egg whites with a fork just until foamy and add to the mixture, folding in delicately.

Roll out pastry and place in a 9-inch pie pan, leaving about 1 inch overlapping. Fill with spinach mixture, smooth out with back of tablespoon. Over the top place either 3 to 4 layers of phyllo pastry dough or regular pastry dough rolled very thin. Tuck the top crust down around the filling, then roll the overlapping crust inward and tuck around the inside edge of the pie pan. Make several slashes in top crust. Brush liberally with oil, bake at 350° for 50 to 60 minutes or until a nice golden brown.

It can be served hot or slightly cooled.

TARTE À LA TOMATE

Tomato Tart

CHOLESTEROL RATING 1
CALORIES PER MAIN COURSE SERVING 325

It's hard to understand why more French restaurants don't serve Tomato Tart. I know of only one, a lively bistro near Les Invalides in Paris, that has made a house specialty of it, and where the regular customers keep it coming from the kitchen in a steady stream. This is a slightly different version of that popular tart, one that could easily become your *spécialité de la maison.*

Small slices of this tart make an unusual starting dish for a special dinner party, but it stars even more as the main dish at lunch. When next having a group of ladies over for tea, try serving *Tarte à la Tomate* rather than sweet things and see how much more it is appreciated.

8 servings as main course
10 servings as first course

½ cup polyunsaturated oil
3 onions, thinly sliced
2 pounds fresh ripe tomatoes (canned won't do here)
1 garlic clove, crushed
2 tablespoons flour
½ teaspoon salt
½ teaspoon pepper
¼ cup plain low-fat yoghurt
¼ cup condensed cream of tomato soup, undiluted
1 tablespoon tomato paste
1 teaspoon basil
large pinch thyme
2 egg whites
1 partially baked 9-inch pastry shell (page 216)
1 tablespoon bread crumbs (optional)
1 teaspoon polyunsaturated oil

Heat ½ cup oil in a heavy skillet and add the onions to simmer gently, covered, for about 15 minutes or until they become very soft, but not brown. Remove 1 cup of the cooked onions and reserve.

Meanwhile, plunge the tomatoes in boiling water for a few seconds and slip off the skins. Cut the tomatoes in half across the middle and gently squeeze out the seeds and excess juice. Chop the tomatoes coarsely and add to the onions in the skillet, mix well, and simmer briskly, uncovered, to evaporate most of the juice. This should take about 15 minutes, depending on the juiciness of the tomatoes. What you want at this point is a thickened mixture that stands up when held in a spoon. Add the garlic, cover, and leave on very low heat for 5 minutes. Remove the skillet from the heat and sprinkle on the flour, salt and pepper, stirring constantly as the mixture thickens. Return to the heat for just another minute. Set aside to cool.

Put the reserved cup of fried onions in the blender with the yoghurt, tomato soup, tomato paste, basil, and thyme and blend to a smooth purée. Add this purée to the cooled tomato mixture, then beat in the egg whites. Spoon this tomato batter into the partially prebaked pastry shell, sprinkle on the optional bread crumbs, and brush the oil on the edges of the pastry shell.

Place the tart in a 375° oven for about 35 to 40 minutes, or until a knife plunged into the center comes out clean. Serve hot, but not right out of the oven. If made ahead, reheat slowly in 325° oven.

MOCK BLINTZES

CHOLESTEROL RATING 1
CALORIES PER SERVING 340

A dairy lunch, or breakfast for that matter, does not have to be forsaken just because egg dishes are not at your disposal. Here is a way to serve up cottage cheese that is good in itself, and not just a substitute for something else. One word of shopping caution: buy the dry, closely packed, skimmed-milk cottage cheese, not the loose, moist kind.

4 to 6 servings

2 cups dry skimmed-milk cottage cheese
¼ cup plain low-fat yoghurt for filling
1 tablespoon sugar
1 teaspoon nutmeg (freshly grated)
24 Uneeda-type crackers
½ to ¾ cup skimmed milk
½ to ¾ cup polyunsaturated oil
¼ cup plain low-fat yoghurt for topping

Put cottage cheese in a deep bowl and mash well with a fork. Add ¼ cup yoghurt, sugar, and nutmeg. Mix well. Put 2 tablespoons of the cheese mixture on a cracker, cover with another cracker, and smooth edges with the back of the spoon. It should now look like a thick cracker sandwich. Repeat, until you have 12 sandwiches.

Pour skimmed milk in a large plate to a ¼-inch depth, the amount of milk depending on the size of the plate. Place the filled crackers in the milk and let the "blintz" soak for 2 minutes, turn them over and let the other sides soak for another 2 minutes. Remove "blintzes" and place them on heavily oiled shallow baking sheet or pie pan. Dribble ½ cup oil over them.

Place in 350° oven and bake for 15 minutes. Turn, dribble on more oil if the crackers seem dry, and bake for 10 minutes more. Spread 1 teaspoon of yoghurt on each "blintz" and bake for another 10 minutes. This may seem like a lot of baking, but it is necessary to give the "blintzes" the desired crispness.

MOZZARELLA IN CARRÒZZA

Fried Cheese Sandwiches

CHOLESTEROL RATING 2
CALORIES PER SERVING 465

Mozzarella in Carròzza literally means mozzarella cheese tucked inside a carriage. The carriage in this case is made of plain white bread. In Italy this popular midday snack is served piping hot with the rich cheese melting inside. Since regular full-fat mozzarella is not used here, nor are there egg yolks in the batter, a few flavor adjustments are made to return some of the original lushness to the hot sandwich.

Frying the sandwiches takes only seconds, assuring crispness when served. The *carròzze,* however, can be prepared ahead, leaving only the final dipping in batter and frying to be done when needed. If you haven't a 4-inch pastry cutter for cutting circles out of the packaged sliced white bread, try using the plastic top from a coffee can, it fits perfectly. Just press it into the bread firmly, pull away the outer edges, and you have a neat 4-inch circle. While on the subject, don't use thin-sliced diet bread. The slices are too thin to hold up in the frying.

Serve with either a hot anchovy, hot tomato, or cold horseradish sauce. All three change the dish completely; each is equally good in its own way. With a salad alongside, *Mozzarella in Carròzza* makes a very substantial luncheon menu.

6 servings

BATTER INGREDIENTS

2 tablespoons flour
salt and pepper
5 tablespoons evaporated skimmed milk
2 teaspoons brandy
2 egg whites

SANDWICH INGREDIENTS

12 slices white bread
8 ounces part-skim-milk mozzarella cheese
salt and pepper
1 teaspoon Worcestershire sauce
¾ to 1 cup skimmed milk
½ cup bread crumbs
polyunsaturated oil for frying

SAUCE: ¾ to 1 cup either Anchovy Sauce (page 239), *Coulis de Tomates* (page 236), or Horseradish Sauce (page 238).

Prepare the batter at least 1 hour before using. Put the flour, salt and pepper in a small bowl and gradually mix in the milk and brandy. When it is thoroughly blended, add the egg whites, and mix with a wire whisk until the batter is smooth. Cover the bowl and let rest.

Meanwhile, cut circles from the slices of bread. Slice the cheese and place on 6 of the bread circles. Leave at least a ¼-inch border around the cheese; it will escape during the frying if placed to the very edge. Sprinkle salt, pepper, and a few drops of Worcestershire sauce on the cheese. Cover the cheese-topped circles with the remaining 6 circles of bread.

Pour about ½ the milk in a shallow dish and put about ½ the bread crumbs in another shallow dish. Working quickly and doing one at a time, dip the sandwiches into the milk, just a second or so on each side. Press the edges of the bread together to seal them. Dip immediately into the bread crumbs, patting the crumbs onto each side of the sandwich. Roll the edges of the sandwich in the crumbs to help seal them even more. Press the edges again and put aside to dry. Continue making the other *carròzze,* adding the milk and crumbs as needed.

Prepare the sauce before starting to fry the sandwiches. At serving time pour oil into a wide skillet to a depth of about ¼ inch and heat until almost smoking. Pour the batter into a dish and dip each sandwich into the batter. Then fry in the hot oil for a few seconds until each sandwich turns a nutty brown; turn to brown the other side. Drain on paper towels and serve piping hot with sauce.

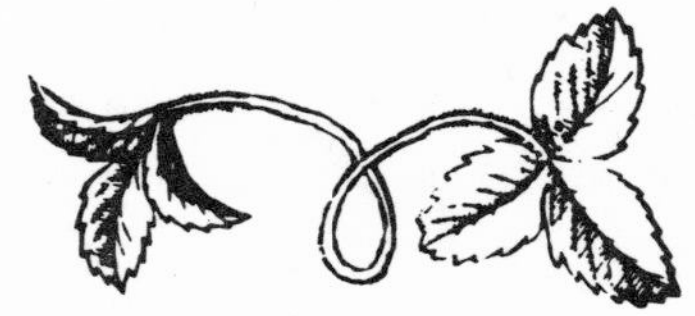

FRIED NOODLES AND ALMONDS

CHOLESTEROL RATING 1
CALORIES PER SERVING 450

There is a touch of the thrifty Chinese housewife in this quickly prepared dish. Although you can use leftover noodles (or any kind of pasta), you'll find enough demand for this crisp dish that you'll be boiling noodles especially for it.

4 servings

1 to 2 tablespoons polyunsaturated margarine
½ cup blanched, slivered almonds
2 tablespoons polyunsaturated margarine
5 cups cooked, drained noodles
1 tablespoon poppy seeds
nutmeg, freshly grated

Put 2 tablespoons of the margarine in a heavy skillet and brown the almonds on a low fire, turning them often. Remove the almonds when they have turned a dark golden color. Add 1 more tablespoon of margarine to the skillet, then the well-drained noodles. Turn the flame up to moderate and fry the noodles until crisp, turning quite often. Add more margarine if necessary.

Just a minute or so before serving, put in almonds, poppy seeds, and a generous sprinkling of nutmeg. Mix all the ingredients thoroughly, flatten the noodles and do not stir again. Turn up the heat so the noodles on the bottom will brown nicely, fry for a minute or two. Reverse the fried noodles (which will resemble a flat pie) onto a serving platter.

POTATO PANCAKES

CHOLESTEROL RATING 1
CALORIES PER SERVING 350

Potato pancakes have long been a Middle European and German favorite. The traditional way of making them means a lot of tedious hand grating of the potatoes. The blender helps here, but one must use it judiciously so that there is still some granular texture to the potatoes—one thing you don't want is a satin-smooth batter. Removing as much of the potato water as possible is a trick to keep the pancakes light; otherwise a lot of flour must be added to absorb the liquid. Naturally, since the pancakes are fried in oil they are not calorically kind to us, but they are good.

4 to 6 servings

2 pounds potatoes
½ cup skimmed milk
½ to ¾ onion, grated
½ cup flour
2 teaspoons salt
2 egg whites
frying oil

Peel potatoes then cut into 1-inch chunks. Put ½ the quantity of milk in the blender, then add ½ the potatoes. Grate in machine quickly, but do not blend too long or you will have a smooth paste rather than a batter with some body to it. Scrape this mixture into a fine sieve to let drip, then do other ½ of potatoes repeating the process exactly. (The milk is put in the blender to help grate the potatoes; it will drip out along with the potato water.) With a wooden spoon, beat the mixture a little while in the sieve to help force out as much of the water as possible.

Put the drained, grated potatoes in mixing bowl, add the finely grated onion, flour, and salt. Mix well, then add egg whites and mix again. Let batter stand about 10 minutes, covered. Don't allow to stand much more than this or batter will turn a little dark.

Heat oil in deep frying pan; there should be about 1-inch depth of oil. When quite hot, fry 1 teaspoon of the batter to taste for salt. Correct if necessary. Keeping oil constantly hot, spoon in 2 heaping tablespoons of the batter, flatten a little to about ½-inch thickness. Place as many pancakes in the pan as can be fried without crowding. If the pan is too crowded, the oil will not remain hot enough and the pancakes will not turn a nice even brown. After 2 to 3 minutes on one side, turn with spatula and fry for the same amount of time on the other side. Remove to hot dish with paper towels to drain; keep warm while finishing the others.

You should get about 12 pancakes, which would serve 4 people amply as a luncheon main course. The pancakes can be fried a little smaller and used to accompany a meat course, then serving 6 people. Applesauce is traditionally passed with the pancakes.

STUFFED CUCUMBERS

CHOLESTEROL RATING 2
CALORIES PER SERVING 240

Unusual, pretty, good to eat and good for you—what else can you ask? Once you get the idea of the dish, experiment with the stuffings; try rice and chopped ham, or olives mixed with rice or kernel corn.

4 to 6 servings

3 to 4 large cucumbers

FILLING

½ pound lean ground beef
2 tablespoons soy sauce
2 tablespoons dried onion soup
1 garlic clove, crushed
2 tablespoons polyunsaturated oil
2 tablespoons finely chopped parsley
1 teaspoon dillweed (fresh or dried)
1 tablespoon Worcestershire sauce
2 pimentos
3 tablespoons dry white wine

SAUCE

1 teaspoon potato flour
1 tablespoon water
⅓ cup dry white wine
½ cup beef broth
½ teaspoon soy sauce
salt and pepper

Choose the largest cucumbers you can find—enough to make 12 1½-inch crosswise slices. Peel the cucumbers, cut into the 1½-inch slices and scoop out their centers with a grapefruit knife. But make certain that the bottom is left intact to serve as a supporting base. For the filling, mix together the beef, soy sauce, dried onion soup, crushed garlic, oil, parsley, dill, and Worcestershire sauce. Mix well, then take small amounts and press into cucumber shells, filling enough to have a nicely rounded top.

Stand the stuffed slices upright in a baking pan. Cut pimento into thin strips and crisscross on top of each piece. Add water to 1/4-inch level in pan (cucumbers will render more liquid), then add the dry white wine. Cover and put in 350° oven for approximately 30 minutes, or until cucumber is translucent. Check water level occasionally to make sure there is about 1/4 inch at all times; if necessary add more wine, water, or beef broth. When finished baking, remove to a hot platter while preparing sauce.

SAUCE

Mix the potato flour with 1 tablespoon water and add to water and juices in the pan, boil briskly while adding 1/3 cup white wine, 1/2 cup beef broth, 1/2 teaspoon soy sauce, salt and pepper to taste, then simmer a few minutes. Spoon 1 tablespoon of sauce over each cucumber slice, then pass the rest in a sauceboat.

This quantity will serve 4 as a main luncheon course, or 6 as first course.

GRATIN D'ENDIVES AU JAMBON

Gratin of Endives and Ham

CHOLESTEROL RATING 2
CALORIES PER SERVING 425

It's too bad endive is so expensive in the United States. It can add great distinction to any meal, either as a cooked vegetable or a raw salad. This always-appreciated luncheon or brunch dish is one way of making the mild-flavored vegetable go a long way. The same recipe can be used for leeks, which for some inexplicable reason, are almost as expensive as imported endive.

6 servings as main course

12 Belgian endives
1 tablespoon salt
6 tablespoons polyunsaturated margarine
1 medium onion, minced
6 tablespoons flour
3 cups skimmed milk
1½ cups condensed cream of celery soup, undiluted
freshly grated nutmeg
1 teaspoon Worcestershire sauce
salt and pepper
1 teaspoon polyunsaturated oil
12 slices lean boiled ham
1 tablespoon bread crumbs or low-fat grated Parmesan cheese (optional)

Trim off the root edges of each endive. Rinse the vegetable. Bring a large quantity of water to a rapid boil, add the salt and the endives. Reduce heat and cook for 10 minutes at a rapid simmer. Drain the endives and plunge immediately into cold water to stop the cooking. Put the endives on the sink board to allow as much water as possible to drain off.

Meanwhile, prepare the sauce. Heat the margarine in a saucepan with the minced onion. Cook the onion slowly for about 10 minutes without allowing it to color. Add the flour and stir well to mix it thoroughly with the margarine and onions: cook for 1 minute. Remove from heat, slowly add the milk, stirring vigorously with a wire whisk. Return to heat and simmer while adding the cream of celery soup, a good pinch of nutmeg, Worcestershire sauce, salt and pepper. The sauce should be rather thick.

Lightly oil a baking dish. Gently squeeze each head of endive between your hands to extract any remaining water. Place each endive on one corner of a slice of boiled ham, and wrap it diagonally rather than straight around so as to achieve a more secure wrapping. Place the wrapped endive in the baking dish, seam side down. Continue with the remaining endives, placing them snugly next to each other in the dish. Spread the sauce completely over the ham-wrapped endives. Sprinkle on the optional bread crumbs or Parmesan cheese. The dish can be prepared ahead to this point and refrigerated.

Just before putting in a 350° oven, check to see if the endive has exuded any more water. If it has, absorb it with a paper towel. Put the dish in the oven for about 30 minutes, or until top is lightly browned. The bread crumbs or cheese will give a darker topping.

CHINESE CHICKEN SALAD

CHOLESTEROL RATING 2
CALORIES PER SERVING 215

As with most of Chinese cooking, a little bit is stretched into something quite filling and tasty. This particular salad tastes as light and fresh as it looks with the thin strips of pink and white meats arranged in a feathery mound on lettuce. It can be served anytime of the year, but in summer the pale colors seem more delicious than ever.

6 servings

4 individual chicken breasts
2 cups chicken consommé
4 ounces thinly sliced lean boiled ham
salt and pepper

3 tablespoons polyunsaturated oil
1½ tablespoons soy sauce
1 teaspoon bourbon
salt and pepper

Put the chicken breasts in a nonaluminum pan that will hold them snugly. Pour in the consommé, enough to barely cover the chicken meat. Put the pan on a low fire and poach the chicken very slowly, keeping the consommé at a slow simmer. Never let it boil. Test for doneness by pressing the center of a breast—it should have some firmness and not be soft and mushy to the touch. Be careful not to overcook. The cooking should take approximately 5 minutes once the consommé is simmering. Cool the chicken in the cooking liquid. This can be done ahead of time.

Remove all the skin and bones from the chicken breasts and, with a very sharp knife, cut the meat into long julienne strips of matchstick thickness. Cut the boiled ham into the same-sized strips. Combine the two meats in a bowl and sprinkle lightly with salt and pepper.

Prepare the dressing by beating together the oil, soy sauce, bourbon, salt and pepper.

Just before serving, pour the dressing over the chicken and ham, toss well, and serve on a bed of crisp lettuce.

BOUDIN BLANC

White Sausage of Chicken and Veal

CHOLESTEROL RATING 2
CALORIES PER SERVING 190

A late-night Christmas or New Year's *reveillon* supper in France without *Boudin Blanc* would be unthinkable. The deliciously mild sausage is unlike any other; there is nothing strong or pungent about it. I tried buying *Boudin Blanc* in the United States and gave up after too many disappointments with the starchy, flavorless variety turned out by French shops here. What else but try to make your own? Success! Then the next step, for me, was to try to reproduce the exquisite flavor of *Boudin Blanc* without all the rich cream and fat. Success again!

Although there are a number of steps, they are stretched out over a few days, and not one of the operations is difficult. An electric meat grinder is a tremendous help. One other suggestion to speed up the work—make two large sausages instead of a dozen small ones, then slice and fry them like patties. Admittedly, individual sausages make a nicer presentation, but the flavor doesn't change, and you might be more encouraged to try them if less time is involved. They are very, very much worth the effort.

12 servings

3 cups sliced onions (2 cups if you prefer milder sausage)
¾ cup polyunsaturated margarine
½ cup rice
1⅓ cups water
1 chicken bouillon cube
½ pound (1 cup) skinless, boneless raw breast of chicken
½ pound (1 cup) lean veal
1 slice white bread, crusts removed
2 teaspoons salt
large pinch white pepper
¼ teaspoon thyme
¼ teaspoon sage
¼ teaspoon freshly grated nutmeg
3 egg whites
½ cup evaporated skimmed milk
For wrapping sausages: cheesecloth, polyunsaturated oil, string

Chop the onions coarsely and simmer slowly in ¼ cup margarine until they are soft and transparent; do not allow the onions to brown. In another pot put the rice, water, chicken bouillon cube, and ¼ cup margarine; cover and simmer until all the liquid has been absorbed (about 30 minutes). Cool both onions and rice.

Meanwhile, put through the finest blade of the meat grinder ¼ cup chilled margarine, then the chicken and veal. Alternately put the cooked onions and rice through the grinder. Then grind the entire mixture once again to achieve a fine texture. Finally, put pieces of the white bread into the grinder. Stop grinding when you see the bread start coming through the blades; this insures that all of the other ingredients have been pushed out.

Add the salt, pepper, thyme, sage, and nutmeg and beat vigorously with a wooden spoon. Then add alternately, in small amounts, the egg whites and the evaporated skimmed milk, beating well between each addition. Fry a teaspoon of the mixture to taste for seasonings; correct if necessary. Chill before forming sausages.

Spread out double layers of cheesecloth on a tray or on aluminum foil. If making two large sausages, the cheesecloth should be approximately 12 × 16 inches for each one; for individual sausages, cut the cloth to 6 × 9-inch pieces. Brush oil over the cheesecloth and form the meat into a sausage shape; put in the center of the cloth. Use half the mixture for each of the two large sausages, or about ½ cup for each of the 4-to-5-inch individual ones. Roll the sausages tightly in their cloths and tie the ends with string. Brush again with oil and refrigerate for 2 days.

To precook the sausages, poach them in a large quantity of salted water kept to just below a simmer. The water should cover the sausages by at least 2 inches and the pot should be covered; a fish poacher is excellent for this. Small sausages will take 25 minutes, large ones 40 minutes. Drain and cool. Refrigerate for a day or two before frying. They can also be frozen.

To serve, carefully remove the cheesecloth wrapping and cut the large sausage in slices about ¾ inch thick. For either the slices or the individual sausages, flour lightly and sauté in polyunsaturated margarine until a light golden brown. This makes an excellent luncheon dish with mashed or fried potatoes and peas or string beans.

FISH

THROUGHOUT MUCH OF EUROPE, THE FISH MARKET IS A WRITHING SEA of every conceivable size and shape of watery creature. The shopper rarely has to inquire about freshness. Such assurance is hard to come by here. But along with the ubiquitous frozen specimens, a good fish shop usually has a regular supply of fresh fish caught locally or nearby. The salesman should be cultivated and his advice sought.

When a really fresh fish is available, do not intrude on its natural sweetness. It needs no more help than being simply poached in a court bouillon (see page 70) or baked with a little polyunsaturated margarine and white wine. The fish will not be overdone if it is cooked for 10 minutes for each inch of measured thickness.

When you cannot get perfectly fresh fish, there are other things to do. The suggestions here range from the delicacy of *Filet de Sole en Turban* to the punch of marinated smoked cod. Several smoked-fish recipes are included, because this is a fish item often overlooked. It is almost always available and delivers a lot of impact for a little bit of money.

Fish presents no problem when it comes to the wine selection. It will be white almost every time. Any of the white Burgundies would be a good choice, like Chablis or Pouilly-Fuissé. A dry Graves, light Riesling, Italian Soave, or Pinot Chardonnay from California are other good choices. When a larger white wine is called for, to serve with the *Darnes de Saumon* for example, one could try a Meursault, Puligny-Montrachet or Chassagne-Montrachet. The one exception where a red wine would be served is when tuna cooked in red wine is on the menu. Then a chilled rosé, Beaujolais, or American Zinfandel would be the choice.

TURBOT SALAD À LA BOUBOULINA

CHOLESTEROL RATING 2
CALORIES PER SERVING 460

This excellent Greek fish salad depends on only one thing—the quality of the ingredients. The higher the quality and the fresher the fish, the better. The larger the piece of fish, the better also, since thin slices will cook too rapidly and toughen. The oil should not be heavy and the pepper should be freshly ground. Another secret is doing it at the last minute so the fish is still slightly warm.

4 to 5 servings

- *2 pounds turbot, hake, or other firm white fish*
- *1 to 2 cups skimmed milk*
- *½ teaspoon salt*
- *¾ cup polyunsaturated oil*
- *juice of 2 lemons*
- *salt and pepper*
- *3 tablespoons finely chopped shallots*
- *3 tablespoons finely chopped parsley*

Select an enameled pan for poaching the fish; gray metals will darken the fish. Put the fish in the pan and pour in enough skimmed milk to reach 3/4 depth of the fish. Add 1/2 teaspoon salt to the milk. Cover and put on a very small flame; you want the milk to heat very slowly. At no point should it boil, but just barely simmer. Depending on the size of the fish, it will take 15 to 20 minutes to cook properly. If you must use frozen filets, 10 minutes should be enough. The fish is done when the flesh is a nice firm white and can be flaked with a fork.

While the fish is poaching, prepare the dressing. With a fork mix together the oil and lemon juice, adding salt and pepper to taste. Also, chop the shallots very fine and put in a mixing bowl, ready to receive the flaked cooked fish.

Remove the fish from the pan as soon as it is cooked. While it is cooling for a few minutes, just enough so you can handle it, warm the bowl containing the shallots by placing in a low oven or passing it over a flame several times.

Remove the skin and bones from the fish and flake it into the warm bowl. The heat of the fish will poach the shallots slightly. Sprinkle over it most of the oil dressing you have prepared. Salt and pepper to taste and toss lightly. Be careful not to mash the fish, but handle it with a light hand. Add chopped parsley and toss again. Taste for seasoning, and add more of the dressing, or salt and pepper, if necessary. Let stand no more than 10 minutes.

Serve on a bed of lettuce, but make sure the leaves are not straight out of the refrigerator and icy cold. Finally you can sprinkle on a little more parsley.

MAQUEREAUX AU VIN BLANC

Mackerel Poached in White Wine

CHOLESTEROL RATING 2
CALORIES PER SERVING 205

It is too bad that more restaurants don't offer this light and low-calorie fish dish. It couldn't be easier to prepare, and since it is best prepared the day before being served, there is no last-minute flurry. Standing for a day also allows the lemony flavor to penetrate the fish.

Maquereaux au Vin Blanc can be an unusual first course at an informal dinner or, served with a large salad, make a lunch a more imaginative affair.

The mackerel can be prepared several ways. I much prefer keeping it whole, if I know my guests won't mind the extra work required. Cooking the entire fish produces a more gelatinous and flavorful sauce. For more finicky diners, the heads can be removed; and the least preferred method is to cook just the filets. If either of the two latter presentations is decided upon, do add the heads and bones to the cooking stock along with the fish, and carefully remove all extra bones before serving.

6 servings

6 medium-sized mackerel, very firm, and very fresh

COURT BOUILLON

1½ cups dry white wine
1 pint water
1 teaspoon salt
½ teaspoon whole peppercorns
2 whole cloves
2 carrots cut in very thin slices
2 onions sliced very thin
1 lemon sliced very thin
⅛ teaspoon thyme
1 bay leaf
1 lemon thinly sliced for garnish

Prepare the court bouillon and let it simmer for 20 minutes. Remove it from the fire and let cool completely. The mackerel should be cleaned and rinsed (whole, without heads, or just the filets) and arranged in a fairly deep oven dish.

Pour the unstrained bouillon over the mackerel. The liquid should reach about ½ the depth of the fish; if not, add more white wine. If heads have been removed, or fish has been fileted, place the heads and bones in the stock around the mackerel.

Place the oven dish on an asbestos pad on top of the stove and bring to a very slow simmer. Cover and place in 350° oven. Keep the bouillon just at the simmering point while it is in the oven, and poach the fish for 10 minutes or so, depending on size. Filets take less time. The fish is done when the flesh flakes easily when pierced with a fork. Remove from oven and let the fish cool in the sauce, still covered. Remove bay leaf.

Refrigerate overnight, but remove far enough in advance of serving to take the chill off. When serving, either on a platter or on individual dishes, spoon carefully over the fish some of the sauce along with the vegetables. Decorate the plate with fresh thinly sliced lemon rounds.

FILETS DE POISSON EN PAPILLOTES

Fish Filets Steamed in Foil Envelopes

CHOLESTEROL RATING 2
CALORIES PER SERVING 305

French *papillotes* are the ruffly papers that hold little candies and cookies. Although large envelopes made of aluminum foil lack the daintiness of the little crinkled cups, they still attract a lot of attention when brought to the dining room. There are other advantages than just the showiness of the presentation. First, all the delicious flavors remain inside the foil, and secondly, the filets stay hot since they are kept in the hot foil almost until the approach of the knife and fork.

Most recipes for *papillotes* suggest presenting them individually on the dinner plates. It doesn't strike me as an attractive way to serve. One doesn't like to eat directly from the foil, and the abundance of liquid can cause splattering accidents. I suggest instead bringing the fish to the dining room in the baking dish just as it comes from the oven. Then the host or hostess opens the *papillotes,* transfers the fish to a warm dinner plate and spoons some of the juices over it. One very large *papillote* can also be made to hold all six servings. But this does mean a *papillote,* not laying the fish into a baking dish and covering with foil. A complete seal is essential.

Fish done this way needs nothing else with it, not even lemon. The flavor is remarkably subtle. With a few *Pommes de Terre à la Vapeur* (Steamed Potatoes), page 180, added to the menu you have a meal of quiet distinction.

6 servings

6 tablespoons polyunsaturated margarine
1 teaspoon regular dark prepared mustard (not hot)
1 garlic clove, crushed
¾ cup minced parsley
½ teaspoon lemon juice
salt and pepper
12 filets of flounder or sole
½ lemon
salt and pepper
aluminum foil

Prepare the seasoned dressing by creaming together the margarine, mustard, crushed garlic clove (remove the center sprout before crushing), parsley, lemon juice, salt and pepper. This mixture should be very soft and thoroughly blended.

Rinse the filets and dry them on a paper towel. Rub both sides of each filet with the lemon half and sprinkle with salt and pepper. Lay out the aluminum foil in a piece large enough to completely fold over the fish like an envelope. Lay one filet on the foil, the skin side against the foil. The difference between the two sides is indicated by the slightly darker and firmer flesh of the outside skin section, and the very white and delicate flesh of the fish's interior.

Spread 1/6 of the seasoned dressing evenly along the entire length of the prepared filet. Cover with another filet and fold the foil over the fish to seal it completely. Roll all seams tightly. Put the *papillote* in a baking dish and continue with the others. (If the filets don't match evenly, fold over the excess and secure with a toothpick.)

The *papillotes* can be prepared ahead of time, put on a baking dish, and refrigerated. Remove from the refrigerator at least 1 hour before baking to bring to room temperature; if there is not time to do this, then increase the baking time by 5 minutes. If the baking dish cannot accommodate all the *papillotes* in a single layer and they must be stacked, the baking time should also be increased by 5 to 10 minutes.

Place the *papillotes*-filled baking dish in a 375° oven for 15 to 20 minutes, depending on the thickness of the filets. Do not overcook. Serve at once directly from the *papillotes.*

FILETS DE SOLE EN TURBAN

Rolled Filets of Sole

CHOLESTEROL RATING 2
CALORIES PER SERVING 193

Good fresh filet of sole does not need much done to it. For a dish of perfect simplicity, it can be sautéed in polyunsaturated margarine, then lightly sprinkled with salt, pepper, and lemon juice. When a more impressive presentation is required, the filets can be rolled around a light stuffing and poached in wine. They arrive at the table looking like a sheik's turban.

6 servings

2 tablespoons polyunsaturated margarine
1 tablespoon minced shallots
¼ pound mushrooms, thinly sliced
salt and pepper
3 tablespoons polyunsaturated margarine
1 teaspoon parsley
½ teaspoon tarragon
6 filets of sole
½ lemon
salt and pepper
¼ cup vermouth
¼ cup dry white wine

Melt 2 tablespoons of margarine in a small skillet, add the shallots, and simmer gently for about a minute. Add the sliced mushrooms, mixing them well with the shallots. Sprinkle with a little salt and pepper, cover the skillet, and simmer gently for about 3 minutes.

In a small bowl, cream together the 3 tablespoons of margarine, the parsley, and tarragon.

Rinse the sole filets and dry on paper towels. Rub each filet on both sides with the lemon half. Lay them on the counter skin side up (this is the darker side). Sprinkle each filet lightly with salt and pepper. Spread some of the herb-flavored margarine over the entire length of each filet, then spread the mushrooms. Do not extend the mushrooms to the very ends. Roll the filet and secure the closing with a toothpick.

Select a heavy nonaluminum pan that will hold the 6 rolled filets snugly. Stand the "turbans" in the pan and pour the wines over them. Put a piece of aluminum foil directly over the filets, tucking it down inside the pan, then place a lid on the pan. The turbans can be prepared ahead and kept in the refrigerator for a few hours; the liquid should not be added, however, until just before cooking.

About 20 minutes before serving, place the pan of "turbans" on a very low fire and heat the wines gently. As they warm up they will begin poaching the filets. Check from time to time to make certain that the wines are not boiling, for that toughens the fish. The wine should be kept just below a simmer. The filets will be poached in about 10 minutes, depending on the size and thickness of the fish. Fifteen minutes should be the maximum. They are done when the flesh is white and flakes if pierced with a toothpick.

Carefully remove the "turbans" to a serving platter, take out the toothpicks, and spoon some sauce over each one. Serve at once.

TRUITES AU PAPRIKA FARCIES

Stuffed Paprika Trout

CHOLESTEROL RATING 2
CALORIES PER SERVING 255

Trout lends itself to many treatments, and this one, with its pale pink sauce, is among the prettiest. The trout heads can be removed if you are finicky about that, or if your plates aren't large enough, but the fish cannot be fileted for this preparation. The stuffing absorbs much flavor from being baked inside the fish; while on the other hand, the trout takes on some mild flavoring from the stuffing. The two work together beautifully.

4 servings

STUFFING

¼ cup minced onions
¼ cup polyunsaturated margarine
½ cup bread crumbs
¼ cup minced parsley
2 teaspoons paprika
salt and pepper
¼ cup dry white wine
4 fresh trout

POACHING

½ onion, thinly sliced
2 teaspoons tomato paste
1 tablespoon paprika
1 cup dry white wine
salt and pepper

SAUCE

2 to 3 tablespoons flour
2 tablespoons polyunsaturated margarine
¼ cup dry white wine
3 tablespoons skimmed milk powder mixed with 2 tablespoons water
2 tablespoons polyunsaturated margarine

Make the stuffing by slowly frying the minced onions in the margarine for just 2 or 3 minutes; the onions should not color at all. Remove the pan from the heat and stir in the bread crumbs, parsley, paprika, and just a little salt and pepper. Pour on the wine and set aside to cool and to allow the crumbs to absorb the wine.

Meanwhile, rinse and dry the trout. Prepare the poaching stock in a deep skillet or pan that can go into the oven. Put in the pan the thinly sliced onion, tomato paste, paprika, wine, salt and pepper and stir until the paprika and tomato paste are dissolved in the liquid.

Stuff each trout with 1 tablespoon of the filling and tie string around the fish in three places to keep the stuffing in place. Put the trout in the poaching liquid and place in 400° oven. Reduce the heat immediately to 350° and poach for about 10 minutes, or until the flesh flakes if pierced with a toothpick. Baste often during the baking. While the fish is poaching, work the flour into the margarine with a fork; this mixture will be used to thicken the sauce later.

Using a long spatula, remove the trout to a heated serving platter, remove the strings and keep the fish warm while finishing the sauce.

Strain the sauce from the poaching pan into a small pot and put on a low fire. Pour ¼ cup white wine into the poaching pan to lift any juices that remained behind and strain this into the pot. Add the flour-margarine blend a little at a time until the sauce thickens, but do not thicken too much. When the sauce coats a spoon, it is just right. While the sauce is simmering, add moistened skimmed milk powder and the 2 tablespoons of margarine. Bring the sauce just to the boiling point and spoon liberally over each trout.

TRUITE À LA GRENOBLOISE

Trout Grenoble

CHOLESTEROL RATING 2
CALORIES PER SERVING 425

Grenoble sits in the shadow of the Alps in southeastern France. The fast-running rivers in the area have traditionally kept the *Grenoblois* well supplied with fresh trout. Recent French laws, however, forbid the sale of wild trout, and only those raised in hatcheries are available in fish stores and restaurants.

The hatchery-produced trout lack the flavor and texture of those that fight the current of turbulent streams. French chefs recognized this lack and experimented with exotic combinations to give the trout a character of some sort. These days the fish is merely a vehicle for everything from raisins to bananas.

The Grenoble preparation is an old recipe using capers that are grown in the Mediterranean area not too far away. I find this a more natural way around the flavor problem than the addition of fruit. The recipe calls for whole trout, which is the best way to prepare them, but, if you prefer, filets can be used instead.

6 servings

6 medium-sized trout
½ cup flour
6 tablespoons polyunsaturated margarine
salt and pepper
¼ cup polyunsaturated margarine
⅔ cup minced mushrooms
2 tablespoons fine bread crumbs
1 cup dry white wine
juice of 1 lemon
2 teaspoons drained capers
salt and pepper

Wash and dry the trout. Spread some of the flour in a large flat dish and lightly flour the trout all over; add more flour as needed. Melt 3 tablespoons of margarine in a heavy skillet. When margarine is hot add the trout (or as many as will fit without crowding), salt and pepper them, and sauté until nicely browned underneath. Add more margarine as needed. Turn trout to brown the other side. Sprinkle with salt and pepper again, and spoon margarine over the trout as the second side cooks. Remove trout to a hot platter and throw out the cooking margarine.

Return skillet to fire and add ¼ cup of margarine. When it is melted, add mushrooms and bread crumbs and stir well while cooking briskly for about 1 minute. Add white wine, lemon juice, capers, salt and pepper. Taste and correct seasoning if necessary. Simmer the sauce briskly for about 2 minutes, then spoon it over the trout and serve at once.

TRANCHES DE POISSON À LA NIÇOISE

Fish Slices with Tomato Sauce

CHOLESTEROL RATING 2
CALORIES PER SERVING 420

When a dish is prepared *à la Niçoise* it will contain tomatoes, at least, and usually several other pungent ingredients like capers, anchovy, olives, and garlic. This may seem like an unusual dressing for fish, but the combination is a resounding success.

It is best to use fish that can be bought in thick slices and has a firm texture—cod for example—but lacking that, thick filets can also be used—haddock would do nicely. Don't use anything as delicate as sole. Serve with *Pommes de Terre à la Vapeur* (Steamed Potatoes), page 180.

6 servings

4 fresh tomatoes
2 tablespoons polyunsaturated oil
1 tablespoon minced onion
1 garlic clove, crushed
6 to 8 anchovy filets
2 teaspoons tomato paste
2 teaspoons capers
½ teaspoon tarragon
½ teaspoon pepper
¼ cup white wine
1 tablespoon lemon juice
6 slices fresh cod about ½ inch thick
¼ cup flour
oil for frying
salt and pepper
6 anchovy filets and 6 parsley sprigs (optional garnish)

Plunge the tomatoes in boiling water for about 10 seconds. Slip off their skins, cut in half, and squeeze out the seeds and inside pulp. Chop the tomato flesh coarsely. Heat the oil in a saucepan, add the onion, cover, and simmer the onion without browning it for about 10 minutes. Add the chopped tomatoes and the garlic, cover again, and simmer for 15 minutes. Add the anchovy filets (6 for a mild flavor, 8 for full fish flavor), tomato paste, capers, tarragon, pepper (no salt at this point since the anchovies are salty), white wine, and lemon juice. Cover and simmer for 10 minutes more. The anchovies will be dissolved by the heat and give the sauce an interesting but indefinable fish flavor. Taste for seasoning and correct if necessary. The sauce can be made in advance.

Rinse the fish slices and dry on a paper towel. Spread the flour in a dish and lightly flour each fish slice. Pour oil in a skillet to a depth of about ¼ inch, heat well, and add the fish slices. Fry until they are nicely browned on both sides, turn carefully with a spatula. Cooking time will depend on the thickness of the slices, but count on about 2 to 3 minutes for each side. Test with a toothpick to see if the flesh is firm, white, and flaky. Sprinkle with salt and pepper. Remove the fish slices to a serving dish and surround with the hot *Niçoise* sauce. Arrange anchovy filet and 1 sprig of parsley on each slice of fish for decoration.

DARNES DE SAUMON BRAISÉES AU VIN BLANC

Salmon Steaks Braised in White Wine

CHOLESTEROL RATING 2
CALORIES PER SERVING 510

Salmon cooked this way is an impressive main course. The vegetable (mushrooms) is cooked with the fish, and the braising creates a lot of sauce that takes no last-minute additions. All that is needed to complete the meal is some rice, which soaks up the sauce. If absolutely necessary, the salmon steaks can be browned ahead and the braising finished at dinnertime.

6 servings

¾ pound mushrooms, sliced
1¼ cups dry white wine
¼ cup lemon juice
1 tablespoon grated onion
grated rind of 1 lemon
¼ teaspoon salt
½ teaspoon white pepper
pinch of saffron
¼ cup polyunsaturated margarine
2 teaspoons minced parsley
½ teaspoon tarragon
½ teaspoon minced chives
3 tablespoons polyunsaturated margarine
6 salmon steaks, 1 inch thick
½ teaspoon fennel seeds
6 thin lemon slices
1 tablespoon minced parsley

An hour before cooking the fish, slice the mushrooms, put them in a small bowl, and pour the white wine and lemon juice over them. Toss well, cover, and put aside.

Grate the onion into a small saucer, add the grated lemon rind, salt, pepper, and saffron. Prepare the herb sauce by creaming together ¼ cup margarine with the parsley, tarragon, and chives.

Rinse the salmon steaks and dry them on paper towels. All of these steps can be done in advance.

About ½ hour before serving the fish, melt 3 tablespoons of margarine in a large heavy skillet that will hold the fish snugly. Add the onion mixture to the melted margarine and stir for half a minute. Turn up the heat and add the salmon steaks so they brown nicely on both sides, giving them about 2 to 3 minutes per side. Turn carefully with a spatula because they are delicate. Once the salmon steaks are turned, add the herb sauce.

When the steaks are browned, add the mushrooms with the lemon-wine marinade and the fennel seeds. Cover the skillet, turn heat to low, and simmer very slowly for 10 minutes. Simmer for 5 minutes more if the steaks are thicker than 1 inch. Baste several times during the cooking. Remove the cover and place a lemon slice on each piece of salmon, baste some of the sauce over the lemon and cook 5 minutes longer uncovered.

To serve, carefully remove the salmon steaks to a platter or individual serving plates, spoon some of the mushrooms and sauce around them and sprinkle with parsley. Pour the extra sauce into a sauceboat to be passed at the table.

SAUMON À LA NORVÈGE

Fresh Salmon Cured with Dill

CHOLESTEROL RATING 2
CALORIES PER SERVING 200

Here is real one-upmanship over boastful friends who have smoking ovens and think there is nothing more chic than home-smoked salmon. Fresh-cured salmon is even more rare and exotic, and it can't be bought at the neighborhood delicatessen at any price.

The fresh delicacy of the flavor of this salmon is hard to describe, except to say that faces light up at the very first mouthful. All the strong flavors used in the curing slowly mellow into a subtle lusciousness. The salmon is not cooked, but cured with a mixture of kosher salt, sugar, pepper, and dill—all working magic over a 4-day period. All you need then is a very sharp knife and lots of time to carefully remove any remaining bones (which will have softened during the marinating) and to slice as thinly as possible. Serve with thin slices of dark bread, lemon wedges, and Mustard-Dill Sauce (page 238).

8 to 10 servings

2 pounds fresh salmon in 1 piece with bones removed
4 tablespoons black peppercorns
4 tablespoons white peppercorns
4 tablespoons kosher salt
4 tablespoons sugar
2 bunches fresh dill (3 is even better)

Select a glass dish that will hold the salmon rather snugly. Put the black and white peppercorns in the blender and grind until they become coarse bits. Thoroughly mix together the pepper, salt, and sugar to make the curing mixture. Put the salmon in the dish, open it to reveal the inside, and rub liberally with the curing mixture; close the salmon and rub the rest of the pepper mixture all over the outside skin surfaces and the ends. All of the mixture must be used; if some remains, rub it on the inside.

Separate the dill into three parts, spread one part on the bottom of the dish, the other inside the salmon, and the third covering the top. Cover the salmon with a piece of clear plastic wrap, then place a really heavy weight on top of the plastic. The weight should cover as much of the surface of the salmon as possible. Refrigerate for 4 or 5 days. Each day turn over the whole piece of salmon, so both sides of the fish are subject to the pressure of the weight. Each day there will be more liquid in the dish as it is forced out of the salmon. Leave the liquid there.

To serve: Lift the salmon from the salty marinating liquid. Spread lots of newspapers on the countertop and scrape onto them all of the pepper marinade from the inside and outside surfaces of the fish and discard. Discard the dill. Then proceed to cut the fish from the skin in thin slices. Lay the slices directly on the serving platter.

SALMON CAKES

CHOLESTEROL RATING 2
CALORIES PER SERVING 430

These savory fish cakes prove that something special can be made of canned salmon. They make a perfect luncheon dish. Or, made quite small, they can be served as a first course at dinner. A more delicate flavor can be achieved by substituting canned tuna. Unlike most fried foods, these cakes should not be served piping hot. They are much better when warm, and best of all cold.

4 servings

- *1 pound can salmon and its liquid*
- *½ cup dry skimmed-milk cottage cheese*
- *1 medium onion, grated*
- *½ cup fine bread crumbs*
- *1 egg white*
- *1 teaspoon soy sauce*
- *¼ teaspoon each salt and pepper*
- *polyunsaturated oil for frying*

Carefully remove all bones from the canned salmon and place it in a bowl along with its liquid. Mash the salmon well with a fork, adding the cottage cheese as you continue mashing. The mixture should be quite smooth and free of lumps. Mix in the grated onion, bread crumbs, egg white, soy sauce, and salt and pepper. Make certain that everything is well blended. Let the mixture rest at least 15 minutes so the bread crumbs will absorb the liquid and act as a binding ingredient.

Pour oil in frying pan to a depth of ½ inch and heat until quite hot. Take 3 tablespoons of salmon mixture and shape it with your hands into a little flat patty almost ½ inch thick. Repeat. Place patties in hot oil and fry 2 to 3 minutes; turn carefully and fry 2 minutes on other side. The cakes should be a nice brown color. Remove to absorbent paper. There should be 7 to 8 patties.

Pass a bowl of homemade mayonnaise along with the cakes.

THON À LA BORDELAISE

Tuna in Red Wine Sauce

CHOLESTEROL RATING 2
CALORIES PER SERVING 405

Unfortunately, fresh tuna doesn't appear very often in fish markets in the United States. When it does, seize the opportunity to make this extraordinary dish. The tuna has dark flesh, which marries beautifully with the red wine and beef stock in the sauce. And, yes, frozen tuna can be used since the preparation calls for covered cooking in a sauce; only the texture of the fish will not be quite so tender.

6 servings

5 tablespoons polyunsaturated oil
1 medium onion, chopped
3 tablespoons flour
2 cups red wine
1 cup beef bouillon
1 tablespoon meat extract (BV) or 3 beef bouillon cubes
3 shallots, chopped fine
3 garlic cloves, chopped fine
1 tablespoon tomato paste
salt and pepper to taste
2 pounds fresh tuna
herb bouquet (4 parsley sprigs tied around 1 bay leaf)
4 fresh tomatoes
½ pound fresh mushrooms (optional)
18 small white onions (optional)
few drops cognac (optional)

In a casserole or pan that can go into the oven, heat the oil. Then put in the chopped onion and cook slowly, but do not allow to brown. Add the flour, stir with wire whisk, cook a few minutes and then add red wine, bouillon and beef extract (or bouillon cubes). Mix well by whisking constantly, and when thoroughly blended add the shallots, garlic, tomato paste, and salt and pepper.

This will make about 1 quart of sauce. Simmer for 10 minutes then add tuna and the herb bouquet. Spoon a little sauce over the tuna. Add more wine or bouillon if it does not reach half the depth of the tuna slice. Cover and put in a preheated 325° oven for 20 to 25 minutes, depending on the thickness of the tuna.

Meanwhile, peel the tomatoes and cut in thick wedges; 5 minutes before tuna is finished add them to pot. At this point you can also add the mushrooms that have been cut in half and browned in a little oil. If another vegetable is desired, you may add small fresh onions that have been boiled, drained, and browned in a little oil.

When tuna is cooked, remove carefully to a hot platter (the fish is delicate and breaks easily, so use a spatula for removing). Remove skin and bones if desired. If desired, add a few drops of cognac to the sauce, then boil it rapidly to reduce a little. Spoon sauce and vegetables around tuna. Serve with rice, and red wine, of course, even though this is a fish dish. A chilled Beaujolais is best.

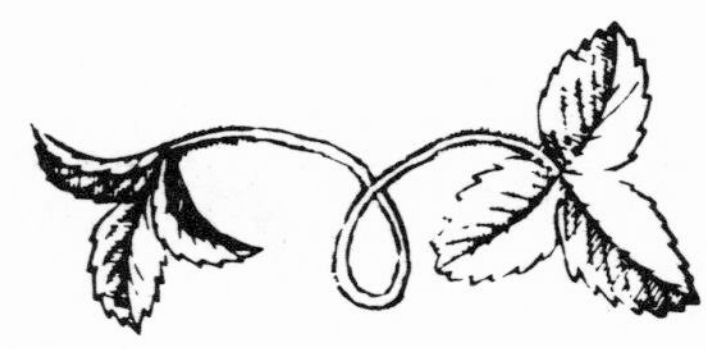

SMOKED HADDOCK SALAD

CHOLESTEROL RATING 2
CALORIES PER SERVING 360

Smoked Haddock Salad is a very unusual first course and one that does not go by unnoticed—its very strong flavor guarantees that. It should not be treated to any sprinklings of parsley or paprika or anything; it needs no help. As economical as this dish is, it goes even further if the cooking liquid is saved and turned into a sort of fish stew that can be the main course of another informal meal. Poach pieces of cod or halibut in the reserved smoke-flavored liquid; do not use a delicate fish since you are working with a strong base. The quantity of the liquid can be increased by adding skimmed milk, and diced boiled potatoes can stretch the stew even further.

6 servings

1 medium onion, sliced thin
1½ pounds smoked haddock
2½ to 3 cups cold skimmed milk
pepper
¾ cup mayonnaise
2 to 3 tablespoons lemon juice
¼ cup bourbon
1½ teaspoons soy sauce
salt and pepper

Select an enameled or copper pot, do not use aluminum or iron. Spread half the sliced onions on the bottom of the pot. Rinse the haddock and place it on top of the onions, then scatter the remaining onions on top of the fish. Pour in the skimmed milk; the amount will depend on the size and shape of the pot, but it should almost cover the fish. Add the pepper. Cover the pot and put it on a very low fire to slowly heat the milk. Once the milk comes to a simmer, reduce the heat, and poach the haddock very slowly for 30 minutes, spooning the milk over it occasionally. Turn off heat and cool the fish in the milk.

Remove the haddock from the liquid and flake the cooked flesh into a bowl, removing any bones or tough outer skin. Make a mayonnaise dressing by mixing the mayonnaise, 2 tablespoons of the lemon juice, bourbon, soy sauce, salt and pepper. Taste. If it seems to lack lemon, add the remaining tablespoon. Pour this dressing over the flaked haddock, mix carefully and well, but do not mash. To serve, line small bowls with crisp lettuce leaves and heap with the prepared haddock.

MORUE MARINÉE

Marinated Smoked Cod

CHOLESTEROL RATING 2
CALORIES PER SERVING 275

This pungent little dish may not sound very *Cordon Bleu,* but it is. Not part of the regular classic study course, to be sure, but one of the pearls that Chef Charles Narcès used to let fall to fill in chopping time. These asides generally ran to bourgeois and home cooking. He was working on a smoked haddock soufflé, which led him to mention that one of the tastiest bits of fish you can put in your mouth, with next to no work at all, is smoked cod that has marinated in a bed of onions. True. Long marinating is important, especially if the fish is kept in a cold refrigerator rather than the cool cellar of a French country house.

I've tried the dish with milder Spanish onions, in deference to onion-timid friends, but it just isn't as good. It is a brand-new way to start off a meal, or if served with cold *Lentilles au Vin Rouge* (Lentils in Red Wine), page 156, or cold *Aubergines à la provençale* (Eggplant Provence Style), page 170, it would make a thoroughly French luncheon.

6 servings as first course

1 pound smoked cod
¾ to 1 cup polyunsaturated oil
2 onions, thinly sliced

Cut the cod into filets about ¼ inch thick. Oil a glass baking dish and arrange a layer of ½ of the filets. Spread ½ the quantity of sliced onions over the fish, then dribble half the oil over the onions. Repeat with the other ½ of the ingredients to make a second layer. Cover tightly and leave in the kitchen for 6 to 12 hours, then put in a cool place (or refrigerator) for one week, or more. Baste occasionally with the oil in the dish.

To serve: Lift the filet from the oil, arrange the filets in the center of a platter surrounded by the onion rings, and pass thinly sliced dark bread. Please don't sprinkle parsley over it for that "touch of color." This is pure fish and pure onion and that's how it should be enjoyed.

MORUE À LA BOULANGÈRE

Smoked Cod with Potatoes and Onions

CHOLESTEROL RATING 2
CALORIES PER SERVING 485

Anytime onions and potatoes appear together in French cooking the dish becomes *à la boulangère,* like the smoked cod here. If fresh cod is used a few anchovy filets can be scattered between the layers to give a snappier flavor. But the smoked cod is so good that nothing has to be added to the recipe. It makes a hearty one-dish dinner.

6 servings

1½ pounds smoked cod
¾ cup polyunsaturated oil
1½ pounds potatoes, thinly sliced
3 cups onions, thinly sliced
freshly ground pepper
powdered basil
1 to 1½ cups skimmed milk

Slice the smoked cod into thin filets and arrange ½ of them in a generously oiled baking dish. Place ½ the potato slices over the cod, then ½ the onion slices. Sprinkle on the pepper, and dribble ½ the oil over the onions.

Repeat with the remaining ingredients, layering cod, potatoes, onions, pepper, and oil. Add a final sprinkling of basil over the top. Pour in enough skimmed milk to reach almost to the top of the onions. Bake uncovered in a 350° oven for about 1 hour or until the potatoes are soft and can be pierced with a sharp knife. Baste often with a bulb baster during the cooking to keep the top layer moist and to blend the cod's smoky flavor into the vegetables.

5

POULTRY

CHICKEN IS A FREQUENT VISITOR TO THE LOW-CHOLESTEROL DINING TABLE, which is no hardship at all. It offers us tasty meat that is always available and comparatively cheap.

Chicken is also wonderfully adaptable. If it is freshly killed, it needs nothing more than plain roasting. But any lower-quality bird (which usually means one bought in a supermarket) can be improved with braising and sauces.

The recipes that follow offer chicken in many guises. The hope is that the family will accept it more often. You can switch from hot to cold presentations, or try the low-cholesterol chicken pâté for something quite new. And for a complete change, there is a chicken-and-veal sausage (*Boudin Blanc*) in the Luncheon chapter.

It was Henri IV who first promised a chicken in every pot, showing that even in sixteenth-century France the way to the citizenry's heart was at the table. It is still a good approach, especially now that chickens are so much better.

Somewhere along the line a rule was set down that white meats and poultry require white wine. It is a rule most gourmets choose to ignore. They find that red wine is more appropriate with these foods of definite character and texture. A light Bordeaux, like Médoc, is what the French usually serve with chicken. One could choose California's Cabernet Sauvignon as a change, or stay in native character when serving chicken in the Italian *Cacciatore* style and pour red Chianti. If white wine is a strong preference, then it should be a full white Burgundy like Meursault.

VOLAILLES EN ESCABÈCHE

Poultry in Lemon Aspic

CHOLESTEROL RATING 2
CALORIES PER SERVING 425

This is a beautiful cold aspic dish for summertime eating. *Escabèche,* Spanish in origin, refers to the lemon-vinegar jelly produced by the cooking.

Like most aspic dishes, the *escabèche* is best prepared at least a day ahead. Two is even better. This allows the flavors to mature and mellow. When selecting a dish for the mold, pick one that fits a serving platter when turned upside down. A fairly deep, round bowl gives the best effect when the aspic is finished. Any sort of fowl can be used. The best, though, are those that are a bit older and larger—they won't disintegrate during the long cooking. You will notice that the whole garlic cloves are not removed, but have no fear; the long cooking turns them quite mushy and sweet.

Serving cold *escabèche* as the main course gives you a chance for a change of pace in planning the menu. A hot dish to begin with could be Mushrooms in Creamy Sour Sauce (page 41) or Stuffed Mushrooms and Grilled Tomatoes (page 188). If it's not a blistering day, a hot dessert could also be served, like Fruit Kebabs (page 198) or Baked Peaches (page 200).

Don't be frightened by the length of the directions. I have been very explicit because I know this may be a new kind of dish for most people. It won't be for long; it usually becomes a hot-weather favorite.

8 servings

2 onions
3 celery stalks
4 large carrots
1 lemon, sliced and seeded
½ red pepper (or 4-ounce jar pimento)
2 green peppers
½ cup polyunsaturated oil
6 to 8 garlic cloves
salt and pepper
1 3-to-4-pound stewing chicken, cut in pieces
1 teaspoon coriander seeds (or 2 teaspoons ground coriander)
2 lemons, sliced and seeded
1 cup dry white vermouth (or 1½ cups dry white wine)
2 tablespoons wine vinegar
2 to 3 cups chicken broth, degreased
1 to 2 tablespoons gelatin
parsley leaves

Slice in even thin slices the onions, celery, carrots, and 1 lemon. The red and green peppers should be sliced in long strips. (If you are using pimento instead of red pepper, it is not used at this point.) Heat the oil in a heavy casserole that can go into the oven, and add the sliced vegetables, the lemon, and the garlic. Cover and simmer very slowly for about 20 minutes or until the vegetables are quite limp, but not browned at all. Sprinkle on a little salt and pepper.

With a slotted spoon remove ⅔ of the vegetables, spreading the remainder evenly in the bottom of the pot. On this place a layer of chicken pieces, using ½ the quantity of chicken. Spread on ½ of the remaining sautéed vegetables. Sprinkle on salt, pepper, coriander, and ½ the uncooked lemon. If pimento is being used instead of red pepper, put some of it in now, cut in thin strips; reserve the pimento juice from the jar. Repeat again with the rest of the chicken and the remaining vegetables, condiments, and lemon slices.

Mix the vermouth (it is preferable to white wine) with the vinegar and pimento juice, if any. Pour this liquid over the chicken, and then pour on enough chicken broth to bring the level of the liquid to where it almost completely covers the ingredients. Use as much liquid as possible so that you will end up with a good bit of aspic.

Bring the liquid to a slow simmer on top of the stove, then place a piece of greased paper or aluminum foil over the chicken and vegetables. Cover with the lid, and place in a 350° oven. Keep at a slow simmer until pieces of chicken are fork tender (about 2 hours, depending on the quality and toughness of the fowl). Remove from oven, uncover, and cool.

Place the chicken pieces in a colander over a deep dish to gather the liquid as it drips. Do the same with the cooked vegetables. Combine this drained stock with the rest of the stock. Chill so that the fat rises to top. Remove the fat. Taste the liquid for salt.

Depending on the jellied consistency of the stock (the bones of the chicken will already have thickened the stock somewhat), add the amount of gelatin necessary.

If the stock is slightly jellied add only one tablespoon of gelatin for each pint. Use a little more rather than less gelatin since there will be some dilution of the aspic from the liquid that remains in the chicken and vegetables. Soften the gelatin in a little water and then heat it thoroughly in the stock until it dissolves. Cool.

When the chicken is cool enough to handle, remove the meat from the bones, discarding the skin and bones. Separate the meat into pieces.

Cook the parsley leaves in rapidly boiling water for 5 to 10 seconds, drain, and plunge immediately into cold water to preserve the deep green color. Drain again and dry on paper towels.

In a round bowl a decoration is now made out of the parsley leaves and the cooked vegetables. Make circles of different colors, or any regular pattern, by placing the assorted vegetables in the bottom of the bowl and along its sides as well. Remember you are working from the outside in, so to speak, since this first layer will form the presentation side when unmolded. Put layers of chicken pieces in the bowl, alternating with layers of the rest of the cooked vegetables. When all is used, pour in enough jelly stock to cover everything and chill well.

At serving time reverse onto a chilled platter. The various vegetable colors held in the lemon aspic is a cool and lovely sight. To slice use a very sharp knife with a sawing motion. Serve with tossed green salad.

POULE AU POT or PETITE MARMITE

Chicken in a Pot

CHOLESTEROL RATING 2
CALORIES PER SERVING 385

Since the time of Henri IV, the French have known the excellence of good chicken, simply prepared. Just a few extra flavors are added to this wonderful Sunday kind of dish that elevates humble boiled chicken to festive dining.

Poule is an old hen, generally a tough bird that needs long, slow cooking; its flavor is better for this dish than a young chicken's. If you can't find a real *poule,* cook the neck, wing, feet, and giblets of your chicken with the beef, adding the chicken itself for the last hour.

8 servings

1 pound lean chuck, with bones
1 3-to-4-pound boiling chicken
2 quarts chicken stock (canned or prepared with bouillon cubes)
cold water
1 cup sliced carrots
½ cup sliced turnips
½ cup sliced celery
½ head cabbage, cut in
1 onion stuck with 2 cloves
4 medium onions, cut in half
3 medium potatoes, quartered
quarters (optional)
herb bouquet (6 parsley sprigs tied around 2 bay leaves)
salt and pepper

Cut meat into 2-inch cubes and plunge into boiling salted water for a few minutes; drain, and put in a large enameled or earthenware pot. Add the chicken, stock, and enough cold water to almost cover the chicken. Slowly bring to a boil, skimming off the foam that rises.

When all foam has subsided, add the vegetables, herb bouquet, and salt and pepper. (If cabbage is included, it is better to cook it separately and add at the end, to heat it.) Cover and simmer very gently for 4 hours. The slow cooking is all-important.

Remove meat and vegetables, discarding the herb bouquet and the clove-studded onion. Strain the broth and let it cool so the fat will rise and can be easily removed. Cut the chicken into serving pieces and return to the pot along with the meat, vegetables, cabbage if included, and broth. Reheat thoroughly. Serve directly from the pot, ladling broth, vegetables, and meats directly into deep soup bowls.

COQ AU VIN

Chicken in Red Wine

CHOLESTEROL RATING 2
CALORIES PER SERVING 520

Even though this popular dish is called *Coq au Vin,* it really isn't. A *coq* is an old chicken that requires long, slow cooking. Few housewives make a point of looking for them. Instead, most use tender young chickens. Even with young chicken the results will still be good if the preparation is altered so that the sauce is cooked for a few hours before the chicken is added. This is done to cook the wine properly. Traditionally, chunks of bacon are used in the sauce, but I find they make the flavor a little coarse. The dish is better and healthier without bacon.

Coq au Vin should be prepared at least two days before being served. This gives the chicken a chance to completely absorb the flavors of the sauce. In fact, I have found that an intermediary reheating helps immeasurably. Reheat the finished dish very slowly, then simmer about 10 minutes before cooling it and returning to the refrigerator. You won't believe the difference it makes.

Vegetables to serve with *Coq au Vin* could be *Pommes de Terre à la Vapeur* (Steamed Potatoes) (page 180) and browned white onions (page 174).

6 servings

1 3-pound chicken, cut in serving pieces
½ to ⅔ cup polyunsaturated oil for frying chicken
salt and pepper
½ cup cognac
few drops gravy color (Kitchen Bouquet)
¼ cup flour mixed with 6 tablespoons cold water

SAUCE

¼ cup polyunsaturated oil
1½ onions, thinly sliced
chicken giblets, neck, wings
5 cups red wine
1 cup beef bouillon
2 garlic cloves, minced
1½ bay leaves
¼ teaspoon thyme
1 tablespoon sugar
2 tablespoons tomato paste
salt and pepper

SAUCE PREPARATION

Heat the oil in a heavy saucepan, add sliced onions, cover, and simmer slowly, about 10 minutes, until the onions are soft. Add the chicken giblets, neck, and wings, turn up the heat and sauté until the chicken parts have browned nicely. Add the wine, beef bouillon, garlic, bay leaves, thyme, sugar, tomato paste, salt, and pepper. Mix well, cover, and let simmer over a very low flame for at least 2 hours, 3 being even better. Skim off any foam that may rise during the cooking. Strain sauce, chill it, and remove any fat that rises to the top.

Rinse the serving pieces of chicken and dry on a paper towel. Heat about ⅓ cup oil in a heavy skillet, add pieces, a few at a time, and brown evenly all over. Keep adding oil as needed. While frying chicken, sprinkle salt and pepper on both sides.

Place browned chicken pieces in a deep heavy pot (preferably not aluminum) and pour in the cognac. Once the cognac is hot, ignite with a match and shake pot vigorously to permit the flames to reach all sides of the chicken. Pour the strained, degreased wine sauce over the chicken. Sprinkle on salt, pepper, and a few drops of gravy color to darken the sauce. Cover and simmer for 35 to 40 minutes, or until chicken is fork tender. Mix flour and water to a smooth paste, add it a little at a time to the simmering sauce and chicken. When the sauce has thickened a little, let it simmer another 5 minutes. The sauce should be about the consistency of very heavy cream. Cool and refrigerate.

The next day remove any fat that has come to the surface. Reheat the *Coq au Vin* slowly again, simmer 10 minutes, cool, and return to refrigerator for at least one more day. At serving time reheat slowly and thoroughly. Arrange chicken pieces on a platter, spoon some sauce over them and pass a sauceboat with extra sauce.

POULET AU CÉLERI

Chicken with Celery

CHOLESTEROL RATING 2
CALORIES PER SERVING 380

No matter how many different chicken dishes you may have eaten, I am willing to bet that this celery combination will be a new one, and one that is sure to become a favorite. You will find that the fresh taste of the celery gives the sauce a very light quality that never seems heavy, even to the most finicky eater.

A few tomatoes are included in the sauce, and the quantity indicated should not be increased. The sauce is mainly a celery sauce and should remain pleasingly pale in color. An easy way to handle the vegetable accompaniment is to put small peeled potatoes to cook in the sauce while it is being reduced. This recipe calls for a long, slow simmering preparation and a cooling of the sauce for degreasing, so it should be started well in advance, or even the day before.

6 servings

1 large bunch of celery
2 teaspoons of salt
¼ cup polyunsaturated oil
1 3-pound chicken, trussed as for roasting
3 onions, minced
salt and pepper
3 ripe tomatoes (or 1 pound can Italian plum tomatoes, drained)
1 teaspoon tomato paste mixed with 2 tablespoons water (optional)
1½ pounds small, peeled potatoes (optional)

Cut off the leaves from the celery and pull the celery stalks apart. With a small sharp knife scrape off the very coarse, heavy fibers on the outside of the larger stalks; the smaller interior stalks will not need any scraping. Cut the celery into 4-inch-long pieces. Meanwhile, bring a large quantity of water to a fast boil, add the salt and the celery pieces. Cook at a fast simmer for 15 minutes, drain and put under cold running water. The celery should still be a little crisp.

While the celery is simmering, pour the oil into a heavy casserole and heat. Dry the chicken and place it in the hot oil to brown on all sides. Once it is nicely browned, remove the chicken and add the minced onions, stirring the onions well with the oil and juices in the pot. Lower the heat, cover, and simmer for 5 minutes or until the onions are limp and take on a light golden color. Return the chicken to the casserole and sprinkle with salt and pepper. Place the celery pieces all over and around the chicken. If using fresh tomatoes, plunge in hot water, slip off the skin, and cut in half. Gently squeeze out the seeds and juice, then lightly crush the tomatoes with your hands and spread them on top of the chicken and celery. If the tomatoes are not of good quality, or if canned tomatoes are used, add the tomato paste mixed with water. Cover and simmer slowly for 1 to 1¼ hours, until tender.

Remove the chicken and reduce the sauce by simmering briskly for about 1 hour. The celery will have given off a lot of liquid that needs to be thickened, and it is better to achieve this reduction by evaporation than by adding flour, which would make a heavier sauce. It is at this point that you can add small potatoes to cook. When the sauce has thickened, remove it from the fire, cool, and skim off any fat that rises to the surface.

Up to this point the dish can be prepared ahead of time, even the day before. When you are ready to serve, cut the chicken into serving pieces, return them to a pot with the sauce and simmer slowly until the sauce and chicken are thoroughly reheated. Put the chicken in the center of a platter and surround it with celery pieces and sauce, as well as the potatoes if they were included.

PÓLLO ALLA CACCIATÓRE

Italian Hunter's-Style Chicken

CHOLESTEROL RATING 2
CALORIES PER SERVING 570

Every Italian housewife has her own way of preparing *Póllo alla Cacciatóre,* but this is one of the easiest and one of the best. I like to prepare it the day before and reheat it when needed. Fingers get licked with this dish. Serve with plain rice and a crisp tossed salad, just as they would in Italy. Chianti would complete the picture.

6 servings

5 pounds cut-up chicken
salt and pepper
1 to 1½ cups polyunsaturated oil
2 garlic cloves
1 onion, chopped fine
1 2-pound 3-ounce can Italian plum tomatoes
12 ounces canned Italian tomato paste
1 cup dry white wine
1 teaspoon sugar
½ teaspoon caraway seeds
¼ teaspoon cinnamon
2 bay leaves

Rinse chicken pieces and dry them thoroughly on paper towels. (Caution: if not dried properly, the chicken will splatter excessively while frying.) Season the chicken with salt and pepper on both sides. In a heavy skillet, heat 1 cup of the oil with the garlic until the garlic cloves turn dark brown and the oil is quite hot. Remove the garlic and brown the chicken pieces a few at a time, starting with the skin side down, turning to brown the other side. Remove the browned chicken to a platter. Add more oil as necessary.

Pour into a deep, heavy pot ¼ cup of the oil used for browning the chicken, heat it slowly and add the onion. Cover and simmer slowly for 5 minutes, or until the onions are limp. Add the canned tomatoes, tomato paste, white wine, sugar, caraway seeds, cinnamon, and bay leaves. Cover and simmer slowly for about 20 minutes.

Add the chicken pieces to the sauce, cover and simmer gently until the chicken is tender, about 45 minutes. Remove the bay leaves and arrange the chicken pieces on a large platter with the sauce liberally spooned over them.

POULET GRILLÉ À LA DIABLE

Broiled Chicken with Mustard Coating

CHOLESTEROL RATING 2
CALORIES PER SERVING 475

Cooking chicken ahead for a dinner party doesn't mean that it has to be a stew of some kind. Crisp and spicy *Poulet Grillé à la Diable* is a more interesting presentation, and it can be done in advance except for the final broiling.

In France, melted butter is used to coat the chicken pieces. But once butter is used with an ingredient as powerful as Dijon mustard, the delicacy of its flavor is completely lost, and oil does nicely. However, the quality of the mustard is important. If Dijon mustard itself isn't used, at least a Dijon-type, or hot, mustard should be. If, by any chance, some chicken is left on the platter, it will make an equally delicious treat when served cold.

8 servings

8 large pieces of chicken, breast or leg
polyunsaturated oil
6 tablespoons strong Dijon mustard
3 tablespoons finely minced shallots
½ teaspoon dried tarragon
½ teaspoon powdered thyme
⅛ teaspoon cayenne pepper
1 teaspoon Worcestershire sauce
3 to 4 cups bread crumbs

Preheat broiler to moderately hot. Place chicken pieces on the rack, skin side down, and sprinkle oil over each piece. Place rack under broiler, about 5 inches away from heat, and broil for 10 minutes (after the first five minutes sprinkle on oil again). Turn chicken pieces and repeat the process on the other side. Remove from oven.

Meanwhile, blend together the mustard, shallots, tarragon, thyme, cayenne pepper, and Worcestershire sauce. Take about ½ cup of the oil drippings from the broiling pan and beat into the mustard mixture. Reserve the rest of the oil drippings.

Put the bread crumbs in a large dish. Then, with a pastry brush, paint each piece of chicken thoroughly until every bit is covered with the mustard mixture. Put the chicken in the bread-crumb dish and carefully pat a thick coating of crumbs over the entire surface. Return the chicken pieces to the broiling rack, again skin side down, and try to let them dry for at least 15 minutes. This much can be prepared ahead of time and refrigerated.

At broiling time, dribble ½ of the reserved drippings over the chicken pieces, place in the broiler, but a little farther away from the heating element this time, about 6 to 7 inches. After 5 minutes dribble on some fresh oil, return for five more minutes. Turn and repeat the process for the other side, using all the drippings you have saved. The chicken is done when the drumstick is tender to the touch, or when juices run clear yellow when meat is pierced with a fork. It is important to have the chicken just done. If overcooked, the meat tends to dry out.

POULET OLGA

Grilled Chicken with Herbs

CHOLESTEROL RATING 2
CALORIES PER SERVING 445

French and Italian chickens have traditionally been of much finer quality and taste than our own, but mass production is beginning to take its flavor toll there, too. An Italian friend, unhappy with American chickens, tried a special recipe of her mother's on frozen supermarket chicken. The results were memorable. Her mother used cognac, but we both feel that whiskey produces an even better flavor, and in a way a less rich one.

There are two ways to do the cooking; on a heavy grill with ridges (the kind some people use for frying bacon) or in a heavy skillet. The ridged grill is better since the chicken comes out crisper, but the flavor is just as good in the skillet.

4 servings

1 3-pound chicken
1 garlic clove
3 tablespoons polyunsaturated oil
salt and pepper
1 teaspoon sage
1 teaspoon rosemary
1 lemon
3 tablespoons whiskey (straight or blended) or cognac
2 tablespoons polyunsaturated oil

Have the chicken split down the back so that it lies flat. This is done by inserting a small sharp knife right beside the tail and cutting along the spine. Remove any visible fat from inside the chicken. Slice the garlic clove very thin, then make small incisions all over the chicken, both inside and on the skin side, and insert the garlic pieces. Rub 3 tablespoons of oil all over both sides of the chicken. Then sprinkle generously with salt and pepper. Mix the sage and rosemary together and crush to almost a powder. Smear this herb mixture all over both sides of the chicken. Lay the chicken flat on its back in a large dish and sprinkle the juice of one lemon and the whiskey over it. Cover and let marinate for 2 or 3 hours. Turn and marinate another 2 or 3 hours.

Heat the oil in either a ridged grill or a heavy skillet, large enough to take the flat split chicken. When quite hot, put in the chicken, skin side down, to brown thoroughly. Turn and brown the underside. Spoon a few tablespoons of the marinade over the chicken, turn down heat to very low, cover, and cook very slowly for about 40 minutes. Turn the chicken 3 or 4 times during the cooking and baste from time to time. (The cooking can be done in a 350° oven, following the same procedure.) Cut into serving pieces.

This same recipe can be used for Rock Cornish game hens, allowing one per person and reducing the cooking time to 25 minutes.

SUPRÊMES DE VOLAILLE

Breast of Chicken

Suprêmes de Volaille, in any guise at all, is one of the most elegant dishes that you can serve. They are perfect for small dinner parties. There is something terribly pure about having just the pale kernel of meat that comes from the chicken breast. Americans have an advantage over the French this time, because poultry men here are used to boning the raw breasts for you. Some supermarkets won't do it, but that presents little problem, since you can buy the chicken breasts separately and remove the meat yourself with a good sharp knife. The skin must also be removed.

One word of caution about *Suprêmes de Volaille*—they must not be overcooked. And that means precision timing, since they are cooked in a matter of minutes. Once you know how little time it takes, you can approach the cooking with confidence. In a hot 400° oven, they are cooked in 6 to 8 minutes. Sautéing in a pan will take a minute or so less. To test for doneness, press the center of a *suprême* with your finger. If the meat is soft and fleshy, it is not done; but as soon as the meat springs back and is slightly resistant to the touch, it is cooked perfectly.

Both methods for cooking the *suprêmes*—in the oven and on the stove—are given below with variations for each. Don't feel limited to these, though; this dish will live up to any garnish you want to use.

All recipes are for 6 servings.

SUPRÊMES DE VOLAILLE POCHÉES

Poached Chicken Breasts

CHOLESTEROL RATING 2
CALORIES PER SERVING 142

In classic French cooking, the *suprêmes* are not usually poached, but I have found that American chickens come out of the oven tastier and more mellow if some liquid is included in the baking dish.

6 raw chicken breasts, boned and skinned
2 tablespoons polyunsaturated margarine
½ lemon
salt and pepper
2 tablespoons dry white wine
½ cup chicken bouillon

Trim the chicken breasts of all skin, fat, and membranes. Using 1 tablespoon of the margarine, liberally grease a baking dish that will hold the 6 *suprêmes* snugly. Place the *suprêmes* in the dish and immediately squeeze a few drops of lemon juice on each one. Sprinkle salt and pepper over the meat, then pour in the wine and chicken bouillon. Cut the remaining tablespoon of margarine into bits and scatter over the breasts. Cover the dish closely, and place in 400° oven for about 6 minutes. Check at that point for doneness *(see above)*. If they are not quite finished, return for just a minute or so more.

Serving Variations for Poached *Suprêmes de Volaille:*

SUPRÊMES DE VOLAILLE À BLANC

Chicken Breasts with White Sauce

CHOLESTEROL RATING 2
CALORIES PER SERVING 175

6 chicken breasts poached (see *master recipe above)*

2 tablespoons flour
3 tablespoons cold water
¼ cup skimmed-milk powder
2 tablespoons cold water
½ teaspoon cognac
½ teaspoon soy sauce
salt and pepper
Poached Mushrooms for garnish (page 173)

Remove poached *suprêmes* to a serving platter and keep warm. Skim off from the poaching liquid as much of the fat as possible. Then pour the remaining liquid into a small saucepot and put on a low fire. Mix the flour with 3 tablespoons of water and add ½ of this to the sauce while stirring with a wire whisk. Mix the skimmed milk powder with 2 tablespoons of water and add to the sauce. If the sauce does not seem thick enough, add more of the flour-water mixture. Season with cognac, soy sauce, salt and pepper. Taste carefully and correct if necessary. Give the sauce one good boil, then spoon it over the *suprêmes*. Have sliced poached mushrooms ready and reheated. Remove them with a skimmer from the pot and scatter them over the chicken.

SUPRÊMES DE VOLAILLE À LA PÉRIGUEUX

Poached Chicken Breasts with Truffle Sauce

CHOLESTEROL RATING 2
CALORIES PER SERVING 282

I have heard some teacher-chefs claim that a good truffle sauce can be made with a superior brand of brown gravy, to which you add Madeira and truffles. I've tried enough of the canned brown gravies to reply that there is no such thing as a superior brand, not even a good one. To my way of thinking, it is a crime to waste expensive truffles on canned gravy. In France, some good small brands of prepared truffle sauce are available, and you may be lucky enough to find one in your fine food shop. Even the best of these canned sauces, though, must be helped along with Madeira and truffle additions. The only other, and the best, way around the problem is to start from scratch with your own brown sauce. It is truly worth it. Served with wild rice, *Suprêmes de Volaille à la Périgueux* is pure luxury.

6 poached chicken breasts (see *master recipe)*

½ cup Madeira or port
2 or 3 canned black truffles and their juice
2 cups brown sauce (page 235)
1 teaspoon meat extract like BV (optional)

Pour the Madeira or port into a saucepan with the juice from the truffles. Boil rapidly until reduced by ½. Add the brown sauce to this reduction and simmer gently. Taste carefully for seasonings, wine, and strength of the sauce. If it seems a little thin, add the meat extract. While the sauce is simmering, slice the truffles and add at the very end. Spoon the sauce over the poached *suprêmes.*

SUPRÊMES DE VOLAILLE À LA FLORENTINE

Poached Chicken Breasts with Spinach

CHOLESTEROL RATING 2
CALORIES PER SERVING 220

6 poached chicken breasts (see *master recipe)*

Spinach Purée (page 187)
White Sauce (page 102)

Make a bed of the spinach purée in the serving platter and arrange the poached *suprêmes* on top of this bed. Spoon the White Sauce over the *suprêmes.*

SUPRÊMES DE VOLAILLE AUX CHAMPIGNONS

Poached Chicken Breasts with Mushrooms

CHOLESTEROL RATING 2
CALORIES PER SERVING 218

6 poached chicken breasts (see *master recipe)*

Poached Mushrooms (page 173)
White Sauce (page 102)

Instead of the white wine used in the master recipe for the poaching liquid, substitute 2 tablespoons of the liquid from the poached mushrooms. Proceed as for *Suprêmes de Volaille à Blanc,* but substitute the mushroom liquid for water in the sauce recipe. Spoon the sauce over the poached chicken breasts and garnish with sliced poached mushrooms.

SUPRÊMES DE VOLAILLE À BRUNE

Sautéed Chicken Breasts

CHOLESTEROL RATING 2
CALORIES PER SERVING 295

6 raw chicken breasts, boned and skinned
¾ cup flour
½ to ¾ cup polyunsaturated margarine
1 tablespoon polyunsaturated oil
salt and pepper

Spread the flour in a dish and roll the *suprêmes* in the flour. Shake off excess flour. Meanwhile, heat half the margarine and oil in a large heavy skillet. When the margarine is hot and foaming, put in as many chicken breasts as the skillet will hold without crowding. Fry quickly, 2 to 3 minutes on each side (*see* cooking note in master recipe). Once the chicken breasts are turned, sprinkle on salt and pepper. As soon as they are done, remove to a serving platter and continue sautéing the other breasts, adding more margarine and oil as needed.

SUPRÊMES DE VOLAILLE AU JUS

Sautéed Chicken Breasts with Cooking Juices

CHOLESTEROL RATING 2
CALORIES PER SERVING 335

*6 sautéed chicken breasts (*see *master recipe)*

½ cup dry white wine
½ cup strong chicken bouillon
2 tablespoons polyunsaturated margarine
salt and pepper

Pour out the cooking fat from the skillet and add the wine and chicken bouillon. Return to a fast fire and scrape coagulated juices from the bottom while the sauce simmers rapidly. When the liquid has reduced by ⅓, add the margarine, salt and pepper, bring to one good boil and spoon over the cooked *suprêmes.*

SUPRÊMES DE VOLAILLE STELLA

Sautéed Chicken Breasts with Tomato Sauce

CHOLESTEROL RATING 2
CALORIES PER SERVING 540

*6 sautéed chicken breasts (*see *master recipe)*

1½ cups Coulis de Tomates *(page 236)*
Petit Pois Filippo *(page 177)*
grated low-fat Parmesan cheese (optional)

Arrange sautéed *suprêmes* on a serving platter, and spoon half the hot *coulis* sauce over them. Carefully spoon the peas around the *suprêmes.* Pass the extra sauce separately.

SUPRÊMES DE VOLAILLE AUX DUXELLES

Sautéed Chicken Breasts with Minced Mushrooms

CHOLESTEROL RATING 2
CALORIES PER SERVING 420

6 sautéed chicken breasts (see *master recipe)*

1½ cups mushroom duxelles *(page 39)*
½ to ¾ cup dry white wine
1 teaspoon cognac

Make a pocket in each *suprême* and fill it with *duxelles.* Close the opening with a toothpick. Then roll the stuffed *suprême* in the flour and proceed to sauté as in the master recipe (*Suprêmes de Volaille à Brune*). Remove the toothpicks from the cooked *suprêmes* and arrange them on a serving platter and keep warm. Pour off the cooking grease and add to the skillet ½ cup of wine, the cognac, and the remaining *duxelles.* Boil the sauce rapidly for a few minutes until it thickens. Add more wine if you would like a thinner sauce. Spoon the sauce generously over the stuffed *suprêmes.*

SUPRÊMES DE VOLAILLE AU JAMBON

Sautéed Chicken Breasts with Ham

CHOLESTEROL RATING 2
CALORIES PER SERVING 365

6 sautéed chicken breasts (see *master recipe)*

3 slices boiled ham
½ cup dry white wine
½ cup beef broth
2 tablespoons polyunsaturated margarine
salt and pepper

Slice each *suprême* in half horizontally and place ½ slice of ham between the two chicken slices. Close both sides of the *suprême* with toothpicks. Proceed to flour and sauté as in the master recipe (*Suprêmes de Volaille à Brune*). Remove toothpicks from the sautéed *suprêmes* and arrange the chicken on a serving platter, keeping it warm. Pour out the cooking grease from the skillet and add the wine and beef broth. Return to a fast fire and scrape coagulated juices from the bottom while the sauce simmers rapidly. When the liquid has reduced by ⅓, add the margarine, salt and pepper. Bring the sauce to one good boil and spoon over the cooked *suprêmes.*

SUPRÊMES PAMELA

Chicken Breasts with Duxelles Sauce

CHOLESTEROL RATING 2
CALORIES PER SERVING 210

This chicken dish was created for an extraordinary lady who knows fine food but eats none of the usual sauces. She declared that this solution gave her the best of both worlds. For Pamela.

6 servings

6 raw chicken breasts, boned and skinned
salt and pepper
¾ to 1 cup dry white wine
1¼ cups duxelles *(page 39)*

Cut the chicken breasts into long strips about ¼ inch thick and place in a heavy enameled or copper skillet. Sprinkle with salt and pepper and pour over enough wine to almost cover the chicken slices. This should take about ¾ cup. Cover the skillet closely with aluminum foil, then place a lid over the foil. Put the skillet on a low fire and very slowly and carefully simmer the chicken until it stiffens and turns almost white, but still with a blush of pink. This will take no more than 2 minutes once the wine reaches the simmering point. Remove the chicken slices with a skimmer and keep warm.

Add the *duxelles* to the wine in the skillet and stir all together. The *duxelles* will absorb most of the wine; if it seems a little thick, add another ¼ cup of wine. Return the chicken to the *duxelles* sauce, give one good boil and serve at once. Serve with rice and grilled tomatoes.

PÂTÉ DE POULET

Chicken Pâté

CHOLESTEROL RATING 3
CALORIES PER SERVING 175

It is hard to eat French pâtés and terrines without being guiltily aware of the enormous amount of fat they contain, most of it pork fat. As much as we all love pâté, the pleasure vanishes in thinking of how horribly they rate on the cholesterol scale. Producing a low-cholesterol pâté worthy of being called pâté became a challenge. Even people who like eating high on the hog praise this version.

A tiny bit of chicken liver is added for its strong aroma (¼ pound spread through 10 servings is not a lot), and it should be used except for the strictest diet.

Don't be timid about trying to make pâté; the procedure is quite easy. You might even add the festive touch of pistachio nuts sprinkled between the layers; the pale green color is pretty when cut.

In France, arguments rage over whether to cool a baked pâté under a weight or not. One school holds that the pressure produces a pâté with firmer and closer texture, one easier to cut. The other school says forget neat slicing and don't squeeze out juices and fat. For low-cholesterol pâtés, the weights must be used both for texture and for the removal of excess fat.

Pâté de Poulet can make a most elegant first course for a gala dinner, or it may be served as a main course following a hot first course.

10 servings

2 pounds chicken meat, dark and light
4 ounces chicken livers (about 4 livers) (optional)
3 shallots, finely chopped
salt and pepper
¼ teaspoon allspice
¼ teaspoon ground basil
½ teaspoon ground coriander
¼ cup Madeira
¼ cup dry white wine
2 parsley sprigs
2 bay leaves
1½ cups sliced onions
3 tablespoons polyunsaturated margarine
2 slices white bread
3 egg whites
2 tablespoons melted polyunsaturated margarine
¼ cup shelled pistachio nuts (optional)

Remove all bits of fat, skin, and nerves from the chicken meat. Take a little less than ¼ the quantity of meat and cut it into long strips about ¼ inch wide (the breast meat is best for this). Put these filets in a small bowl. Cut the rest of the chicken meat into pieces and put it in another bowl with the chicken livers. Then sprinkle all the following seasonings on the meats in the two bowls, giving a larger share to the bowl with chicken pieces and livers—chopped shallots, salt and pepper, allspice, basil, and coriander. Pour the Madeira over the breast filets and the white wine over the other meat. Mix up the contents of each bowl with your fingers. Tuck the parsley and bay leaves into the bowl with the pieces. Marinate at least 3 hours, and turn the meat from time to time.

Meanwhile, in a small covered pan, simmer the onions slowly in 3 tablespoons of margarine.

After the marinating period, remove the parsley and bay leaves from among the chicken pieces. Lift the pieces out of the marinade and put them through the finest blade of a grinder with the cooked onions. Pass the ground mixture through the grinder once again, and put through the grinder last of all the bread slices. By grinding the bread last you are sure that all the other ingredients have been worked through. Combine the marinade from the two dishes, put in a small pan and boil briskly to reduce by half, and add to the ground mixture. Melt two tablespoons of margarine in the same pan and add it, too, to the ground mixture. Add the egg whites, and beat well with a wooden spoon. Fry a teaspoon of this mixture, let it cool, and taste for seasoning. Correct if necessary.

Oil a 6-cup pâté mold well and put ⅓ of the ground mixture in it. Over this place rows of the breast filets, using half the quantity, and sprinkle on some pistachio nuts, if desired. Repeat with the ground mixture, filets, and nuts. Finish with the last ⅓ of the ground mixture.

Put the cover on the mold. Place a piece of aluminum foil over the cover. Pierce a hole in the foil over the vent hole in the mold cover. Place in a pan and pour in enough water to reach about halfway up the side of the mold. Bring the water to a slow boil on the stove, then place in a 350° oven. The water in the pan should simmer very slowly. Bake for about 1¼ hours. Test by inserting a skewer through the vent hole to the center of the pâté, remove and touch it to the inside of your wrist—if hot, the pâté is finished.

Remove the pâté mold from the pan of water and let it cool for 15 minutes. Remove the mold cover. Cover the pâté with aluminum foil and place a heavy weight on it, covering as much of the surface as possible with the weight. Almost anything will do for a weight—heavy copper pots, dishes filled with marbles, even cans of fruit juice. Cool overnight with the weights in place. Pour off the accumulated juices, then refrigerate for one day with the weights. Let the pâté mature in the refrigerator for at least 3 days before serving.

To serve, remove the pâté to a platter and garnish with watercress. Slice with a very sharp knife, using a sawing motion.

MOUSSE DE FOIES DE VOLAILLE

Chicken Liver Mousse

CHOLESTEROL RATING 4
CALORIES PER SERVING 205

Chicken livers are not meant to be a regular item on a low-cholesterol diet. Their occasional appearance on the dining table does make good sense, though, when they are tasty enough to take the place of some other treat that would be far higher in cholesterol.

Traditional French mousses absorb a lot of cream and butter in the making. This recipe obviously does not, but polyunsaturated margarine is worked into it instead, and careful seasoning is used to substitute for the forbidden items. At least 24 hours of marinating is necessary to achieve the smooth flavor that this mousse should have. Most people won't believe that it is not wickedly rich.

The mousse can be put into one large jelly-lined mold, or into individual custard cups with a layer of jelly to decorate the top. When serving the mousse as a first course, the individual portions are much prettier.

6 servings

½ pound chicken livers
¼ teaspoon salt
⅛ teaspoon pepper
¼ teaspoon allspice
⅓ cup Madeira or port wine

Carefully pick over the chicken livers and remove any clinging fat and membranes. Put livers in a small nonmetal bowl, sprinkle with salt, pepper, and allspice. Pour on the wine and mix well. Cover and let stand for 24 hours, mixing occasionally.

ASPIC

1 can undiluted beef broth
1 tablespoon gelatin
2 tablespoons Madeira or port wine
6 1-cup custard cups

Heat the broth in a small pot, while softening the gelatin in the wine. When the broth is hot, add the softened gelatin and stir until it dissolves. Cool.

Spoon 1 tablespoon of the cooled aspic into each of 6 custard cups. Place them on a tray and put in the refrigerator. Keep the rest of the liquid aspic handy for the mousse recipe.

MOUSSE

2 tablespoons polyunsaturated margarine
1 tablespoon chopped shallots
1 teaspoon cognac
4 tablespoons polyunsaturated margarine
pinch thyme
½ teaspoon Madeira or port wine
½ teaspoon cognac

Drain the livers, reserving the marinade, and pat them dry on paper towels. Heat 2 tablespoons of the margarine in a heavy pan and add the shallots. Fry for about 1 minute on a slow fire, keeping the shallots from browning. Turn up the heat and dump in the livers. Fry them quickly, turning constantly for 1 or 2 minutes only. Scoop them into a blender, scraping in all the sauce. Return the pan to the fire, pouring in the marinade and teaspoon of cognac. Boil quickly to reduce by ½, then scrape this reduction into the blender. Return pan to fire and melt the remaining 4 tablespoons of margarine. Pour the melted margarine into the blender and add the thyme. Blend until smooth.

Force the mixture through a fine sieve, thus removing any remaining membranes (there always are some). Taste for salt and seasoning, correct if necessary, and add the extra ½ teaspoon of cognac. Add 4 tablespoons of the liquid aspic, and stir again. Refrigerate the remaining aspic to set it.

The aspic in the custard cups should be completely set before you spoon in the mousse. Spoon the mousse into each cup, tap the cups sharply to settle the mixture into them, cover and refrigerate.

Refrigerate for at least 2 days; this will mellow the flavor and improve it greatly. To serve, unmold onto individual serving dishes. Chop the leftover aspic into small pieces and spoon around the mousse. Serve with thin slices of toast.

6

MEAT

MEAT IS BEYOND A DOUBT THE MOST BASIC AND BEST-LOVED PART OF THE American diet. Good heart health, however, calls for restricting our exaggerated consumption of meat.

All meats, except veal, are high in saturated fats, no matter how lean the cut. It is true that lean cuts, trimmed of all fat, have less flavor than heavily marbled meat wrapped in fat. But the lean cuts don't have to taste less good. A little oil added to lean ground beef, for example, gives it back some of the moisture it otherwise lacks. Braising with stock, wine, or beer and spices can also make the difference between something that tastes like health food and a dish that pleases the fussiest gourmet. Most of the time the diner will not suspect that these dishes have been made without the aid of fats and butter.

Veal is the best meat to use in a low-cholesterol diet. But unfortunately, it is not very popular on the American table. The veal recipes in this chapter present six different ways to cook that delicate meat, using different cuts for greater variety of flavor. In Europe, veal is given a place of honor in fine dining, an attitude that we could very well import.

How much meat you eat is a matter between you and your doctor, but when you do eat it—enjoy it. Here are some recipes I think will help your enjoyment.

The wine to aid that enjoyment will almost always be red. With veal dishes one could choose Beaujolais, a light Bordeaux (particularly Médoc) or a California Cabernet-Sauvignon. Rosé is another good choice with veal. Beef needs something fuller and heavier like Pomerol, Nuits-Saint-Georges or Aloxe-Corton from Burgundy; Saint-Émilion from Bordeaux; Pinot Noir or any of the better Burgundy-type wines from California. If one is watching pennies, try Côtes-du-Rhône. When ham and pork dishes are served any of the following do nicely: Beaujolais, Médoc, rosé, or a luscious white like Chassagne-Montrachet, Hermitage, or dry Graves. Cold dishes in aspic call for rosé, Beaujolais, Médoc, or any of the Pinot Chardonnay whites from California.

GRENADINS AU VERMOUTH

Veal Grenadins with Vermouth

CHOLESTEROL RATING 2
CALORIES PER SERVING 505

The grenadin is really a cut of veal rather than a particular portion. The meat comes from the topside of the young calf and is cut into small, round, thick collops that resemble beef tournedos. French butchers automatically encircle the grenadin with a strip of pork fat (which is immediately removed for this recipe). If you cannot get the real grenadin, then slices of boned and rolled veal rump can be substituted.

The delicacy of the veal is not overwhelmed by the vermouth. This is a dish of great subtlety that is merely coated with a discreet amount of sauce, not bathed in it. Whether you are lucky enough to get the plump grenadins or have to use another cut, this is a presentation of distinction.

6 servings

- *6 veal grenadins or rump steaks at least ¾-inch thick*
- *¼ cup flour*
- *3 tablespoons polyunsaturated margarine*
- *½ teaspoon grated lemon rind*
- *½ cup dry white vermouth*
- *3 tomatoes*
- *12 small white onions*
- *herb bouquet (4 parsley sprigs tied around 1 bay leaf)*
- *¼ teaspoon thyme*
- *½ teaspoon basil*
- *salt and pepper*
- *1 tablespoon flour mixed with 2 tablespoons cold water*
- *1 tablespoon polyunsaturated margarine*
- *1 teaspoon cognac*

Remove any fat from around the veal and lightly flour the meat. Heat the margarine in a heavy skillet and brown the veal on both sides over medium heat. While the veal is browning, grate the lemon rind into the vermouth and pour over the veal. Cover the pan at once and remove from the fire. Shake the pan to loosen the juices that have fried to the bottom. Let the covered pan stand for 5 minutes off the fire to infuse the meat with the vermouth.

Meanwhile, cut the unpeeled tomatoes in quarters, lengthwise, and squeeze out the seeds and pulp. Peel the onions and prepare the herb bouquet.

Return the skillet to the fire and add the tomatoes, onions, herb bouquet, thyme, basil, salt and pepper. Cover and simmer over very slow heat for 30 to 40 minutes, or until the onions are soft when pierced with a sharp knife. Baste several times during the cooking.

Discard the herb bouquet and arrange the veal and vegetables on a serving platter; keep them warm while finishing the sauce. Turn up the heat under the skillet and add the flour-and-water mixture, a little at a time, to thicken the liquid slightly. The sauce should be the consistency of heavy cream. Add the margarine and cognac, give one good boil (about a minute), then spoon the sauce over the veal and vegetables.

CÔTES DE VEAU AU VIN BLANC

Veal Chops in White Wine

CHOLESTEROL RATING 2
CALORIES PER SERVING 375

When veal is served with a sauce, the sauce is generally loaded with cream and egg yolk. Ugh. Instead offer a browned white-wine sauce, liberally laced with onions, and you'll find that this unusual presentation gets more attention, and just as many compliments.

The quantity of onions may seem excessive at first, but they cook down considerably and turn quite sweet during the process. The whole dish can be prepared well in advance, even the day before, and reheated slowly at serving time. The only thing to keep in mind is to allow for the extra heating time—by not cooking too long in the original preparation. Overcooking will turn the chops rather dry.

6 servings

½ cup polyunsaturated oil
4 medium onions, sliced in thin rings
6 1-inch-thick veal chops, trimmed of any fat
salt and pepper
1 cup dry white wine
herb bouquet (6 parsley sprigs tied around 2 bay leaves)
1 garlic clove on toothpick for easy removal
2 teaspoons meat extract (BV)
2 tablespoons cornstarch
½ cup water
1 tablespoon cognac

Heat the oil in a heavy pan, add onions, cover, and simmer very slowly until transparent, about 15 minutes. Remove all onions with a skimmer and keep in a dish. Dry chops on paper towel. Turn up heat under the pan and *quickly* brown each veal chop on both sides over fast flame. Salt and pepper after turning. Add more oil if necessary during the browning of the chops. Remove chops to a side dish and pour out the oil.

Return the pan to fire and pour in white wine, scraping bottom with a wooden spoon to work coagulated meat juices into the wine. Simmer 1 minute. Return chops along with any juice that collected in the dish. Add the cooked onions. Tuck the herb bouquet into the sauce, and add the garlic clove stuck on a toothpick. Salt and pepper lightly.

Place aluminum foil directly over the meat, then cover the pan. Simmer very slowly for about 30 minutes.

Remove meat to a side dish. Also remove the bouquet and the garlic clove and discard. Add the meat extract. Mix the cornstarch with water and add ½ of this mixture to the sauce and stir. If the sauce does not seem thick enough, add more cornstarch as needed; the amount will vary depending on quality of meat and how much juice it releases during cooking. Add cognac. Taste and correct seasoning with salt and pepper if necessary. Simmer 2 to 3 minutes. Return chops to pan to reheat.

If the dish is prepared ahead of time, let the sauce cool before replacing the chops in the pan. Keep covered until needed, and reheat very slowly.

Serve with sauce and onions liberally spooned over each chop.

VEAU GENDARME À LA GELÉE

Cold Roast of Veal Studded with Pistachio Nuts, Aspic Garnish

CHOLESTEROL RATING 2
CALORIES PER SERVING 455

I suppose the unusual name for this veal roast comes from the *baton,* or nightstick, carried by French *gendarmes.* The rolled roast has the shape of the weapon, and its inside is studded—but with tasty pistachio nuts instead of heavy lead.

If veal were more popular in the United States, perhaps a finer quality would be more readily available. At its best, veal should be pale, almost white-pink, a color that comes from milk feeding the calf. This quality is not easy to find, and although the darker-fleshed veal can be used in this recipe, some of the original subtlety will be lost.

Veau Gendarme can be served hot, like any other roast, but I find its flavor comes through best when it is cold. The cold presentation is more unusual and more festive than hot, especially when surrounded with a glistening circle of chopped *gelée* (aspic). The meat is easier to slice when cold, and the pattern made by the pistachio studs is quite pretty. For an even more elaborate pattern, the roast can also be studded with lean Canadian bacon and black truffles. With all three items inserted into the meat, the slices are an attractive mosaic of pale pink meat, green pistachio nuts, black truffles, and deep pink Canadian bacon. Your butcher can lard these items into the roast, but if you have a long larding needle and can do it yourself, you then have the opportunity to marinate the nuts, truffles, and bacon in brandy before inserting them. The added flavor does help.

An impressive menu is *Veau Gendarme à la Gelée, Concombres Crémeux* (Cucumbers in Creamy Sauce), page 33, and cold *Petits Pois Clamart* (Pea Purée), page 177, or *Purée de Laitue* (Lettuce Purée), page 171.

8 servings

3-pound rolled veal roast, without the layer of fat wrapped around it
¼ cup shelled pistachio nuts
¼ pound lean Canadian bacon and/or 1 black truffle (optional)
¼ cup cognac
¼ cup white wine
4 ounces polyunsaturated margarine
salt and pepper
2 garlic cloves, cut in half
1 medium onion, thickly sliced
1 bay leaf broken in half

With a larding needle insert the pistachio nuts, and optional Canadian bacon and truffles, into the roast, or have your butcher do it. Place the veal roast in a baking pan and pour the cognac and wine over it. Spread ½ the margarine over the entire surface of the roast, sprinkle on salt and pepper, and scatter the garlic, onion slices, and bay leaf around the meat. Insert a meat thermometer into the thickest part of the roast and place in a 325° oven. Roast slowly, basting quite often, until the thermometer registers 160°, which will leave a slightly pink center to the roast. Count on about 30 minutes per pound, or 1½ hours. Halfway through the roasting time spread the remaining margarine on the meat. Frequent basting is most important in keeping the meat moist, since there is no fat on it.

Remove the roast from the oven and take out the thermometer. Let the veal cool in the pan, basting from time to time while it cools. The veal can be roasted in the morning to serve for dinner; however, it should not be refrigerated.

At serving time, remove the roast from the pan and, with a sharp knife, cut it into thin slices, no thicker than ¼ inch; thin slices look nicer. Arrange the slices down the center of the serving platter, overlapping them a little. Sprinkle some chopped aspic along the middle of the row of veal slices, and spoon the rest of the chopped aspic all around the meat. No parsley please; there is enough color contrast on the platter.

ASPIC

2 cups strong chicken consommé

2 tablespoons gelatin

Soften the gelatin in ¼ cup of the chicken consommé, while heating the rest of the consommé in a small pot. Once the consommé is quite hot, add the softened gelatin and stir until it completely dissolves. Cool, then pour into a bowl and refrigerate. It needs about 3 hours to jell completely, but can be made long in advance.

Chill a chopping board or large dish. Scoop the aspic onto the chilled board and, with a long sharp knife, chop into small pieces. Hold the knife at both ends and use it as a chopper working with an up-and-down motion. The finer the aspic is chopped, the prettier. Return the chopped aspic to the bowl and refrigerate until needed.

PAUPIETTES AUX PISTACHES

Veal Birds with Pistachios

CHOLESTEROL RATING 2
CALORIES PER SERVING 340

A *paupiette* listed on a French menu rarely says that it is veal, but it always is. Long, very thin slices of the pale meat are pounded until almost paper-thin; a stuffing is spread over the veal, which is then rolled, tied, and braised. You will find that the veal is so thin it will not weigh much on the pocketbook, despite its premium price in the butcher shop.

Generally the stuffing is made of pork sausage meat, which I feel overwhelms the delicacy of the veal. You are offered here, instead, a light aromatic stuffing. When this *paupiette* is cut, you'll see pretty swirls of almost-white meat and dark filling, with pale green pistachios peeking through.

6 servings

2 tablespoons polyunsaturated margarine
2 tablespoons minced shallots
½ cup finely minced fresh mushrooms
2 tablespoons minced parsley
3 tablespoons bread crumbs
salt and pepper
1 tablespoon dry white wine
½ cup shelled pistachio nuts
2 egg whites, unbeaten
6 thin veal scallops
salt and pepper
½ cup flour
2 tablespoons polyunsaturated margarine
½ cup dry white wine
¼ to ½ cup water
1 to 2 teaspoons Madeira, according to taste

Melt the 2 tablespoons of margarine in a small skillet. Add the minced shallots and simmer, uncovered, for about 3 minutes. Keep stirring so the shallots do not brown. Add the minced mushrooms, cover, and simmer slowly for 5 minutes. Remove the skillet from the heat and add the parsley, bread crumbs, salt, pepper, and wine. Mix these ingredients until they are well blended, then add the pistachios and the egg whites. Mix well again. This is the stuffing for the veal birds.

Lay out the veal scallops and trim off any visible fat or gristle. Sprinkle lightly with salt and pepper. Spread the stuffing evenly on the scallops, but not all the way to the edges. Roll the scallops, tucking in the sides as you roll; then tie securely with string.

Spread the flour in a dish, and flour each *paupiette* on all surfaces, shaking off excess flour. Melt 2 tablespoons of margarine in a heavy skillet just large enough to hold all the *paupiettes.* When the margarine is hot and foaming, add the *paupiettes* and fry until they are a dark golden color—a matter of minutes. Do not brown them too much; the whole point of this dish is its subtlety.

When all the *paupiettes* are browned, add the wine, reduce the flame, cover, and simmer very gently for about 40 minutes, turning the meat often.

When ready to serve, remove the *paupiettes* to a warm serving platter. Add the water to the sauce, the amount depending on how much liquid the meat has absorbed. You need enough for just a light coating of sauce. Add the Madeira and simmer for a few minutes while you remove the strings from the *paupiettes.* Spoon the sauce over the *paupiettes* and serve immediately.

OSSOBUCO

Italian-Style Veal Shanks

CHOLESTEROL RATING 2
CALORIES PER SERVING 305

Unlike most versions of *Ossobuco,* this one does not call for a heavy tomato sauce. It is instead a more aromatic and interesting way of preparing the veal, and another example of the great finesse of serious Italian cooking. For a pretty presentation see the introductory note of *Petits Pois à la Niçoise* (Peas with Tomatoes), page 178.

6 servings

6 veal shanks, at least 1¼ inches thick
¼ cup polyunsaturated oil
1 medium onion, chopped fine
¾ cup dry white wine
salt and pepper
2 teaspoons tomato paste
1 cup water
1-inch strip of lemon peel
1 garlic clove
½ onion
¼ cup parsley leaves
1 teaspoon rosemary
1 teaspoon sage

Score the sides of each veal shank in one or two places to prevent them from curling during the cooking. Heat the oil in a heavy skillet and brown the shanks evenly on both sides. Push the veal to one side and add the finely chopped onion, mixing it well with the oil and juices in the pan. Simmer for about 10 minutes until the onions turn a light brown. Add the white wine, salt, and pepper and mix well. Turn the meat several times to thoroughly imbue it with the onions and wine. Cover and simmer for about 30 minutes, or until the wine has almost completely evaporated. Dilute the tomato paste in the water and add to the cooking pan. Cover again and continue cooking 30 minutes more.

Meanwhile, prepare an herb addition called *gremolata:* chop together as finely as possible the lemon peel, garlic, onion, and parsley leaves and put in a small bowl; if you are using dried rosemary and sage, crush them between your fingers or with a pestle until they become powdery; if using fresh herbs, chop them until they resemble powdery bits. Mix the herbs with the chopped vegetables until all the flavors are completely blended. Sprinkle this mixture over the simmering veal and turn the shanks a few times to coat them with the *gremolata.* Cover and cook for 10 minutes more. If the pan looks a little dry, add some white wine, but keep in mind that this preparation of *Ossobuco* does not come with a lot of sauce, just a bit more than a tablespoon per serving.

WIENER SCHNITZEL

Veal Scallops, Vienna Style

CHOLESTEROL RATING 2
CALORIES PER SERVING 475

A perfectly done Wiener schnitzel should be extremely thin, crisp, and dry. All this is easily achieved by following the steps outlined. American veal is, however, a problem. A twelve-week-old calf just cannot produce the pale, moist delicacy of European milk-fed veal, which is slaughtered much younger.

Since the flavor of American veal has a stronger character, the best thing to do is capitalize on it by frying the veal in oil subtly flavored with garlic.

Cloves of garlic are heated very slowly in the frying oil until the oil is hot and the garlic turns a dark brown. The slow heating is very important; it allows the garlic to give off a more mellow, cooked flavor than the pungent, sharp flavor that results from burning it with high heat. In fact, if you let the garlic steep in the oil for at least an hour before turning on the heat, the flavor will be still better. How many cloves of garlic depends on how large a frying pan you are using and how much oil. A good rule of thumb is 1 clove for each 3 cups of oil.

When buying veal scallops, plead, cajole, beg—do anything to get the butcher to cut them thin, thin, and then, no matter how thin he cuts them, before starting to prepare the veal, put the scallops between two sheets of waxed paper and pound them thinner yet.

Even though Wiener schnitzel must be a last-minute operation, don't be afraid to do it for company. The veal fries in a matter of seconds, so a whole platterful can be done in a few minutes.

The lemon shouldn't be omitted either. The tang of the lemon flavor is essential.

1 large veal scallop per person, very thin
salt and pepper
½ to 1 cup flour spread on a plate
1 egg white plus 1 teaspoon water for each 3 to 4 scallops
1 to 1½ cups fine bread crumbs spread on a plate
garlic cloves
polyunsaturated oil for frying
very thin lemon slices, 2 per scallop

Sprinkle salt and pepper on one side of each scallop, dip into flour and pat a generous quantity on both sides; shake off excess. Beat together very lightly the egg white and water, pass each scallop through the egg white and immediately place it on bread crumbs, patting crumbs in well and covering every bit of meat. Let dry at least 15 minutes, longer if possible.

Heat the garlic cloves in the oil very slowly; when they have turned dark brown remove from the oil. Place one or two scallops at a time in the hot oil, depending on the size of the pan. Fry about ½ minute on one side, then turn for another ½ minute; remove to absorbent paper. Keep the oil hot while continuing to fry the other scallops.

Place on a warm platter and put the paper-thin slices of lemon (cut across) on top of each. The lemon slices are meant to be pressed into the scallop with the back of a fork.

BIFTECK BERCY

Steak with White Wine Sauce

CHOLESTEROL RATING 3
CALORIES PER SERVING 540

When selecting a steak for grilling, there is just no getting around the fact that the more marbled with fat it is the better it tastes. On the other hand, when selecting meat for a low-cholesterol diet, the leanest meat possible is what is looked for. Lean meat is best when served rare to medium rare. Long cooking toughens the meat.

But the eating can be just as good if the flavor comes from a good sauce instead of fat. In fact, French chefs created any number of well-known sauces to spoon over beef largely for one reason: French beef traditionally was lean, grass fed, and lacking in flavor.

6 servings

6 steaks, top round or lean sirloin, ¾-inch thick (about ½ pound each)
polyunsaturated oil for grilling
salt and pepper
2 tablespoons polyunsaturated margarine
6 shallots, finely minced
1 cup dry white wine
salt and pepper
2 tablespoons polyunsaturated margarine
1 tablespoon minced parsley

Pan-broil the steaks to the desired degree of doneness. Sprinkle salt and pepper on steaks after they have been turned. Remove the steaks to a warm platter and keep them warm while making the sauce. Pour the cooking fat from the pan, add 2 tablespoons of margarine to the pan and return it to the fire. Add the shallots and sauté them over a brisk fire for about 1 minute, stirring constantly so they do not brown and scraping up the meat juices from the bottom of the pan while stirring.

Pour in the wine, turn up the heat, and boil the sauce rapidly until it reduces by about ⅓. Add salt and pepper, reduce the heat to very low, and add the other 2 tablespoons of margarine. When the margarine melts turn off the heat, add the parsley, stir well, and spoon the sauce over the steaks. The sauce is made in about 3 minutes.

BIFTECK, MARCHAND DE VIN

Steak with Red Wine Sauce

CHOLESTEROL RATING 3
CALORIES PER SERVING 540

6 servings

6 steaks, top round or lean sirloin, ¾-inch thick (about ½ pound each)
polyunsaturated oil for grilling
salt and pepper
2 tablespoons polyunsaturated margarine
6 shallots, finely minced
1 cup red wine
salt and pepper
½ teaspoon Worcestershire sauce
2 tablespoons polyunsaturated margarine
2 tablespoons minced parsley

Pan-broil the steaks according to the recipe for Bifteck Bercy. Remove the steaks to a warm platter and keep them warm while making the sauce. Pour off the cooking fat from the pan, add 2 tablespoons of margarine, and return the pan to the fire. Add the shallots and sauté them over a brisk fire for about 1 minute, stirring constantly so they will not brown and scraping up the meat juices from the bottom of the pan while stirring.

Pour in the wine, turn up heat and boil the sauce rapidly until it reduces by about ⅓. Add salt, pepper, and Worcestershire sauce. Reduce the heat to very low and add the other 2 tablespoons of margarine. When the margarine melts, turn off the heat. Add the parsley, stir well, and spoon the sauce over the steaks. The sauce is made in about 3 minutes.

STEAK MORVANDIAU

CHOLESTEROL RATING 3
CALORIES PER SERVING 495

The name of this sauce is taken from a cattle-raising area in France, the Morvan. Dijon, which lends its famous mustard to the sauce, is not far away.

6 servings

6 steaks, top round or lean sirloin, ¾-inch thick (about ½ pound each)
6 shallots, finely minced
1 cup dry white wine
2 teaspoons strong Dijon mustard
salt and pepper
2 tablespoons polyunsaturated margarine
polyunsaturated oil for grilling

Combine the shallots, wine, and mustard in a small heavy pot and simmer gently until the mixture is reduced a little, say for about 10 minutes. (This can be prepared well in advance and reheated at serving time.)

Rub a thin layer of oil on both sides of each steak. Preheat the broiler and quickly broil or pan fry the steaks to the desired degree of doneness. Sprinkle salt and pepper on the steaks after they have been turned.

Reheat the sauce, adding the margarine. Remove steaks to a heated serving platter and spoon sauce over each one.

STEAK AU POIVRE

Pepper Steak

CHOLESTEROL RATING 3
CALORIES PER SERVING 560

This is a fiery way to serve steak that also permits you to use cheaper cuts of meat. The peppercorns that are pressed into the meat cure it enough to tenderize it a little. French chefs often add large dollops of heavy cream to the sauce to cut the strength of the pepper. But if you're going to make *Steak au Poivre* in the first place, why diminish its impact?

6 servings

1 1-inch slice of round steak, about 3 pounds, or 6 individual steaks at least 1 inch thick
2 tablespoons polyunsaturated oil
2 tablespoons peppercorns, black and white
polyunsaturated oil for grilling
salt
1 cup dry white wine
1 cup beef broth
2 teaspoons cornstarch
¼ cup cognac
2 tablespoons evaporated skimmed milk
3 tablespoons polyunsaturated margarine

Trim the meat of all fat and gristle and dry it on paper towels. Rub 2 tablespoons of oil into the meat on both sides. Crush the peppercorns slightly, but not too fine; a blender can be used for this. Press the crushed peppercorns into all surfaces of the meat and put it aside for at least 2 hours.

Pour enough oil into a heavy skillet to film the bottom and put it on the stove to get quite hot. Add the meat and sauté it on both sides according to the degree of doneness desired. Salt the steak after it has been turned. Remove the steak to a warm platter and keep it warm while preparing the sauce.

Pour out all the oil from the frying pan and add the white wine and ¾ cup of beef broth. While the liquids begin to simmer, mix the cornstarch with the other ¼ cup of beef broth and add it to the sauce, stirring with a wire whisk and scraping up the coagulated juices from the bottom of the pan. When the sauce has thickened, add the cognac and milk. Simmer the sauce for another ½ minute, remove from the heat and add the margarine. Stir until the margarine is melted, then spoon the sauce over the steak.

BIFTECK HACHÉ À LA TOULOUSAIN

Ground Beef with Red Wine Sauce

CHOLESTEROL RATING 3
CALORIES PER SERVING 530

The "Toulousain" part of the title refers to the tasty and very fatty sausage meat from Toulouse that is often served with a simple country wine sauce. Such sausage meat, of course, is not used in this book, but the sauce is retained. And by adding extra flavor to the sauce one easily compensates for the use of a less spicy meat. Bread crumbs are at the base of this sauce and provide the starch vehicle that absorbs the liquid, red wine in this case. The principle of bread crumbs as a base for sauces can easily be adapted for use with beef broth or chicken broth in a variety of dishes. But note that the sauce will be slightly granular.

6 servings

1½ pounds lean ground beef
¼ cup dried onion soup
¼ cup polyunsaturated oil
1½ tablespoons Worcestershire sauce
1 teaspoon powdered coriander
salt and pepper
⅓ cup polyunsaturated oil
½ cup fine bread crumbs
3 cups red wine
½ teaspoon powdered thyme
2 bay leaves
4 parsley sprigs
1 tablespoon sugar
2 teaspoons powdered coriander

Mix the beef with dried onion soup, ¼ cup oil, Worcestershire sauce, 1 teaspoon coriander, salt and pepper. Work the mixture well and separate it into 6 thick patties. The flavors will mingle better if this is done at least ½ hour before cooking time. Heat oil until smoking in a heavy skillet and quickly brown patties on each side. Allow no more than 1 minute per side because the cooking will be finished later, in the sauce. Remove patties.

Take the skillet off fire and stir in bread crumbs; return to fire and keep stirring as the crumbs turn a dark brown color. Add at once 1 cup of red wine, mix to smooth, and slowly add the rest. The sauce will thicken as the crumbs absorb the wine. Add thyme, bay leaves, parsley, sugar, two more teaspoons of coriander; cover and simmer very slowly for 15 minutes. (Can be turned off at this point until ready to serve.) Remember, at any point you can increase the quantity of the sauce by slowly stirring in more bread crumbs and wine, but the crumbs are really best if browned at the beginning.

At serving time remove the parsley and bay leaves from the sauce. Taste for salt and pepper. Bring to a fast simmer, add patties, cover and cook 2 to 3 minutes on each side depending on thickness of meat and degree of doneness desired. Place patties on serving dish and pour sauce over them.

BOEUF BOURGUIGNON

Beef Stew in Red Wine Sauce

CHOLESTEROL RATING 3
CALORIES PER SERVING 650

The care taken to prepare the stewing sauce properly for this dish will pay off in the full flavor that slowly cooks itself into each piece of meat. This is another one of the classic French dishes that benefits from being made well ahead of time, even a day before, so that all the flavors can properly marry. And even without the traditional chunks of bacon, the flavor is no less *Bourguignon* (Burgundian). Serve with boiled noodles, steamed rice, or steamed potatoes, any of which can absorb the sauce on the plate.

6 servings

3 tablespoons polyunsaturated oil
1 sliced onion
1 sliced carrot
3 pounds lean stewing beef, cut in 2-inch pieces
¼ cup cognac
3 tablespoons flour
2 tablespoons tomato paste
1 tablespoon red currant jelly
3 cups red wine
3 cups beef stock or broth
2 garlic cloves, mashed
½ teaspoon thyme
herb bouquet (4 parsley sprigs tied around 2 bay leaves)
1 teaspoon salt
½ teaspoon pepper
½ pound small white onions
1 pound fresh mushrooms

Heat the oil in a heavy casserole that can go into the oven later. Slowly brown the sliced onion and carrot in the oil, and then remove them with a slotted spoon. Reserve.

Dry meat on paper towels. Turn up heat under the casserole and quickly brown the beef. Brown just a few pieces at a time so the heat will not be reduced too much. Remove the pieces of meat to another dish as they are done.

Pour out cooking oil, reduce flame, and return the casserole to the fire. Pour in the cognac, scraping up the residue on the bottom with a wooden spoon. Add flour and mix with wire whisk. Add tomato paste and currant jelly while continuing to whisk. Slowly add red wine and beef stock. Bring to a rolling boil. Then add mashed garlic, thyme, herb bouquet, and sprinkle on the salt and pepper.

Boil for five minutes, then return the browned vegetables and meat to the casserole. Cover and place the casserole in the oven that has been preheated to 325°. Regulate heat so liquid is constantly simmering. Cook for 3 to 4 hours, depending on the cut of meat (top round will take less time than lean chuck); meat is done when it is fork tender. Taste carefully and correct seasoning.

While the meat is cooking, peel the onions, boil until almost tender, and drain immediately. Fry the mushrooms in a small amount of oil until brown; remove from pan. Fifteen minutes before meat is done, add the onions and mushrooms to the casserole. If the dish is prepared the day before and refrigerated, add the vegetables when reheating the stew. Remove the herb bouquet.

Serve the stew right from the casserole, which gives an authentic note, or place it in a deep platter with plenty of sauce.

CARBONNADES À LA FLAMANDE

Beef and Onions Braised in Beer

CHOLESTEROL RATING 3
CALORIES PER SERVING 630

Belgium is well known for brewing fine beer, and the *Flamande* (Flemish) in the title indicates that beer is used in the braising of this full-bodied stew. Do not be afraid of the quantity of onions (2 pounds) because in the slow braising they are reduced almost to a purée.

6 servings

3 pounds of lean chuck, rump, or eye of round
1 cup flour
polyunsaturated oil for frying
2 pounds onions, thinly sliced
salt and pepper
5 garlic cloves, crushed
1 cup beef bouillon
1 bottle beer
1 tablespoon Dijon mustard
2 tablespoons dark brown sugar
herb bouquet (4 parsley sprigs tied around 2 bay leaves)
2 tablespoons cornstarch
2 tablespoons wine vinegar
½ cup beer

Trim all fat off the beef. Slice the meat into pieces about ½ inch thick, 2 inches wide and 4 inches long. Dredge the slices in flour to dry them and for a nice coating when browned. Pour enough oil into a heavy skillet to coat the bottom well. Heat oil until hot and fry a few pieces of meat at a time, browning each side quickly, and removing to a side plate.

If the flour has burned in the oil, pour out and use fresh oil to sauté the onions, again filming the bottom of the pan well. Keep heat moderately low for the onions, which you should cook slowly and covered. Turn the onions occasionally and continue cooking until they are limp, but not cooked through (about 10 minutes). Add salt, pepper, and garlic, then cover again and cook for 3 minutes more.

In a small pot combine the bouillon, 1 cup of the beer, mustard, and brown sugar. Bring to a slow boil to dissolve the mustard and sugar.

Select a deep casserole that can go into the oven and put in a layer of ½ the browned meat pieces. Sprinkle on salt and pepper. Spoon ½ the quantity of cooked onions over the meat. Repeat the procedure, using the remaining ½ of the meat and onions.

Pour the heated stock over the meat and onions, adding enough beer to bring the liquid level almost to the top of the onions. Bury the herb bouquet, cover the casserole, and put in the oven preheated to 325°. Cooking time should be 1½ to 2 hours, depending on the cut of the meat. Test for doneness by piercing with a small sharp knife. When the meat is thoroughly tender, drain off the remaining liquid into a saucepan. Be careful doing this since the casserole will be heavy and hot; hold the cover firmly in place and let the liquid pour out of the side.

Put the cornstarch, wine vinegar, and ½ cup of beer in a small bowl and mix to a smooth paste. Slowly add this paste to the drained stock and simmer slowly while whisking vigorously to keep the sauce smooth. Return the sauce to the casserole and stir well while reheating the meat thoroughly. Serve with boiled potatoes or noodles.

EL LAHM EL M'QALI

Lamb with Lemon and Olives

CHOLESTEROL RATING 3
CALORIES PER SERVING 600

One expects French cuisine to be excellent in Paris, and it is, but, unexpectedly, so are other national cuisines served there. French chefs really know about food and they apply their knowledge and taste to exotic preparations. With its former ties to North Africa, it follows that Paris has a healthy number of North African restaurants. This popular Moroccan specialty has an advantage for home and restaurant use—the basic preparation must be done the day before so all the chilled fat can be removed, and even when completely finished, it reheats beautifully.

6 servings

½ cup polyunsaturated oil
½ teaspoon ground ginger
½ teaspoon turmeric
1 teaspoon ground coriander
¼ teaspoon powdered saffron
1 teaspoon finely chopped garlic
2 teaspoons salt
2 cups finely chopped onions
2½ pounds boneless leg of lamb, trimmed of all fat, cut into 1-inch cubes
4 cups water
2 to 3 lemons, cut lengthwise in quarters
30 to 40 ripe green olives, pitted, medium size
¼ cup parsley

Pour the oil into a heavy 4-quart casserole, then mix into it until smooth the ginger, turmeric, coriander, saffron, garlic, and salt. Turn on the heat and add chopped onions, mixing thoroughly. Cover and simmer for a few minutes until the onions begin to soften, then add the lamb and water and bring to a boil. Lower heat and add lemons, then cover, and simmer for about 45 minutes or until the lamb is tender. With a skimmer, remove any foam that rises to the top. Cool and refrigerate overnight. The next day remove all the fat that has solidified on top of the liquid.

Using a slotted spoon, remove the lamb and lemons to a bowl. Turn up the heat and boil the sauce briskly, uncovered, until it reduces and thickens slightly. This should take 10 to 15 minutes. Return the lamb and lemons to the sauce. Meanwhile, thoroughly drain and rinse the olives under cold running water (none of their vinegar must remain). Add the olives and simmer the stew for about 3 minutes, covered. Taste for seasoning and correct if necessary. Remember this should have a rather aromatic flavor; it is not a subtle dish. Just before serving, mix in the chopped parsley, which adds a nice touch of bright color. Serve with rice or flat Arab bread.

RÔTI DE PORC DE CHEF NARCÈS

Chef Narcès's Pork Roast

CHOLESTEROL RATING 4
CALORIES PER SERVING 790

Pork on a low-cholesterol diet? Of course, when it is the leanest possible cut, like the loin used here, with all traces of fat removed. Even so I would still suggest limiting the frequency of its appearance on the table. But when you decide it's time for pork, I can think of no tastier and more sensible way to prepare it.

I salute Chef Charles Narcès of Paris's Cordon Bleu for this superb dish. In my many years of attending the famed school, this pork dish was one of the very few pork dishes that Chef Narcès prepared. Pork is not considered refined enough for *haute cuisine.* (Have you ever seen it on a menu in a fine *classique* restaurant?) But when the master chef did turn his attention to lowly pork, he knew precisely what to do with it. This recipe proves that.

Because of the covered cooking, the meat remains juicy while imparting its flavor to the delicious sauce, a thinned purée of the cooking vegetables. Few people will guess how you achieved such a remarkable nonfatty sauce.

One indispensable ingredient is the pork bones removed from the loin. Make certain the butcher keeps them for you. They go into the pot to give extra flavor.

6 servings

3 pounds boned, rolled loin of pork, center cut, trimmed of all fat (reserve bones)
½ cup polyunsaturated oil
4 onions, cut in half
4 or 5 garlic cloves
3 ripe tomatoes, cut in quarters
salt and pepper
½ to 1 cup beef stock
few drops gravy coloring (Kitchen Bouquet)
1 teaspoon flour
3 teaspoons water
2 teaspoons cognac

Heat the oil in a heavy pot that can go into the oven. Once oil is quite hot, put in the rolled pork loin and brown well all over, including the ends. Remove the meat, pour out the oil and rinse the pot. Return meat to the pot and add the reserved bones, onions, garlic, tomatoes, and salt and pepper. Cover tightly and put in a 325° oven for about 1½ hours, or until the meat thermometer reads 185°. (You can prepare the meat ahead to this point, but then cook a little less, only about 1¼ hours with the thermometer reading 170°, and finish cooking at serving time.)

Remove meat from pot and throw away the bones. Pour the cooking liquid and vegetables into a food mill that is placed over a saucepot. Purée the vegetables through the mill and into the liquid. Let the pot stand for 5 minutes so the fat will rise and remove it with a spoon or by pulling paper towels across the surface.

Place the pot on a slow fire, add a few drops of gravy color to darken the sauce, and ½ to 1 cup of beef stock depending on how thin you would like the sauce. If you want a lot of sauce, add the full cup and thicken the sauce with the necessary amount of flour and water mixed together. Add cognac and taste for salt and pepper.

While the sauce is simmering, remove the string from the rolled pork and cut the meat in slices. Arrange sliced meat on the serving platter to resemble the uncut loin. Spoon some of the sauce over the top of the meat and pass the rest in a sauceboat.

TRANCHES DE JAMBON MORVANDELLE

Ham Slices Morvandelle

CHOLESTEROL RATING 4
CALORIES PER SERVING 660

The Morvan region is about one hundred fifty miles southeast of Paris and is famous for its Charolais beef and its delicious ham. A pink cream sauce was created to spoon over the ham and compliment its special, slightly smoky flavor. Ham, one of America's better products, becomes a real party dish when embellished with *Sauce Morvandelle*. Rice and poached mushrooms are good choices to serve with the ham.

6 servings

2 tablespoons polyunsaturated margarine
¼ cup minced onions
2 tablespoons flour
1 cup beef bouillon
½ cup evaporated skimmed milk
½ cup Madeira
1½ tablespoons tomato paste
1 teaspoon sugar
pinch of nutmeg
1 teaspoon meat extract (BV)
6 slices lean ham, ¼ inch thick, tenderized or canned
¼ cup polyunsaturated margarine
1 teaspoon cognac

Melt the margarine in a heavy saucepan, add the onions. Slowly cook the onions without browning them. Stir in the flour and cook for 1 minute before slowly adding the beef bouillon while mixing with a wire whisk. Add the evaporated skimmed milk, Madeira, and tomato paste. Continue stirring until the sauce thickens, then add the sugar, nutmeg, and meat extract. (The sauce can be made ahead to this point.)

Trim all fat off the ham slices. At serving time heat the margarine in a skillet and quickly brown the ham slices on both sides. Arrange them on a warm serving platter.

Reheat the sauce, add 1 teaspoon of cognac, and spoon some of the sauce over the ham, passing the rest in a sauceboat.

HAM À LA MARCELLA

CHOLESTEROL RATING 4
CALORIES PER SERVING 740

Ham is a popular dish in Central Europe. A Czech friend serves it in steaks with an onion and sweet wine sauce. I much prefer sherry to the heavier wine, but port or Madeira can be substituted.

4 servings

3 medium onions, sliced thin
½ cup polyunsaturated oil
2 pounds lean ham steak
pepper
1 cup sherry

Slice the onions thin while heating the oil slowly in a heavy skillet. Add the onions, cover, and simmer slowly until they are soft and translucent, being careful not to brown them. This should take 15 to 20 minutes. (This step can be done ahead of time.)

Dry the ham slice on paper towels. Push onions into a pile on one side of the skillet and move it a little so that the onions are not over direct heat. Increase heat and when the oil is very hot, but not smoking, add the ham slice and brown quickly on both sides. Pepper the ham, but do not add any salt.

Drain off the oil. This can be done by firmly holding a lid over the skillet and tipping it carefully. Add sherry, cover, and simmer a few minutes, turning the ham once or twice. Shake the skillet vigorously to loosen the browned bits of ham that stick to the bottom. Cut into serving portions and arrange on platter with onions spread on top.

JAMBON PERSILLÉ

Mold of Ham and Parslied Aspic

CHOLESTEROL RATING 4
CALORIES PER SERVING 725

Burgundy has almost as many food specialities as it has varieties of wine. *Jambon Persillé* is one of its most famous dishes and a traditional item on the Burgundian Easter table. Parisian restaurants that feature it generally buy it in Burgundy. One friendly restaurateur gave me the address of his supplier in Chalon-sur-Soâne. It was hard to believe that something as carefully prepared as this ham dish could come from that unattractive industrial town. I used to deliberately avoid the city when driving to Geneva. But this time I plunged into town, found the tiny, very unpromising-looking *charcuterie,* and with great misgivings ordered the *jambon,* convinced that I had the wrong address. A dumbwaiter sent it up from the basement-kitchen, and there it was, just as I had admired and enjoyed it in Paris. It did make one wonder what other treasures that kitchen contained. Trips to Geneva became more frequent.

Here in the United States you cannot buy prepared *Jambon Persillé,* but good ham is available, and so is parsley. Our country hams like Virginia or Smithfield, once they are desalted, closely approximate the French hams. But even store-bought tenderized hams can produce a fine *persillé.* Canned hams won't do.

The pork rind and other fatty ingredients in the classic version have been omitted in this recipe.

A lot of the complexities of the French version have been simplified to encourage you to try it. I don't think you'll be disappointed.

10 to 12 servings

1 7-pound slightly smoked ham, bone in
1 large onion, cut in quarters
2 carrots, sliced
2 garlic cloves
1 celery stalk with leaves
1 fresh or dried tarragon
½ teaspoon basil
½ teaspoon sage
2 bay leaves
1 teaspoon peppercorns
8 parsley sprigs
½ cup dry white wine
½ cup white vermouth
3 tablespoons plain gelatin (possibly 2 more)
2 tablespoons dry white wine
¼ cup tarragon vinegar
1½ tablespoons fresh or dried tarragon
1 garlic clove, crushed
pepper
1 cup firmly packed, finely chopped parsley

Cook the ham the day before assembling the dish. Cut away the rind and all fat from the outside of the ham. Rinse the ham thoroughly and put it in a large pot, covering it with water and turning on the fire to bring the water to a slow boil. Add the onion, carrots, garlic, celery, tarragon, basil, sage, bay leaves, peppercorns, and parsley. Simmer the ham for 20 minutes per pound if it is a tenderized ham. Cook a local or country ham according to the directions. Remove any foam that may rise to the surface.

When cooked, lift the ham from the stock, and as soon as you can handle it, take off the meat, leaving behind all the bones and fat. Put the pieces of meat in a bowl and pour on the white wine and vermouth, mix thoroughly, cover and let stand overnight in a cool place. Do not refrigerate. Mix the meat pieces from time to time. Strain 6 cups of the cooking liquid and refrigerate.

The next day remove and discard all the fat that has risen to the top of the stock and congealed. The stock itself should be rather gelatinous. If it is, the 3 tablespoons of gelatin will be sufficient to make the aspic; if not, 2 more tablespoons will be required. In a small bowl soften the gelatin in the 2 tablespoons of white wine and the tarragon vinegar. Drain the wine marinade from the meat into the stock and pour it into a pot. Put the stock on the stove and heat slowly, adding the tarragon, garlic, and pepper. When the stock is hot, add the softened gelatin and stir to dissolve completely. Take a spoonful of the stock and cool it before tasting for seasonings; flavors are always less strong when a dish is chilled. Correct if necessary. This is now an aspic. Cool the aspic and test for firmness by chilling 2 tablespoons of it in a small saucer. If it does not jell solidly in ½ hour, reheat the stock and add the extra gelatin to it. The ham and parslied aspic will be combined in the same dish from which it is served. Select a wide, moderately deep bowl, approximately 10 to 12 inches in diameter and 4 to 5 inches deep. Do not use a regular mixing bowl since it is too deep; salad bowls are more suitable.

Put the ham pieces in the bowl, but do not pack them in tightly since the aspic should seep in between the pieces. Also try not to put the ham too close to the edges of the bowl, allowing some room for an aspic coating. Chill thoroughly.

Chill the stock-aspic separately until it just begins to jell, then add the chopped parsley. If the parsley is added when the stock is a liquid the leaves will not be held in suspension but will float to the top. As soon as the parsley is in the thickened stock, carefully spoon the stock into the bowl, all around and over the ham. There should be enough aspic to completely cover the ham with about a ¼-inch layer on top. Chill at least overnight. One or two days is much better.

To serve, use a very sharp knife with a sawing motion. Slice at the table directly from the bowl into pie-shaped wedges. Serve as a main course with salad and perhaps cold *Purée de Laitue* (Lettuce Purée), page 171.

(Note: Clarified stock is prettier still, but not essential. To do this, heat the stock with an egg white and bring to a boil while whisking. Strain through a very fine cloth, then proceed with adding the gelatin.)

PÂTÉ À LA GELÉE

Jellied Lamb and Veal Pâté

CHOLESTEROL RATING 3
CALORIES PER SERVING 270

The recipe for this pâté does not follow the classic method, as others in this book do. Instead the meat is cooked first, ground, and then molded. This procedure permits the removal of the greatest amount of fat. But even though it is a different kind of pâté, it should still mature in the refrigerator for at least two days before eating, just like any other pâte. The well-flavored meats are held in a jellied suspension that gives a pretty shine to each slice. It makes an impressive main course in winter or summer. A nice accompanying dish would be cold *Petits Pois Clamart* (Pea Purée), page 177.

10 servings

1½ pounds lamb shoulder with bones
1½ pounds veal shoulder with bones
2 bay leaves
2 teaspoons salt
6 peppercorns
1 onion, quartered
1 celery stalk
½ pound lean ham
1 onion
½ teaspoon ground pepper
½ teaspoon ground ginger
½ teaspoon allspice
½ teaspoon ground coriander
1 tablespoon gelatin
1 cup dry white wine
1 tablespoon cognac
½ teaspoon gelatin
2 tablespoons dry white wine
For garnish (optional):
blanched parsley leaves, thin carrot slices, thin lemon slices, green pepper rings, olives

Remove all fat from the lamb and veal, put them in a large pot, and add water to cover the meat completely. Place on the fire and slowly bring to the boiling point. Reduce the heat and simmer for 15 to 20 minutes, skimming off the foam that rises. When the foam subsides, add the bay leaves, salt, peppercorns, quartered onion, and the celery. Cover the pot and simmer gently for 2½ to 3 hours, or until the meat is tender when pierced with a fork.

Place a colander over a dish and remove the meat to the colander to drip, adding this liquid to the stock. Strain the stock and chill it, which makes it easy to remove the fat that rises and congeals on top. Return the stock to the pot and boil rapidly to reduce to a little more than a quart. Reserve ½ cup of this reduced stock to use for a jellied topping.

Take the meat off the bones, removing any fat or gristle. Cut the meat into chunks and put them through the finest blade of a meat grinder; then grind the ham and 1 onion. Add the ground mixture to the stock, plus the ground pepper, ground ginger, allspice, and ground coriander. Cover and simmer gently for 20 minutes. Cool a teaspoon of the mixture and taste for seasonings; correct if necessary. Soak 1 tablespoon of gelatin in 1 cup of wine, then add to the hot mixture to dissolve the gelatin. Cool the mixture a little before adding the cognac.

Spoon the mixture into a lightly oiled 9 × 5 × 3-inch loaf pan, or any 6-cup mold, or even a soufflé dish. Chill overnight.

Heat the reserved ½ cup of strained stock in a small pot while softening ½ teaspoon of gelatin in 2 tablespoons of white wine. Add the softened gelatin to the hot stock and stir to dissolve. Chill until the stock is syrupy then spoon over the chilled pâté to form a jellied topping. Return the pâté to the refrigerator to set the topping a little, then decorate it before the jelly sets completely, using any of the garnishes you decide upon.

To serve, remove from the mold and place on a serving platter and slice with a very sharp knife.

You may find it easier to remove the pâté from the mold before adding the decorative coating of jelly on top. In that case, prepare the aspic, chill until syrupy and then brush on with pastry brush in several layers, chilling to allow each coating to set firmly before adding more.

PÂTÉ DE VEAU ET JAMBON

Veal and Ham Pâté

CHOLESTEROL RATING 4
CALORIES PER SERVING 315

I am particularly proud of this recipe. We all know that typical French pâtés achieve their rich flavor through generous use of pork fat. The enormous amount of fat in the pâtés makes them very smooth and luscious, but it also means they are forbidden to anyone concerned about cholesterol.

In this adaptation, the principles and procedure of making pâté were saved, but all the fat, butter, and eggs were eliminated. Still, this recipe produces a firm-textured pâté that is rich in flavor and still can be enjoyed by people on a low-cholesterol diet. I know of no other pâté that does this.

(Please see the note about the weighting of pâtés under *Pâté de Poulet* [Chicken Paté], page 108.)

12 servings

2 pounds lean veal
1 pound lean ham
2 ounces prosciutto or other cured ham
3 shallots, minced
½ teaspoon thyme
½ teaspoon sage
½ teaspoon basil
1 teaspoon ground coriander
salt and pepper
½ cup Madeira
½ cup cognac
4 garlic cloves
2 bay leaves, each broken in half
8 sprigs parsley
½ cup polyunsaturated margarine
2 onions, coarsely chopped
2 slices white bread
4 egg whites
1 tablespoon polyunsaturated oil
2 tablespoons pistachio nuts (optional)
2 bay leaves

Trim the veal of any fat or gristle. Cut ¼ of the veal into long thin strips, about ¼ inch wide and put them in a pie dish. Cut the remaining veal into pieces and put them in a bowl. Do the same with the ham, trimming it, cutting strips that are placed in the dish beside the veal strips, and the pieces into the bowl with the veal pieces. Trim the cured ham of all fat, cut into small pieces, and add to the bowl with the meat pieces.

Scatter the minced shallots over all the meat, then sprinkle with thyme, sage, basil, and coriander. Grind pepper over all the meat, but add salt just to the veal strips since the ham is already salted.

Pour the Madeira and cognac over the meats and separately mix the dish and bowl of meats with your hands so the spices and wines reach all pieces. Tuck among the meats the garlic, bay leaves, and parsley. Cover the two dishes and put aside for at least 3 hours, 6 if possible, and mix from time to time.

Meanwhile, melt ¼ cup of margarine in a skillet, add the chopped onions, cover, and fry gently until the onions are soft and translucent; do not allow them to brown. All the preceding steps can be done in advance and refrigerated.

To prepare the pâté, discard the bay leaves and parsley from both dishes. Lift the chunks of meat and all of the garlic out of the marinade and put through the finest blade of the grinder, along with the onions. Pass the ground mixture through once again if you have an electric grinder. Break the bread into pieces and put through the grinder. The bread will push through all the meat ahead of it, as well as help act as a binding agent.

Combine the marinade from the two dishes, put in a small pan, and boil briskly to reduce by ½. Add this to the ground mixture. Melt ¼ cup margarine in the same pan and add it, too, to the bowl. Add the egg whites and beat the mixture with a wooden spoon until all ingredients are thoroughly blended. Take a teaspoon of this stuffing and fry it. Let it cool, then taste for seasoning. Correct if necessary.

Grease a 6-cup pâté mold or loaf pan with the tablespoon of oil. Layer into the mold ⅓ of the stuffing, arrange over it ½ of the veal and ham strips, plus a few pistachio nuts if you are using them. Repeat with another ⅓ of the stuffing, the rest of the strips and pistachios. The final layer will be the last ⅓ of the stuffing. Lightly press the bay leaves on the center of this top layer.

Put the cover on the mold, then over that a piece of aluminum foil. Pierce a hole in the foil over the venthole in the mold cover. Place in a pan and pour in enough water to reach halfway up the side of the mold. Bring the water to a slow boil on the stove, then place in a 350° oven. The water in the pan should simmer very slowly. Bake for about 1½ hours. Test by inserting a skewer through the venthole to the center of the pâté, remove, and touch it to the inside of your wrist—if hot the pâté is finished.

Remove the pâté mold from the pan of water and let cool for 15 minutes. Remove the mold cover and cover the pâté with aluminum foil, and place a heavy weight on it, covering as much of the surface as possible with the weight. Almost anything will do for a weight—boxes of salt, heavy copper pots, dishes filled with marbles, even cans of fruit juice. Cool overnight with the weights in place. Pour off the accumulated juices, then refrigerate for one day with the weights still in place. After a day the weights can be removed, but let the pâté mature in the refrigerator for at least 3 days before serving.

To serve, remove the pâté to a platter and garnish with watercress. Slice with a very sharp knife, but do not slice too thin.

7

VEGETABLES

The Great Red Artichoke

ONE OF AMERICA'S RICHES IS ITS YEAR-ROUND SUPPLY OF FRESH VEGETABLES. With each change of season, something else comes along to add variety to the staples. The aim of this chapter is to show how many roles our fresh vegetables can be given in planning low-fat meals. At times, they can be made important enough to star by themselves, they don't always have to play second fiddle to meat and fish.

New interest can be given to ordinary vegetables through unusual flavor combinations (peas with dill), different cooking methods (oven-braised onion slices), or even making a hot vegetable out of a salad green (puréed lettuce).

Vegetables can be both fun to serve and healthful to eat. With a little study of the following recipes, the chef will no longer ask "What vegetable can I serve with the roast?" but rather "What main course would do justice to the *Céleri Provençal*?"

ARTICHOKES

CHOLESTEROL RATING 1
CALORIES PER SERVING PLUS SAUCE 55

One of the most festive things that can be placed on the table at the beginning of a meal is a whole, flowerlike artichoke. Sitting there like some elegant jewel, it seems to carry the promise of a special occasion. Too often, though, this noble vegetable is reserved just for important occasions. Its infrequent appearance on the American table is due to timidity and fear on the part of the housewife: What do you do with something as strange looking as that? How do you eat it? Is it worth the trouble?

It's time to put myths and prejudices aside. The artichoke's strange appearance seems less so when one realizes that it is really a thistle. In a way, it is the lush flower of a rather spindly bush, which accounts for its exotic showiness among vegetables of the root and runner variety.

Eating it can be a delightful (and time-consuming) ritual as each petal is plucked free, dipped in a sauce, and pulled between the teeth to get the fleshy morsel at its base. Dozens of petals later on, the artichoke's heart is revealed; more sauce is spooned on, and it is eaten with knife and fork. There is a hint of sweet corn to it, and also something of a sweet nut. But one shouldn't look for comparisons when enjoying a flavor as delicate and refined as that of a fresh artichoke.

SELECTING: Choose firm, heavy artichokes with a bright olive-green color. There will always be a few brownish petals at the bottom from handling and shipping bruises, but that is all right. However, if the upper leaves (petals) are brown and dried looking, pass it up. The leaves should be rather tightly closed, a sure sign of freshness.

6 servings

STOCK

1 medium onion, sliced
1 carrot, sliced
1 bay leaf
leaves from one celery rib
few sprigs of parsley
1 tablespoon juniper berries (optional, but recommended)
½ lemon, thinly sliced
4 tablespoons salt
1 tablespoon peppercorns
6 fresh artichokes
1 cup sauce

A stock is prepared to insure good flavor even if the artichokes are not of the best quality. Select a pot that will hold at least 8 quarts of water in addition to the artichokes. Add all vegetables except the artichokes to the water, bring to a boil and simmer for 15 to 20 minutes.

TRIMMING: Meanwhile, prepare the artichokes. Do not cut off the stems, but break them off. This will pull out some of the stiff fibers that have grown into the heart. Snap off some of the lower leaves, and trim the stems to provide a steady base. Put each artichoke on its side and with a sharp knife slice about ½ inch off the pointed top. With scissors, cut about ⅓ off each leaf, thus removing all the sharp points. If you are preparing artichokes long before boiling them, drop them into a large basin of cold water with the juice of one lemon squeezed in. This will prevent discoloration.

COOKING: Cover the pot, bring the stock to a rapid boil and drop the artichokes in one at a time, waiting a few seconds between each one to give the water a chance to come back to a boil. Remove the cover once the water is boiling strongly; after a few minutes reduce heat so that the water keeps boiling, but not so ferociously. Cook for about 30 to 45 minutes, depending on the size of the artichokes. As the water level recedes, add more hot water. Test for doneness by inserting a small, sharp knife into the center of the heart, on the bottom. If it is tender and no real resistance is felt, the artichokes are done. Be sure not to overcook or they will be mushy. Remove them from the pot with a long-handled skimmer and put them on sink board upside down or on their sides to drain. If you are serving them warm or cold, let them cook in this manner, turning them a few times. Even if they are to be served hot, drain them for at least 5 minutes.

REMOVING CHOKE: It's always nice to remove the choke for your guests. This is no problem when you are serving the artichokes warm or cold. But if the vegetable is to be served hot, you could never get all of them done and still have any warmth left. The way around that is to remove the chokes after the artichokes cool and to reheat them in the oven, standing the artichokes in a shallow roasting pan with ¼ inch of water in the bottom. To remove the choke, gently spread the top leaves at the center of the artichoke, reach in to the center cone, hold it firmly and twist a little. It will come out all in one piece. Then with a teaspoon gently scoop out the fuzzy choke that lies on top of the heart. Turn the cone upside down and put it back into the center of the artichoke. This is a universal sign that someone has taken the care to remove the choke.

SAUCES: If the artichokes are served warm, pass Hot Vegetable Dressing (page 242). With cold artichokes, serve Herbed French Dressing I with the shallots or without (page 243); Herbed French Dressing II (page 243), or Mayonnaise Dressing (page 242).

Provide a large bowl for the leaves in the center of the table, paper napkins, and plenty of time for leisurely enjoyment before the next course is brought on.

FONDS D'ARTICHAUTS

Artichoke Bottoms

CHOLESTEROL RATING 1
CALORIES PER SERVING WITHOUT SAUCE 48

The pale green artichoke bottom can be used as a beautiful shell for all sorts of fillings, like *duxelles* (*see* page 30). When used to hold a prepared stuffing, the artichoke bottom does not have to be trimmed down while it is still raw. It makes better economic sense to cook the whole artichoke and serve the leaves as a first course to the family the day before you need the bottoms. Serve them with lots of French dressing and everybody can eat the leaves to his heart's content, but must promise not to dig into the heart.

But if your family isn't cooperative about eating just the leaves, or if the artichoke bottom is to be cooked as a vegetable as in *Fonds d'Artichauts à la Barigoule* (Artichoke Hearts, Provence Style), page 151, then the vegetable must be trimmed while still raw.

Break off the stem—do not cut it—and begin snapping off the leaves by bending them away from the artichoke. Continue breaking off the leaves until you begin to see the curve of the bulbous heart. At this point the leaves, which are now quite thin, begin tapering to a cone. Hold the artichoke firmly on a cutting board and with a very sharp knife slice across the artichoke just above the top of the bottom. Trim the bottom with a small sharp knife to smooth out the ragged edges.

While holding the artichoke bottom start trimming away the green leaves that surround it. Keep trimming until you begin to see the white of the heart. Rub with ½ a lemon and drop into a bowl of cold water with lemon juice. Unless the artichoke bottom is going to be cooked as a vegetable, leave the fuzzy choke in and remove it after the cooking.

FOR THE COOKING

½ cup flour
1 cup cold water
juice of ½ lemon
1 tablespoon salt

Using a nonaluminum pot, bring several quarts of water to a rapid boil. Mix the flour and cup of cold water to a smooth paste, then gradually beat this paste into the boiling water. Add the lemon juice and salt and finally drop in the artichoke bottoms. Simmer for 30 to 40 minutes, or until they are tender when pierced with a sharp knife. Cool the artichokes in the cooking liquid. If they are to be held in the refrigerator, keep just enough of the liquid to cover them, and close the container tightly with a lid or aluminum foil.

Before serving, gently remove the fuzzy choke with a teaspoon. The artichoke bottom can be served by itself as an always-appreciated first course with some Herbed French Dressing I or Herbed French Dressing II, page 243, spooned over.

FONDS D'ARTICHAUTS À LA BARIGOULE

Artichoke Hearts, Provence Style

CHOLESTEROL RATING 1
CALORIES PER SERVING 190

Barigoule is a cooking term derived from the old Provençal word *barigoulo,* a name given to stuffings or garnishes that include mostly bacon and onions. I was never particularly fond of greasy bacon with delicate artichoke hearts and found that the recipe is much better without it. *Artichauts à la Barigoule* makes a particularly appealing first course when served barely warm; or it can be served hot as a vegetable with meat.

6 servings as first course
8 servings as vegetable course

6 fresh artichoke bottoms (or 2 boxes frozen artichoke hearts)
½ cup polyunsaturated oil
20 small white onions, peeled
1 cup dry white wine
hot water
juice of ½ lemon
1 garlic clove (on toothpick for easy removal)
1 bay leaf
¼ teaspoon each thyme, savory, rosemary
salt and pepper

Prepare the artichoke bottoms according to instructions on page 150, but scoop out all the fuzzy choke as well. Keep the artichokes in cold water with lemon juice until ready to be used.

Heat the oil in a heavy pan and add the small onions to color them slowly; not too much but just enough to give them a blush of gold. Remove artichoke bottoms from water, dry on a towel, and cut in quarters. Add the artichokes to the onions and color them as well. This should take about 3 to 4 minutes while they are turned with a wooden spoon. Pour in the wine and enough hot water to cover. Add the lemon juice, garlic, bay leaf, herbs, salt and pepper. Cover the pan and cook very slowly for about 1 hour or until the artichokes are tender when pierced with a sharp knife. Remove the bay leaf and garlic before serving.

Lacking fresh artichokes, you may substitute frozen artichoke hearts. In this case, precook the onions for about 20 minutes before adding the artichokes, which need less cooking time than fresh ones.

ARTICHAUTS À LA CLAMART

Artichoke Hearts and Peas

CHOLESTEROL RATING 1
CALORIES PER SERVING 135

In French culinary language, *Clamart* always means that peas are included in the dish. In this version they are mixed with artichoke hearts to make a rather glamorous vegetable dish. It is so good, in fact, that it can be offered as a separate course. I've done this often, following a cold main dish with this hot vegetable course.

6 servings

1 10-ounce package frozen artichoke hearts
2 tablespoons polyunsaturated oil
1 tablespoon finely chopped shallots
2 10-ounce packages frozen peas
1 cup water
½ teaspoon sugar
¼ teaspoon fresh or dried tarragon
1 teaspoon salt
¼ teaspoon pepper
2 tablespoons polyunsaturated margarine
herb bouquet (4 parsley sprigs tied around 1 bay leaf)

Thaw the artichoke hearts. If they are whole cut them in half, lengthwise, then dry them on a towel. Heat the oil in a heavy skillet and add the artichoke hearts to brown quickly, turning them often so they brown evenly. Reduce the flame, add the chopped shallots, cover, and simmer for 1 minute, just to soften the shallots without browning them. Add the frozen peas, water, sugar, tarragon, salt, pepper, margarine, and the herb bouquet.

Cover the skillet and simmer very slowly for about 25 minutes, or until the peas are tender. If you are making this dish in advance, simmer for 20 minutes and finish cooking at serving time. Discard the herb bouquet and spoon into a deep serving bowl.

HARICOTS VERTS AUX AMANDES

String Beans with Almonds

CHOLESTEROL RATING 1
CALORIES PER SERVING 185

It has always been a puzzle to me why anyone would serve frozen string beans with almonds when they are so tasteless and expensive. We don't get the shoestring-thin French string beans here, but once ordinary beans are dressed up with flavored almonds, it almost doesn't matter.

6 servings

1½ pounds fresh string beans
1 tablespoon salt
2 tablespoons polyunsaturated margarine
½ to ¾ cup slivered almonds
2 garlic cloves
2 toothpicks
3 tablespoons polyunsaturated margarine

Cut off the ends of the beans and remove any strings. Meanwhile, bring a large quantity of water to a rapid boil, add the salt, and then plunge in the beans. Cook at a fast simmer until they are tender, but not mushy. This should take about 15 minutes. Drain immediately and plunge them into a pan of cold water. Drain again and put aside.

In a small heavy skillet, slowly melt 2 tablespoons of margarine. Add the almonds and the garlic cloves which have been stuck on the toothpicks (for easy removal later). Cover the skillet and sauté the almonds very slowly until they turn a dark golden color. Turn often, so the almonds will brown evenly. Remove from fire and put aside.

At serving time, heat 3 tablespoons of margarine in a 2-quart pot. When the margarine has melted, add the string beans; remove the garlic cloves from the almonds and add the almonds to the beans. Gently mix up the beans, almonds and margarine, cover the pot and reheat very slowly for about 5 minutes. Remove to a deep vegetable bowl and serve at once.

PURÉE DE HARICOTS VERTS

String Bean Purée

CHOLESTEROL RATING 1
CALORIES PER SERVING 105

This is a relatively little known way of preparing a vegetable that is available almost the whole year. It has a very delicate flavor that goes well with subtly prepared meats or fish. This dish is also a way around the quality of domestic string beans, which at times leaves much to be desired. If canned string beans are used, rinse them well under running cold water.

6 servings

1 pound fresh string beans
2 teaspoons salt
½ to ¾ cup evaporated skimmed milk
1 cup canned chick peas, drained
½ teaspoon meat extract (BV)
1 tablespoon polyunsaturated margarine

Remove the ends and strings from the beans and rinse under running cold water. Bring a large quantity of water to a fast boil, add the salt and the beans. Cover the pot until the water comes back to a rapid boil, then remove the lid. Boil the beans for about 40 minutes, which is a much longer cooking time than usual. Drain the beans.

Put ½ cup of the evaporated milk in a blender, add the beans, and purée. Add the chick peas and purée again. The mixture will be rather thick and should be stirred a few times. If absolutely necessary, add more skimmed milk. Put the purée in a pot, add the meat extract and margarine, and reheat slowly until the margarine melts. Taste for salt and pepper and correct if necessary. Serve hot, but it is also good cold.

If not using a blender, pass the cooked beans and chick peas through a food mill. Then add the milk, meat extract, and margarine before heating.

HARICOTS BLANCS PROVENÇAL

Stewed White Beans, Provence Style

CHOLESTEROL RATING 1
CALORIES PER SERVING 290

In America, too few women bother to cook beans. It seems so easy just to dump them out of cans. But believe me, no matter how much doctoring up you do, you can never disguise the overly starchy, too sweet flavor of canned beans.

If just once you prepare white beans as they do in southern France, you'll renounce Boston's version forever. This stewed bean recipe is very easy to prepare, and for best flavor should be done at least a day ahead. Serve these beans along with any meat, roasted or grilled. With the addition of some leftover baked ham, roast beef, or roast lamb, you'll have a hearty main course, sort of a left-handed *cassoulet.*

6 servings

2 cups dried white beans
2 tablespoons salt
herb bouquet (6 parsley sprigs tied around 2 bay leaves)
½ teaspoon basil
½ teaspoon thyme
1 clove stuck into an onion
1 stalk of celery, with leaves
1 garlic clove, minced
2 tablespoons polyunsaturated oil
1 onion, chopped
½ cup tomato sauce
1 cup liquid reserved from beans
1 teaspoon meat extract (BV)
1 garlic clove, crushed
salt and pepper

Put the beans in a deep pot, cover with hot water, and let stand overnight. Drain off the water, then cover with boiling water, add 2 tablespoons of salt and bring to a boil. With a skimmer remove any foam that may rise during the first 5 minutes of boiling. When all the foam has subsided, add the herb bouquet, herbs, the onion with the clove stuck into it, celery stalk, and the minced garlic clove. Simmer the beans until they are tender, but still firm. This should take about ¾ to 1 hour depending on the beans. Remember, they get further cooking, so do not overdo them at this point.

Drain the beans, reserving the liquid. (Any liquid left over is excellent for soups, stocks, sauces, and so on.) Remove the onion, herb bouquet and celery. Put the 2 tablespoons of oil in a heavy skillet or small heavy casserole and heat. Add the chopped onion, cover, and simmer 4 to 5 minutes. Add ½ cup tomato sauce, cover, and simmer 5 minutes more. Add 1 cup of the liquid from the beans, 1 teaspoon of meat extract, and 1 crushed garlic clove. Add salt and pepper, tasting carefully first; the amount will depend on the kind of tomato sauce you use. Add the beans to this sauce, mix well, cover and simmer slowly for 20 minutes. Taste again for seasoning. The beans should be tender, but not mushy. If possible, prepare them the day before and reheat slowly at serving time.

LENTILLES AU VIN ROUGE

Lentils in Red Wine

CHOLESTEROL RATING 1
CALORIES PER SERVING 165

No bistro in France would make up a winter menu without lentils somewhere on the list. Chunks of bacon are usually added, but you'll find that they are not at all necessary. A few extra herbs and spices more than make up the difference. *Lentilles au Vin Rouge* makes an excellent accompaniment to game, guinea hen, or Rock Cornish hen.

6 servings

1½ cups lentils
6 cups red wine
3 medium carrots
3 medium onions
3 garlic cloves, crushed
1 teaspoon coriander
3 teaspoons salt
1 teaspoon pepper
herb bouquet (6 parsley sprigs tied around 2 bay leaves)
3 whole cloves stuck into a small onion

Today's lentils do not have to soak for hours; a thorough rinsing under cold water will do. Place the lentils in a large, heavy pot. Pour on the red wine. Cut the carrots in quarters lengthwise, then slice them thinly crosswise and add to pot. Chop the onions fine and add them along with the crushed garlic cloves. Add the seasonings, herb bouquet, and the small onion that holds the cloves.

Cover the pot and bring to simmer. Cook for about 1½ hours, or until the lentils are soft, but not mushy. Stir rather frequently during the cooking, mixing the lentils so those no longer in the liquid exchange places with those that are. If you feel that the liquid is boiling off too rapidly, add a little more wine or water. Even when the lentils are completely cooked, there should be a little bit of liquid remaining. Remove herb bouquet and the small whole onion with cloves. Serve hot but it is also an excellent cold vegetable.

CHOUX DE BRUXELLES AUX MARRONS

Brussels Sprouts and Chestnuts

CHOLESTEROL RATING 1
CALORIES PER SERVING 230

This pretty vegetable combination is best served in late fall when both Brussels sprouts and chestnuts can be bought fresh. The chestnuts and the sprouts are about equal in size, and once nicely browned, they look almost like two versions of the same vegetable. Fortunately, the hunting season is on at the same time and this dish is a natural with venison, pheasant, or wild duck.

Although canned unsweetened chestnuts can be substituted if necessary, I warn against using frozen Brussels sprouts: their waterlogged consistency ruins the crispness of the dish.

6 servings

- *1½ pounds fresh, firm Brussels sprouts*
- *salt*
- *¾ pound boiled chestnuts (or canned, unsweetened)*
- *1 celery stalk*
- *½ cup polyunsaturated margarine*
- *¾ cup strong beef broth*

Trim the Brussels sprouts and soak them in salted water for 15 minutes. Drain, then boil them in salted water for no more than 10 minutes. Do not overcook the sprouts at this stage since they will be cooked again later. Meanwhile, prepare the chestnuts by slashing them a little on the flat side, and boiling them for a few minutes until their skins begin to pull away. Drain and peel the chestnuts as soon as you can handle them. Now boil the peeled chestnuts in lightly salted water to which a celery stalk has been added. When tender but not too soft drain, then dry them on a towel. If canned chestnuts are used, be certain they are not sweetened; drain them thoroughly and dry on a towel. Canned chestnuts must be handled gently since they can break easily.

Heat 2 tablespoons of the margarine in a heavy skillet, add the chestnuts and fry briskly to brown them evenly. Turn the chestnuts carefully, adding margarine as necessary. Add the Brussels sprouts and the rest of the margarine and brown the sprouts quickly. Pour in the beef broth, partially cover the skillet and simmer for 5 to 8 minutes, or until the sprouts have finished cooking and the liquid is reduced. Remove carefully to serving dish.

BRAISED CABBAGE

CHOLESTEROL RATING 1
CALORIES PER SERVING 175

Americans too often ignore the wonderful possibilities of plain old cabbage. French bistros don't make that mistake. The lowly vegetable is dressed up with a meat stuffing, or cooked under a roasting duck to catch all the dripping fat and juices. It is also boiled plain to go with boiled beef, and often braised to be served with game, pork roasts, or ham.

Chunks of bacon are usual in braised cabbage. To me this seems superfluous when cabbage is served with meat; it also makes the dish too greasy. An extra texture, however, is nice to have, so use poppy seeds which also add an intriguing flavor. White wine helps a lot, too, and its softness is not at all lost to the cabbage flavor; instead the wine elevates this inexpensive, always-available vegetable to a dish worthy even of pheasant.

6 servings

1 medium head cabbage, 2 to 2½ lbs.
⅓ cup polyunsaturated oil
3 medium onions, thinly sliced
1 cup water
1¼ cups white wine
2 garlic cloves, crushed
1 beef bouillon cube
½ teaspoon celery salt
¼ teaspoon powdered basil
¼ teaspoon powdered thyme
salt and pepper to taste
herb bouquet (6 sprigs parsley tied around 3 celery stalk tops and 2 bay leaves)
1 tablespoon poppy seeds

Shred the cabbage with a knife and blanch in a large quantity of boiling salted water for 2 minutes. Drain and immediately put under cold running water. Leave the cabbage in a colander to drain thoroughly. Heat oil in a heavy pan and add the sliced onions. Cover and simmer for 5 minutes.

Meanwhile, squeeze the cabbage, a handful at a time, to remove all water. Add the cabbage and mix well with the onions. Pour the water and 1 cup of the white wine over the cabbage. Add garlic, beef bouillon cube, celery salt, basil, thyme, salt and pepper, and herb bouquet. Cover and simmer for 15 minutes. Add the poppy seeds and the remaining ¼ cup of white wine, cover, and simmer for another 15 minutes.

CHOUX, TOUT EN ROUGE

Red Cabbage, Braised in Red Wine

CHOLESTEROL RATING 1
CALORIES PER SERVING 140

Cabbage may not be served in fancy restaurants, but French bistros and country inns know how to take advantage of the spicy deliciousness of the vegetable. This particular version uses red cabbage all dressed up in red wine and by the time it comes to the table it has taken on a most attractive color. Adding a few spices and a few tart apples, along with the wine, gives lowly cabbage all kinds of flavorful airs.

During the cooking, the apples will disintegrate completely, just lending their tart flavor to the dish. This cabbage recipe is best made the day before and reheated slowly when needed. It is a natural with baked ham, any game, roast or grilled lamb. Served with Potato Pancakes, page 58, it would make a hearty, homespun luncheon or supper.

6 servings

2 tablespoons polyunsaturated oil
2 medium onions, thinly sliced
2-pound head red cabbage
¼ cup water
1 teaspoon caraway seeds
2 garlic cloves, crushed
2 tart apples, peeled and thinly sliced
2 tablespoons dark brown sugar
1¼ cups red wine
1 teaspoon ground coriander
salt and pepper
½ lemon

Select a large pot for cooking the cabbage because at the beginning there will be a lot of bulk. In this pot heat the oil and add the sliced onions. Simmer them gently, uncovered, until they begin to soften, about 10 minutes. Meanwhile shred the cabbage and add to the onions. Add the water, caraway seeds, and garlic, and mix everything together. Cover the pot and simmer for about 10 minutes or until the cabbage begins to wilt.

Now add the apples, brown sugar, red wine, coriander, salt and pepper. Squeeze in the juice from the ½ lemon and then toss in the lemon shell itself. Mix again quite thoroughly, cover, and simmer very gently for about 1 hour, stirring a few times during the cooking. The liquid should be almost completely absorbed by the end of the cooking period. Remove the lemon shell before serving.

If this dish is prepared ahead and reheated, you may have to add a little red wine or water to keep the cabbage from scorching. But add no more than just the amount necessary, since there should be almost no liquid at the end.

CAROTTES BRAISÉES

Braised Carrots

CHOLESTEROL RATING 1
CALORIES PER SERVING 118

Carrots are among the more dependable vegetables in the market. If you are lucky enough to find tiny spring carrots, you will enjoy them as never before. But even those that are no longer at their young, sweet best can be greatly improved by this simple braising method.

6 servings

1½ pounds carrots, peeled or scraped
½ cup polyunsaturated margarine
1 tablespoon sugar
salt and pepper
¾ to 1 cup water
1 chicken bouillon cube

If you are using tiny spring carrots leave them whole; cut large carrots in half lengthwise. Heat the margarine in a heavy skillet and add the carrots. Sprinkle on the sugar, salt, and pepper, while keeping the heat rather high to caramelize the sugar onto the carrots. Turn often to prevent burning. When the carrots are all nicely browned pour in enough water to come almost to the top of the carrots. Crumble the chicken bouillon cube into the water, stir thoroughly, cover the skillet, and let the carrots simmer for 20 to 30 minutes, depending on size.

If they are not to be served immediately, turn off the heat while a little liquid remains in the skillet. At serving time turn up the heat to reduce the remaining liquid to a thick syrup, while carefully mixing the carrots to coat them with the syrup.

CAULIFLOWER PAPRIKA

CHOLESTEROL RATING 1
CALORIES PER SERVING 120

There is a bit of Hungary in this tangy vegetable dish. Depending on how you want to serve the cauliflower, cook it either whole or in large flowerets. It looks prettiest whole, with the paprika-colored sauce poured over it. But the whole version makes it more difficult for a guest to serve himself because he will have to cut down into the stem. If the cauliflower is to be placed on a buffet table, or passed and held for serving, then it should be left intact. Otherwise, the flowerets are more easily served.

6 servings

1 medium cauliflower
5 tablespoons polyunsaturated margarine
2 good pinches pepper
pinch of salt
2 tablespoons lemon juice
1 teaspoon paprika
¼ teaspoon Worcestershire sauce
¼ cup chopped parsley

the cauliflower (whole or in flowerets) in a large quantity dly boiling salted water. Meanwhile, put all other ingredi-ents, except the chopped parsley, in a small sauce pan, cover, and heat very slowly until the contents bubble. If heated quickly, the paprika will burn, turn black instead of red, and lose its mild flavor.

At the moment of serving, drain cauliflower well (if not drained well enough, the water exuding from the vegetable will dilute the sauce), and put in serving bowl. Pour on the sauce which adds a very pretty color and a flavor that is a perfect note with the cauliflower's natural, strong taste. Sprinkle on chopped parsley.

CÉLERI PROVENÇAL

Braised Celery, Provence Style

CHOLESTEROL RATING 1
CALORIES PER SERVING 170

Celery should come out of the salad bowl more often and appear at the table as a cooked vegetable. Since it is in year-round supply, you can count on having it anytime you decide to prepare this exceptionally tasty version of cooked celery. It is substantial enough to be served French style, as a separate course, following a fish dish, for example. But it can be used just as successfully to accompany a roast of any kind. Or try it with Wiener schnitzel, page 124.

6 servings

- *3 large bunches of celery*
- *2 teaspoons salt*
- *¼ cup polyunsaturated oil*
- *6 small white onions, or 3 medium onions cut in half*
- *4 carrots, cut in ½-inch pieces*
- *1 garlic clove, crushed*
- *1 to 1½ cups dry white wine*
- *1½ tablespoons tomato paste*
- *⅓ cup water*
- *1 bay leaf*
- *salt and pepper*

Break off the tough outer stalks from the celery bunches, and use them in soups. With a sharp paring knife, scrape off the heavy fibers on the outer stalks that remain.

Cut off the leaves and tops, leaving about a 6-inch stalk section. Trim off a little of the heavier root ends. Meanwhile, bring a large quantity of water to a rapid boil, add the salt, and blanch the celery bunches for 10 minutes. Drain at once and plunge them into cold water to stop the cooking. Drain again and gently squeeze out as much water as possible from each bunch. Cut each bunch in half and tie in 2 or 3 places with string.

Meanwhile, heat the oil in a heavy flat skillet or casserole and add the onions and carrots. Brown the vegetables gently in the oil, turning often to color them evenly. When they are browned, push them to one side of the skillet and put in the celery bunches to brown. If the skillet won't hold all the vegetables, remove the carrots and onions for the time being. Once the celery bunches are browned, return the other vegetables, add the crushed garlic clove, cover the skillet and reduce the heat to allow the vegetables to give off some moisture. This should take about 10 minutes.

Add 1 cup of the wine, the tomato paste mixed with the water to thin it, bay leaf, salt and pepper. Cover and gently simmer the vegetables for about 1 to 1½ hours, or until a small sharp knife pierces the celery center easily. The cooking time will vary with the vegetable season; at some times celery is tougher than at others. Baste and turn the vegetables several times during the cooking, adding more wine if the cooking liquid begins to reduce too much.

To serve, place the vegetables on a serving platter and remove the strings from the celery bunches. While doing this, turn up the heat to reduce and thicken the sauce. Spoon the sauce over the vegetables, discarding the bay leaf, and serve.

MARRONS GLACÉS

Glazed Whole Chestnuts

CHOLESTEROL RATING 1
CALORIES PER SERVING 245

There's more to chestnuts than wintertime roasting or dessert making. They are especially good, and unusual, when served as a garnish for roast turkey, game birds, or venison. There is, however, a nuisance factor to consider—peeling. Only fresh chestnuts can be used for this preparation, since all the flavor penetrates the nut during the cooking process. Everyone has his favorite way of getting rid of the shells (children are a great help), but one more way is described in the recipe for *Choux de Bruxelles aux Marrons* (Brussels Sprouts with Chestnuts), page 157. Remember, also, that chestnuts are a rich food, so don't count on too many per person.

6 servings

24 chestnuts (about 1¼ pounds)
2 cups beef bouillon
1 tablespoon potato starch or cornstarch
¼ cup Madeira
2 tablespoons polyunsaturated margarine
1 celery stalk, cut in half

Place the peeled chestnuts in a baking dish in a single layer. It is important that they not be stacked, which would cause them to cook unevenly and would bruise the chestnuts. While the bouillon is heating in a small pan, mix the starch and Madeira together into a smooth paste and add it to the bouillon. Then add the margarine and simmer for two minutes. Pour this stock into the baking dish until the chestnuts are completely covered; if there isn't quite enough, add some water. Tuck the two pieces of celery among the chestnuts.

Cover the dish and bake in 350° oven for about one hour or until the chestnuts are tender. Do not stir them during the cooking because they become quite fragile and break easily. By the time the chestnuts are cooked almost all of the liquid should be evaporated with only a thick syrup remaining; if not, remove the cover for faster evaporation. At the end, remove the celery stalks and gently roll the chestnuts around in the syrup to give a shiny glaze to each one.

Serve the chestnuts hot and promptly after baking.

MARRONS SAUTÉS

Sautéed Whole Chestnuts

CHOLESTEROL RATING 1
CALORIES PER SERVING 285

This is a fast and easy way to present whole chestnuts. Only minutes are required to finish them off. Again, fresh ones are best to use, but canned chestnuts can be substituted. You'll find this garnish excellent with poultry or meats of all kinds.

6 servings

1½ pounds boiled, peeled whole chestnuts (or canned, unsweetened)
⅓ cup polyunsaturated margarine
nutmeg, freshly grated
salt and pepper
⅓ cup dry sherry

Drain the chestnuts and dry on a paper towel. Melt the margarine in a skillet, and once the margarine is foaming, add the chestnuts. Sprinkle on some freshly grated nutmeg, salt and pepper. Mix carefully to brown evenly on all sides. When the chestnuts are nicely browned, pour in the sherry, cover, turn up the heat, and let simmer for 1 minute. Remove the cover and boil rapidly to reduce and strengthen the sherry. Remove carefully to serving dish.

CORN FRITTERS

CHOLESTEROL RATING 1
CALORIES PER SERVING 360

Until recently, most of Europe regarded corn strictly as something to feed the livestock. Only in America was eating corn, on or off the cob, known for the sweet pleasure it is. As American agricultural experts improved corn strains, especially to withstand long-distance shipping, Europeans slowly began to shed their long-cherished prejudice against the vegetable. Now they are cultivating it there to eat themselves.

Once a French chef starts working with a food product, he will almost always manage to add new flair to it. This has been done with good old American corn fritters. The trick is to use a minimum amount of batter, adding lots of freshly grated nutmeg, and frying the fritters in just a little fat, instead of deep frying. Of course the French would use eggs in the batter and butter in the frying pan. Neither is essential, as you will see.

Corn fritters go beautifully with roast chicken or veal, and make a nice brunch dish when served with grilled tomatoes and fried mushrooms.

6 servings

2 egg whites
2 1-pound cans whole kernel corn
½ teaspoon salt
½ teaspoon freshly grated nutmeg
½ cup flour
polyunsaturated oil for frying

Put two egg whites in the blender. Drain corn well and add to the egg whites. Blend on slow speed for just a few seconds. The mixture should not be too smooth; in fact, it is better to leave a few kernels whole to give a nice firmness to the fritters. Scoop the corn into a mixing bowl and add salt and freshly grated nutmeg. Don't be afraid of the nutmeg—it should almost announce itself when cooked.

Add the flour, mix well, and let the mixture rest at least 15 minutes so that the flour will absorb liquid. Pour a little oil into a frying pan; the oil should coat the pan well but not be really deep. The fritters are to be fried gently on each side, not deep fried. When the oil is hot, spoon in 2 tablespoons of the batter for each fritter and flatten them with the back of a spoon. The fritters should not be crowded in the pan or they will not brown evenly and will be difficult to turn. Fry them to a nice brown on one side, then turn and fry the other side. Remove to absorbent paper, keeping fritters warm while finishing the rest of them. Add oil as necessary. There should be 14 to 16 fritters, depending on how large they have been made. If you want to make them ahead of time, fry the fritters to a light golden color, drain on paper, and place on a cookie sheet. At serving time, reheat them in a 375° oven for 3 to 4 minutes.

CUCUMBERS WITH HERBS

A cold dish

CHOLESTEROL RATING 1
CALORIES PER SERVING 25

Cucumbers are almost exclusively reserved for the salad bowl. But there is no reason at all why they shouldn't be served as a vegetable with meat or fish. If they were just thought of as another kind of squash there would be no prejudice against using them in that way. In fact, once they are cooked, cucumbers take on a deliciously delicate flavor that is a surprise to everyone.

To have the prettiest presentation, scoop out the solid, fleshy part of the cucumber with a melon-ball knife. If you lack the patience to do that, quarter the cucumber lengthwise, remove the seeds and pulp, and cut the solid part of the vegetable into ½-inch chunks.

As they are cooked, the cucumbers turn a pretty pale green, then sprinkle on the herbs to add a contrasting dark green touch. If available, fresh herbs, of course, are best. Include this unusual dish on any menu with cold meat or fish.

6 servings

5 cucumbers, peeled and cut into balls; or cut lengthwise, seeds and pulp removed, and cut into ½-inch chunks
3 quarts boiling water
2 teaspoons salt
2 teaspoons dillweed
1 teaspoon finely chopped tarragon
salt and pepper
parsley leaves for garnish

Bring the water to a fast boil and add 2 teaspoons salt. Dump in the prepared cucumbers and cook for about 6 minutes, or until they are slightly transparent and a sharp knife pierces them easily. Do not overcook. Drain immediately and blanch with cold water to stop any further cooking. Let the cucumbers drain thoroughly in a sieve or colander. Mix carefully from time to time with a wooden spoon, trying not to crush the cucumber pieces.

Add seasonings about 30 minutes before serving time. If the cucumbers are cooked much in advance, they will continue to render water, which should be drained off before seasoning. Sprinkle on salt and pepper, the dill and tarragon, and mix thoroughly but carefully. Heap into a bowl for serving and add a small bouquet of fresh parsley leaves on top. The contrast between the deep and the pale green is very pretty and refreshing.

SAUTÉED CUCUMBERS

CHOLESTEROL RATING 1
CALORIES PER SERVING 74

This is a way to serve cucumbers as an unusual hot vegetable. Like the cold cucumbers, they go equally well with meat or fish. The vegetable is prepared just as in the preceding recipe with two small changes. Boiling time should be reduced to about 4 to 5 minutes, or until the cucumber is still rather firm when pierced with a sharp knife. The cooking will be completed later. Also, after having been thoroughly drained in a sieve or colander, the pieces must be dried on a towel. If this step is ignored, the cucumbers will end up stewing in their own juice, instead of frying and browning nicely.

6 servings

5 cucumbers prepared as in preceding recipe
3 tablespoons polyunsaturated margarine
salt and pepper
1 tablespoon dried dillweed

Place the partially cooked cucumbers on a towel to dry. Select a fairly large skillet that can hold the cucumbers in a single layer. Melt the margarine in the skillet and bring to a good hot temperature. Pick up the towel and dump the cucumbers into the skillet. Keep the temperature hot. Immediately sprinkle on salt, pepper, and dill and toss the pieces with a wooden spoon or spatula so that they brown lightly all over. This frying should take about 3 minutes.

CONCOMBRES AU RIZ

Cucumber Shells filled with Rice

CHOLESTEROL RATING 1
CALORIES PER SERVING 155

Anyone turning out meals day after day soon begins looking for new and interesting ways to present vegetables. These pretty cucumber shells, filled with seasoned rice, will liven up that part of the menu immediately. They look pretty, too, as the cooked cucumbers turn a translucent pale green. At dinner this would be a good choice with roast chicken or roast meats, but it could also be the main course at lunch with Grilled Tomatoes, page 188.

6 servings

¾ cup rice
1 tablespoon salt
3 medium-sized cucumbers
⅓ cup plain low-fat yoghurt
2 tablespoons prepared mustard, Dijon preferably
2 tablespoons polyunsaturated oil
¼ teaspoon curry
salt
1 tablespoon minced parsley
6 tablespoons fine bread crumbs
paprika
2 tablespoons polyunsaturated margarine
½ cup water

Rinse the rice and cook it for 10 minutes in a large quantity of rapidly boiling water with 1 tablespoon of salt. Drain the rice immediately and rinse well under cold running water. While the rice is cooking peel the cucumbers, cut in half lengthwise, and scoop out the inside seeds and pulp (a grapefruit knife works well here).

In a small bowl mix together the yoghurt, mustard, oil, curry, and a sprinkling of salt. Add this sauce to the rice and mix well. Add the parsley and gently mix again. Fill the cucumber halves with the seasoned rice. Sprinkle 1 tablespoon of crumbs over each cucumber, then follow with a light powdering of paprika.

Place the cucumbers in a baking dish and dot each one with 1 teaspoon of the margarine cut into small pieces. Pour the water into the dish and put in a 375° oven. Bake for about 45 minutes, or until the cucumber shells are tender, but not mushy. Taste a grain of rice to be sure that it is completely cooked.

EGGPLANT NEAPOLITAN

Eggplant Baked with Onions and Tomato Sauce

CHOLESTEROL RATING 1
CALORIES PER SERVING 290

Naples is the capital of the tomato-growing region of Italy. There, tomatoes are combined with everything from pasta to fish to fresh vegetables, which also abound. The Neapolitans can't resist adding layers of creamy cheese to this dish, but if the sauce is made tasty enough by the addition of red wine and saffron, it isn't necessary. Many good canned tomato sauces are on the market, but the best are the imported Italian brands. They do have a way with tomatoes. This is an excellent side dish with meats of all kinds. Or it can make a luncheon main dish served with a large tossed salad.

6 servings

2 eggplants, approximately 1 pound each
2 tablespoons coarse salt
flour
⅓ cup polyunsaturated oil
2 cups thinly sliced onions
1 garlic clove, crushed
extra oil for frying
1 cup tomato sauce
⅓ cup red wine
1 teaspoon Worcestershire sauce
pinch saffron
salt and pepper
¼ cup grated low-fat cheese

Slice the unpeeled eggplants across in ⅓-inch-thick slices. Salt them liberally and let them stand for ½ hour to get rid of excess moisture and bitterness. Pat the slices dry. Put flour in a large dish, dip in the eggplant slices, patting flour in well and then shaking off the excess.

Meanwhile, heat ⅓ cup oil in a large skillet. Add onions, cover and simmer for about 15 minutes until the onions are transparent. For the last 5 minutes add the garlic. Remove onions from the skillet with a skimmer, leaving behind as much oil as possible. Add more oil only if necessary for frying the eggplant slices. But at no point should there be more than a heavy film of oil in the skillet. If there is too much oil used, the eggplant will absorb it excessively. Turn up the heat and quickly fry the eggplant slices until they are golden brown on both sides. Keep adding oil a little at a time as necessary. Remove to a plate.

Prepare the sauce by mixing together the cup of tomato sauce, wine, Worcestershire sauce, saffron, salt and pepper. Lightly oil a 1-quart casserole dish that can go into the oven. Put in the dish ½ the eggplant slices, then ½ each of the onions, sauce, and grated cheese (sprinkled on) in that order. Repeat the procedure using the other ½ of the ingredients. Cover the casserole tightly with a lid and bake in a 350° oven for 20 minutes.

AUBERGINES À LA PROVENÇALE

Eggplant, Provence Style

CHOLESTEROL RATING 1
CALORIES PER SERVING 370

This is a variation of a flavorful dish served in one of France's famed restaurants near Avignon. Eggplant, Provence Style, can be served at just about any point during the meal. When cold it can be a first course at dinner, or it can be heaped on a crisp bed of lettuce for a luncheon main course. When served hot it goes well with roasts or poultry.

If you prepared a quantity of *Coulis de Tomates* (page 236) for your freezer, you can have the perfect sauce to put over the eggplant. If not, the recipe below comes mighty close to it. As for the quantity of garlic in the sauce, remember this is a Provençal dish, and in Provence cooks are not timid with garlic.

6 servings

1½ pounds eggplant
2 tablespoons coarse salt
⅔ to ¾ cup polyunsaturated oil
2½ cups sauce or prepared Coulis de Tomates *(page 236)*

SAUCE

2½ pounds fresh tomatoes, or canned Italian plum tomatoes
¼ cup polyunsaturated oil
½ cup white wine
3 to 5 garlic cloves, crushed
1 tablespoon tomato paste
orange peel, 1 × 2 inches
1 teaspoon salt
½ teaspoon pepper
¼ teaspoon sugar
3 tablespoons chopped parsley

Cut unpeeled eggplant lengthwise in slices about ¼ inch thick and spread them out on sink board or on a large chopping board. Rub coarse salt into both sides and let eggplant stand for about 1 hour so excess water will be drawn out. Rinse slices and dry well on a towel. Pour oil into a frying pan, about ¼ inch deep. Heat well, and quickly fry a few eggplant slices at a time until they are well browned. Remove slices to paper towels to drain off oil. Continue frying, adding oil as necessary.

If fresh tomatoes are used for the sauce, peel them and remove seeds and juice; then chop coarsely. If canned tomatoes are used, drain off the juice and chop the pulp coarsely. Heat ¼ cup oil in a heavy pan, add tomatoes, white wine, garlic, tomato paste, orange peel, salt, pepper, and sugar. Mix well, cover, and simmer for 20 minutes. Stir often during the cooking, mashing the tomato pulp against the sides of the pan as you stir. Add the chopped parsley, return cover and simmer for another 20 minutes.

Arrange eggplant slices in a single layer in a baking dish. Cover the slices completely with the tomato sauce and reheat in 325° oven for 20 minutes. (If preparing the dish in advance, do not spread the tomato sauce over the eggplant until just before putting it in the oven. In this way the two separate flavors will remain more distinct.)

PURÉE DE LAITUE

Lettuce Purée

CHOLESTEROL RATING 1
CALORIES PER SERVING 52

It was in the excellent restaurant of the Hotel Ritz in Paris where I first encountered this delicious lettuce purée. In fact, I have never seen it anywhere else. There is great delicacy to the dish, which comes through even if it is served cold to accompany a cold main course.

I have tried different varieties of American lettuce and found that, for this recipe, romaine approaches most closely the flavor of French lettuce. While on the subject of purées, I might mention that several of France's finest restaurants make a specialty of serving with the meat course a side dish holding three different kinds of purées. The suave harmony of flavors is beautifully orchestrated.

6 servings

1 large head romaine lettuce, approximately 1½ pounds
1 teaspoon salt
1 shallot, sliced thinly
½ teaspoon sugar
salt and pepper
¾ to 1 cup beef bouillon
¼ cup skimmed milk
½ boiled potato (about ½ cup), cut in pieces
1 tablespoon polyunsaturated margarine
½ teaspoon soy sauce
½ teaspoon Worcestershire sauce
salt and pepper

Discard any bruised or brown lettuce leaves. Separate the remaining leaves and rinse them under cold running water. In the meantime, in a large pot bring a large quantity of water to a rapid boil and add 1 teaspoon of salt. Plunge in the lettuce, cover and as soon as the water returns to a boil, uncover the pot and boil the lettuce for 1 minute. Drain immediately and put under cold running water to stop the cooking. A handful at a time, squeeze out the excess water in the lettuce, then chop the leaves coarsely.

Put the chopped lettuce in a heavy skillet or pan, add the sliced shallot, sugar, salt, pepper, and just enough beef broth to almost cover the lettuce. Cover the pan, bring to a simmer, and cook slowly for 30 minutes. Drain off the broth (it can be saved and used for soups and stews) and when cool enough to handle, squeeze out the excess water from the lettuce.

In a blender put the milk, potato and lettuce. Blend until smooth, then return to the pot. Add the margarine, soy sauce, and Worcestershire sauce. Taste for salt and pepper before adding any more. Reheat slowly.

POACHED MUSHROOMS

CHOLESTEROL RATING 1
CALORIES PER SERVING 43

Fresh mushrooms just aren't on the dining table often enough as a hot vegetable. There is no reason for that since they can be prepared quite easily. Once cooked, they will keep in the refrigerator for 4 or 5 days. When making a casserole or some other recipe that calls for mushrooms, try this recipe instead of reaching for a can. Canned mushrooms will merely add bulk but fresh ones will give you flavor as well. And as the vegetable cooks it renders a lot of juice. Guard it preciously, even after all the mushrooms have been eaten. This juice can be boiled down a little to concentrate the flavor and added to any number of sauces. The juice freezes perfectly. French chefs are forever slicing poached mushrooms to add to sauces, especially fish sauces.

A word about buying mushrooms: they must be fresh. By this I mean tight, white fresh. Tight, because the cap must be closely attached to the stem. As mushrooms age the natural moisture evaporates and the cap pulls away from the stem. This is when you see the fluffy brown underside. The whole mushroom darkens as it loses its freshness. Older mushrooms are all right for adding to hearty stews, but won't do where delicateness is required.

6 servings

1 pound fresh mushrooms
juice of 1 lemon
salt and pepper
1 tablespoon polyunsaturated oil
½ cup cold water

Clean the mushrooms under running cold water. Cut in half, or quarters if they are large. Put them in a heavy pot that just holds the quantity, the more closely they are packed the better. Sprinkle on the lemon juice, salt, pepper, and oil. Then pour on the water last. Place a piece of aluminum foil directly on top of the mushrooms to cover the surface completely. Put a tight-fitting lid on the pot and place on high heat. Once the water begins to boil (you can hear it), reduce heat and simmer for 2 minutes.

PETITS OIGNONS SAUTÉS

Sautéed White Onions

CHOLESTEROL RATING 1
CALORIES PER SERVING 125

Here is one vegetable that we can enjoy much more than the French. Small white onions are a springtime item there and are difficult to find the rest of the year. But when he does have them, the French cook knows what to do with them: he rarely buries their natural sweetness under a blanket of thick, white sauce—the usual preparation here. Most often, they come to the table just boiled and added to various stew-type dishes; or boiled, then sautéed to a crisp brown, and served separately. A sprinkling of sugar when sautéing helps caramelize and brown the onions, while adding a delicious extra sweetness.

6 servings

2 pounds small white onions
salt
½ cup polyunsaturated margarine
2 teaspoons sugar
salt and pepper

Peel onions, cutting a small cross into the bottom of each one so the centers will not pop during the cooking. Drop them into a large quantity of boiling, salted water. Cover and simmer gently until the onions are almost soft, about 20 to 25 minutes. Drain and immediately run cold water over them to stop the cooking. Dry on towels. (This much can be done in advance.)

Heat ½ the margarine in a heavy skillet until it is foaming; add the onions and fry for a few minutes until they are heated through. Sprinkle on the sugar, salt, and pepper and shake the skillet vigorously so that all surfaces of the onions are coated with the sugar. Add margarine as needed. Sauté until the onions have turned a deep brown.

BAKED SPANISH ONIONS

CHOLESTEROL RATING 1
CALORIES PER SERVING 108

Most people love onions—as long as they are cooked, and with good reason. In this original recipe the Spanish onion becomes a delicious vegetable by itself rather than just an addition to something else. All the sweetness of the onion comes out in the long, slow cooking. Although the quantity and thickness of the slices may seem like a lot, the bulk reduces greatly in the baking.

6 servings

4 large Spanish onions, peeled
1 cup beef broth
salt and pepper
1 teaspoon powdered thyme

Cut off the ends of the onions so that the slices will be flat. Slice onions horizontally ½ inch thick and put in a single layer in a large baking dish. Pour in enough beef broth to come to ½ the depth of the slices, spooning some broth over each slice. Sprinkle on salt, pepper, and powdered thyme. Cover and place in a 325° oven for 45 minutes.

During the baking baste occasionally and watch the level of broth, which should always be at least ⅛ inch deep; add more water if necessary. Remove the cover and bake 15 minutes more. This will evaporate most of the water and reinforce the onion flavor. The onions will have turned a dark golden color and be quite limp. If you are preparing them ahead of time, remove the dish from the oven before the final uncovered baking. At serving time, pour in ¼ cup water, uncover, and reheat for 10 minutes in 350° oven.

SHEPHERD'S MARKET ONION RINGS

CHOLESTEROL RATING 1
CALORIES PER SERVING 175

London is full of friendly pubs where you can have a first-rate meal, especially cold buffets. One of the best in the city is in Shepherd's Market, just off Curzon Street. All the food is prepared on the premises, including this easy-to-make, zippy onion relish. You will find it an interesting accompaniment to roasts and chops, a wonderful addition to an antipasto platter, and even a brand-new picnic item. The recipe is deliberately presented for a large quantity because it keeps for weeks in the refrigerator, and goes quickly.

16 servings

3 pounds Spanish onions
3 cups granulated sugar
2 cups vinegar

Cut the onions in very thin slices and put in a large nonmetal bowl, separating the slices into rings. Pour sugar and vinegar over the onions and mix well. Cover and let steep at room temperature for at least 12 hours (24 is better yet), stirring occasionally. The bulk of the raw onions will reduce as they wilt and soften. They are now ready for the refrigerator and continual snacking enjoyment.

PERSIL FRIT

Fried Parsley

CHOLESTEROL RATING 1
CALORIES PER SERVING 85

This little emerald-green garnish is proof again of how French chefs can make something quite special out of practically nothing. In fine restaurants, fried fish is often accompanied with a powdering of crisply fried parsley. It takes seconds to do, costs almost nothing, and adds glamour to the most ordinary dish.

6 servings

1 bunch regular parsley, not the flat-leafed variety
polyunsaturated oil for frying
salt

Pick off only the leaves from the parsley, saving the stems to flavor soups and stews. Wash the parsley leaves under cold running water and dry thoroughly, really thoroughly. If any moisture clings to the leaves it will splatter like Vesuvius in the hot oil. One master chef confided that at times he puts the parsley leaves in a barely warm oven for just a few seconds to insure absolute dryness. It's a great tip, but care must be taken not to warm the leaves too much or they will become limp.

Heat frying oil in a deep pan until it's almost smoking. Put the dried parsley leaves in a wire basket and plunge it into the hot oil for no more than 5 seconds. Remove the basket and drain the parsley on paper towels. Sprinkle with salt and serve immediately.

Lacking a deep-fry basket, you can toss handfuls of the parsley into the pan of hot oil and quickly remove the fried leaves with a skimmer and place them directly onto the absorbent paper.

PETITS POIS CLAMART

Pea Purée

CHOLESTEROL RATING 1
CALORIES PER SERVING 173

Something really good can be made from frozen peas. This preparation also gives them a more subtle place on the menu. The blending of the lettuce, shallots, and onions along with the peas brings out the flavor that in other versions must come from butter and cream.

6 servings

2 10-ounce packages frozen peas
6 large lettuce leaves, shredded
1 chopped shallot
1 medium onion, sliced thin for faster cooking
4 tablespoons polyunsaturated oil
4 parsley sprigs
1 teaspoon sugar
salt and pepper
½ cup chicken stock, mushroom juice, or water
½ teaspoon Worcestershire sauce

Put the peas in a saucepan with the shredded lettuce, shallot, onion, oil, parsley, sugar, salt, pepper, and stock or water. Cover and bring to a boil, then reduce heat and simmer until tender, about 10 minutes. When cooked, remove the parsley and put the rest in a blender. Blend to a fine purée, then return to pot and reheat. Add Worcestershire sauce, taste for salt and pepper, and correct if necessary. If the purée is a little thin, boil rapidly, uncovered, until some of the liquid boils off; if it's too thick, add 1 to 2 tablespoons skimmed milk and cook for a few minutes. It is also good served cold.

PETITS POIS FILIPPO

Peas with Dill

CHOLESTEROL RATING 1
CALORIES PER SERVING 200

The sweet flavor of tiny Italian peas is unforgettable. All other peas should be measured against that standard. When at their best, Italian peas are served *au naturel* with a dollop of butter. Those of slightly lesser quality are often given a boost with a strong flavoring of fresh dill. It is a taste combination not too different from our own peas with mint, but somehow more respectful of nature's harmony. Fresh dill, of course, gives far better results than dried. While the addition of a small amount of onion adds a snap, it is almost undetectable if minced or grated fine enough. Frozen peas really improve with this treatment.

6 servings

½ cup water
2 10-ounce packages frozen peas
½ teaspoon sugar
¼ teaspoon salt
3 tablespoons polyunsaturated oil
¼ cup onion, very finely chopped or grated
¼ cup polyunsaturated margarine
1½ tablespoons chopped fresh dill (dry if necessary)

Bring ½ cup of water to a boil, add the frozen peas, sugar, and salt, cover, and simmer gently for 3 to 4 minutes. Do not overcook at this point because the peas are reheated later. Drain peas thoroughly.

Meanwhile, heat the oil in a small pot and add the finely chopped or grated onions. Cover and simmer gently for 5 minutes, stirring often so the onions do not brown. (These steps can be done ahead of time.) At serving time, heat the cooked onions, add the drained peas and margarine, and mix well until the margarine is melted. Sprinkle on the dill and gently mix all together. Cover and simmer slowly for 1 minute.

PETITS POIS À LA NIÇOISE

Peas with Tomatoes

CHOLESTEROL RATING 1
CALORIES PER SERVING 185

The first time I came across these peas in tomato sauce, they were peeking out from between two layers of rice. The chef had made a sort of layer cake presentation by forming a layer of cooked rice about 1 inch thick and 8 inches in diameter. The peas-in-tomatoes were carefully spooned on top of the rice. Then another rice layer was gently arranged on top, and a sprinkling of chopped parsley finished it off. The layered effect was very pretty. At other times, the same chef makes a whole meal of this dish by placing veal Ossobuco (page 123) on the very top. The idea can be used for any meat prepared with just a little sauce.

6 servings

¼ cup polyunsaturated oil
½ cup onion, chopped very fine
2 fresh tomatoes
1 tablespoon polyunsaturated margarine
2 10-ounce packages frozen peas
salt and pepper

Heat the oil in a small heavy pot, add the chopped onion, cover, and simmer gently for about 5 minutes without browning the onion. Meanwhile, plunge the tomatoes into boiling water for a few seconds and slip off the skins. Cut the tomatoes in half horizontally, discard the seeds and chop coarsely. Add the tomatoes and the margarine to the onions. Simmer briskly for about 15 minutes. You should now have a nice, fairly thick tomato sauce. Add the frozen peas, salt, and pepper, cover, and simmer very slowly for about 30 minutes or until the peas are tender.

POIVRONS AUX OIGNONS

Green Peppers and Onions

CHOLESTEROL RATING 1
CALORIES PER SERVING 115

Green peppers are one of the most popular early fall vegetables all through Central Europe. Many versions can be served hot or cold after having been grilled, stuffed, done in oil, fried, or braised. This particular dish is a hearty vegetable when served hot, but it can also be chilled and come at the beginning of a meal with just a little extra oil poured over. When red and yellow peppers are in season, you can make a pretty color contrast by mixing in a few.

6 servings

¼ cup polyunsaturated oil
2 medium onions, thinly sliced
5 green peppers
1 cup white wine
1 cup water
1 or 2 garlic cloves, crushed
1 teaspoon oregano
1 bay leaf
1 teaspoon salt
½ teaspoon pepper

Heat oil in a skillet, add the sliced onions, cover, and simmer slowly for about 10 minutes or until onions are limp. Meanwhile, remove seeds from the green peppers and cut in long strips, about ¼ inch wide. Add the pepper strips to the onions, mix well, and pour on wine and water. Add the garlic, oregano, bay leaf, salt and pepper. Cover and simmer for about 20 minutes, or until the peppers are soft. Stir a few times during cooking. Remove bay leaf and serve hot as a vegetable or cold as first course.

POMMES DE TERRE À LA VAPEUR

Steamed Potatoes

CHOLESTEROL RATING 1
CALORIES PER SERVING 93

The difference between steamed potatoes and boiled potatoes is like the difference between caviar and lumpfish. Not even pressure-cooked potatoes approach the mellowness of potatoes steamed slowly and steadily. But you don't have a potato steamer? Who does, and who wants an extra pot cluttering the cupboard? Any deep pot and a colander or sieve will do. The only other thing necessary is a dish towel for enveloping the potatoes. The towel prevents the potatoes from coming in contact with the metal, so they do not turn gray. Also, since they are closely wrapped, the heat is concentrated to cook the potatoes more evenly. They are at their very best when just finished, but the timing will vary with different potatoes, so precooking may be necessary. Still, don't steam them so long in advance that they cool completely before being reheated at serving time. The best potatoes to use are the small, red-skinned new potatoes.

6 servings

2 pounds small red-skinned potatoes, peeled
water
1 teaspoon salt
2 tablespoons chopped parsley

Choose a deep pot in which you can place a colander or large sieve so that it is suspended above the bottom. There should be at least 1 inch of space between the bottom of the colander and the bottom of the pot. Put in just enough water to almost reach the colander and add salt to the water.

Wring out a dish towel with cold water and line the colander with it, leaving the ends of the towel hanging over the colander. Put the peeled potatoes in the towel and cover them completely with the rest of the towel; then put a lid on the pot.

Bring the water to a rapid boil, then lower the heat to keep the water at a constant rapid simmer. Check the water level from time to time and, if necessary, add more hot water. Also make certain that the top of the towel doesn't dry out; if it begins to, pour some water over it. This is important.

After about 45 minutes check the potatoes for doneness by piercing the center of one with a sharp knife. There should be no resistance when they are finished. Potatoes about the size of a small egg should take approximately 1 hour, larger ones 1¼ hours. The heat can be reduced to slow down the remaining cooking time.

Just before serving, sprinkle chopped parsley over the steamed potatoes.

POMMES SAVONETTES

Baked Potato Slices

CHOLESTEROL RATING 1
CALORIES PER SERVING 160

Here is a novel way to prepare potatoes, one invented in the kitchens of a posh Parisian hotel. The name *Savonette* comes from the shape of the slices, since each one originally was trimmed to resemble a small oval bar of soap, *savon*. A nice touch, but not necessary.

In this method, thick slices of potatoes are almost completely covered with water and slipped into a hot oven. As the water boils off, the interior of the potato becomes moist and extremely tender. Any slices that are left over can be resliced in half and turned into the best fried potatoes you ever had.

The original recipe calls for butter, but with the addition of a bit of chicken bouillon cube one arrives at equally good results without it. Idaho potatoes of uniform size are the best to use.

6 servings

4 Idaho potatoes
¼ cup polyunsaturated margarine
water
salt and pepper
1 chicken bouillon cube, crumbled

Peel the potatoes and cut off a slice from each end. Then slice them horizontally into 1-inch-thick pieces. It is important that all slices are of the same thickness so that they will cook uniformly. Place in a single layer either in a heavy skillet or a baking dish. Choose one that holds the slices snugly; do not use too large a dish.

Spread ½ teaspoon of margarine on each slice, pour in enough water to come almost to the top of the slices, sprinkle on salt and pepper, and sprinkle the crumbled chicken bouillon cube into the water. On top of stove (with asbestos pad if using a glass baking dish) bring water to simmer. Then place the dish in 425° oven for about 45 minutes. At the end of this time the water should have almost completely boiled off and the potato slices should be soft when pierced with a sharp knife. If not, add a little more water and bake for 10 minutes more.

The potatoes can be baked ahead of time and reheated in the oven, again with a little water added to the dish.

FLEMISH POTATO CASSEROLE

CHOLESTEROL RATING 1
CALORIES PER SERVING 185

Belgian cuisine is divided quite clearly between the delicate and the hearty. The subtle, lightly sauced dishes have much in common with French cooking of the highest order. But since much of Belgium endures a long and austere winter, a real stick-to-the-ribs tradition of eating has also evolved. Potatoes, naturally, figure importantly in the kitchen, and no cooks anywhere use onions quite so liberally. The two vegetables are used together in this satisfying casserole, which can easily become a main course with the addition of some diced leftover beef or lamb.

8 servings

⅓ cup polyunsaturated oil
2 cups thinly sliced onion
8 medium potatoes
salt and pepper
¼ cup grated low-fat cheese
¾ cup canned beef broth
¾ cup water

Heat the oil in a heavy pot. Add onions, cover, and simmer about 10 to 15 minutes very slowly until the onions are transparent but not at all colored.

Meanwhile, peel the potatoes and slice them ¼ inch thick.

Lightly oil a 2-quart casserole. Put in a layer of potatoes using about ⅓ of the entire amount, then ⅓ of the onions, a light sprinkling of salt, pepper, and cheese. Repeat for the second layer. Finally, layer in the last ⅓ of the potatoes and press lightly with the palms of your hands. Mix the beef broth and water together and pour over the potatoes to the level where you can just see the liquid under the potatoes. Finally put in the last of the onions, salt, pepper, and cheese.

Place the casserole on top of the stove and heat until the liquid begins to bubble. If the casserole cannot take direct heat, place an asbestos pad under it. Once the liquid is bubbling, cover the casserole and place it in an oven preheated to 325°. Bake for 1½ hours or until a knife pierces the potatoes easily.

The long, slow baking gives a better and more uniform flavor to the potatoes. In fact, this is one vegetable dish that is even better if baked the day before until the potatoes are only ¾ done and is then finished when needed. In either case, check from time to time to make sure that liquid remains in the dish. It will diminish, but it should never go below the ¼ level.

Serve directly from the casserole.

PUB POTATO SALAD

CHOLESTEROL RATING 1
CALORIES PER SERVING 290

The chef in a popular pub just off Curzon Street in London prepares and serves by himself one of the best cold buffets in town. His particular version of potato salad has a flavor and texture like none other. The crushing, rather than mashing, of the cooked potatoes is crucial, as is working with them while they are still too hot to handle . . . well, almost. Homemade mayonnaise is also necessary since the prepared variety is much too sweet. Serve with any cold meat or vegetable plate.

8 servings

2 pounds potatoes, preferably new potatoes
3 tablespoons finely cut chives; or 2 tablespoons sweet Spanish onions; or 2 tablespoons shallots
1 to 1½ cups mayonnaise
salt and pepper
2 tablespoons chopped parsley if onions are used instead of chives

Cook the potatoes in their skins in large quantity of boiling salted water. Meanwhile, cut chives fine into a mixing bowl. When the potatoes are cooked, peel them as soon as you can handle them, cutting into large chunks directly into the chives while the potatoes are still hot. This will help poach the chives a little. When all the potatoes are skinned, crush the chunks lightly. They should not be mashed into creaminess, but should retain a firmer consistency. You might call this a somewhat lumpy texture.

Let the potatoes cool a little, then mix in the mayonnaise with a wooden spoon, adding a heaping tablespoon at a time. The exact amount of mayonnaise added will depend on the quality of the potatoes, but there should be enough for the potatoes to become shiny and form a large mass. If Spanish onions or shallots are used instead of chives, let the salad cool thoroughly then add the chopped parsley to give some color.

This salad is best if made a few hours before using, so flavors can mingle. If made the day before and refrigerated, remove it from the cold long enough in advance to let it come almost to room temperature.

POMMES DE TERRE À L'HUILE

French Potato Salad

CHOLESTEROL RATING 1
CALORIES PER SERVING 170

Parisians like to go to cafés for after-theater supper, and one of the most popular of all is Lipp, that venerable institution in St.-Germain-des Prés. One of the favorite dishes served the late diner at Lipp is grilled sausages with *Pommes de Terre à l'Huile.* As with so many simple French dishes the careful preparation makes the difference between ordinary eating and dining *à la française.*

There are three simple rules to follow here: (1) good quality boiling potatoes, red-skinned new potatoes being especially good; (2) preparing the potatoes while they are still warm; (3) good homemade salad dressing. It's not at all complicated and is an excellent dish served with any cold meat or *Morue Marinée* (Marinated Smoked Cod), page 84).

8 servings

2 pounds boiling potatoes
1 tablespoon salt
¼ cup dry vermouth or dry white wine
2 tablespoons polyunsaturated oil
½ cup Herbed French Dressing I (page 243)

Scrub the unpeeled potatoes while bringing a large quantity of water to a rapid boil. Add the salt to the water, then the potatoes, and boil until tender, or about 30 minutes, depending on the size of the potatoes. Drain at once.

As soon as the potatoes are cool enough to handle, peel and cut them into slices about ⅛ inch thick. Put the potato slices in a deep mixing bowl.

Pour the vermouth or wine over the potatoes and toss carefully so as not to break the slices. Dribble on the oil and toss more. Cover and set aside for 5 minutes.

Just before serving, pour on the salad dressing and mix carefully. The potatoes are best if they are served while still warm, but leftovers will be almost as good.

PRUNES FOR GARNISHING

CHOLESTEROL RATING 1
CALORIES PER SERVING 107

Strictly speaking, prunes don't belong in the vegetable chapter, but they can fill the bill usefully. They are especially helpful when a final decorative touch is needed to improve the look of a meat platter from "family" to "company." Even when the ever-present parsley is pressed into service, platter arrangements often look underdressed. But with the addition of plump hot prunes, not only do you add decoration, but you add one that can be eaten. Wine-cooked prunes go especially well with roast game, lamb, or chicken, or as an unexpected touch with *Poulet Grillé à la Diable* (Chicken Grilled with Mustard), p. 98.

6 servings

½ pound large pitted prunes
1 cup dry white wine
1 clove
½ cup water
2 tablespoons sugar

Rinse the prunes under cold water and place in a small enameled pot or a bowl. In another small pot heat the wine almost to the boiling point and immediately pour it over the prunes. Add the clove, cover, and set aside for at least 3 hours, or overnight.

When you are ready to cook the prunes, add the water and sugar to the pot, cover and bring to a low simmer. Cook the prunes on this heat for about 10 minutes or until they are soft and plump. The exact timing will depend on their quality. Do not overcook or they will not remain plump but will flatten out. The prunes can be cooked ahead of time and reheated at serving time. Remove them from the pot with a skimmer and arrange around the meat on a platter.

RICE

CHOLESTEROL RATING 1
CALORIES PER SERVING 130

There is no great mystery about cooking rice properly. And still the mastery of the few needed principles eludes too many women. Nothing could be simpler than the method used by Paris's Cordon Bleu where fluffy, individual grains of tender rice are *de rigueur.* No guesswork is involved; the procedure is almost scientific. Proportions are important—exactly twice the amount of water as rice. Timing is equally important—exactly 20 minutes in a constant 350° oven.

The possibilities of varying the basic dish are limitless. A finely chopped onion can be sautéed in the oil; chicken or beef broth can be used for the liquid; and a variety of vegetables, fish, or meat can be added to create substantial main courses. In short, the rice can become a vehicle for your imagination and your leftovers. So say goodbye to sticky, clumped-together rice, which is good for only one thing: eating with chopsticks.

6 servings

¼ cup polyunsaturated oil
1½ cups long grain rice, unwashed
3 cups hot water
salt and pepper

Heat oil in a heavy pan that has a lid and can go into the oven. Add the dry, unwashed rice and stir with a wooden spoon until the translucent grains turn white. This cooking of the starch in the rice prevents it from being released in the water, which causes stickiness. As soon as the rice is opaque and white, pour in the water, salt, and pepper and bring to a boil. Cover at once and put in oven preheated to 350°. Leave in oven for 20 minutes without ever removing the lid. At the end of this time the liquid will be absorbed. Remove from the oven, but do not remove the lid for another 10 minutes. Fluff rice with a fork. If the rice is cooked ahead of time, it can be reheated at serving time by sprinkling on 2 tablespoons of cold water, fluffing again with fork, covering, and heating in a slow oven.

PURÉE D'ÉPINARDS

Spinach Purée

CHOLESTEROL RATING 1
CALORIES PER SERVING 65

Spinach purée is a very handy recipe. You'll find it a fancy way to serve a vegetable that is often considered quite ordinary. In addition, it opens menu planning to a whole list of dishes called "à la Florentine," the culinary term for dishes containing spinach. An impressive presentation can be made by preparing a bed of puréed spinach on top of which is put anything from poached fish to ham braised in Madeira. You can even use *Gratin d'Endives au Jambon* (Gratin of Endives and Ham), page 60.

Fresh spinach, of course, makes the best purée and can be used in this recipe. However, directions are given for frozen spinach since that is probably what will most often be available.

4 servings

½ cup water
¼ cup thinly sliced onions
½ teaspoon salt
1 10-ounce package frozen whole-leaf spinach, or 1 pound fresh
5 tablespoons skimmed milk
½ boiled potato (about ½ cup), cut in pieces
1 tablespoon polyunsaturated margarine
large pinch nutmeg
¼ teaspoon sugar
½ teaspoon lemon juice
salt and pepper
1 tablespoon margarine, ¼ cup skimmed milk (optional)

Put the water, onions and salt in a pot, cover and bring to a boil. Add the spinach and cook for 5 minutes after the water returns to a boil. Drain the spinach and onions thoroughly, then, a handful at a time, squeeze the excess water out of it. Chop the spinach coarsely.

Put the squeezed spinach and onions, milk, and boiled potato in a blender. Purée until smooth. Return the purée to the pot and add the margarine, nutmeg, sugar, lemon juice, salt and pepper. Reheat slowly and taste for seasoning; correct if necessary. This makes a fairly thick purée. If you would like it thinner, add the extra margarine and skimmed milk.

GRILLED TOMATOES

CHOLESTEROL RATING 1
CALORIES PER SERVING 42

Grilled tomatoes are one of the handiest, easiest, and most colorful vegetable dishes that can be brought to the table. Most European cooks would dribble butter over them instead of oil, but the small touch of curry in this recipe turns the tomatoes into something different in which butter has no place at all. Besides, even flavorless winter tomatoes get an extra boost this way. How much curry you use depends on your taste and what else is being served. Sprinkling, though, is better than splashing.

6 servings

6 medium firm tomatoes
salt and pepper
curry powder
2 tablespoons polyunsaturated oil

Select tomatoes that are still firm or they will render too much juice. Remove the stems carefully and cut the tomatoes in half crosswise. Place tomatoes, cut side up, on oiled baking dish. Sprinkle with salt, pepper, and curry. Just before slipping under the broiler, sprinkle on some oil. Place about 5 inches away from flame, so the tomatoes will cook through more slowly. After about 4 to 5 minutes, place closer to flame to brown a little.

COURGETTES FRITES ARMÉNIENNE

Fried Zucchini, Armenian Style

CHOLESTEROL RATING 1
CALORIES PER SERVING 165

Next time you think of serving French fried potatoes, switch to fried zucchini instead. They are much, much lighter to the taste and digestion, and needless to say, they are certainly more unusual. The zucchini arrive at the table long and crisp and are meant to be eaten with fingers. The Armenian style is to dip the crunchy sticks into a garlic-flavored yoghurt, which, though good, might be a bit potent for most tastes. The traditional recipe is given, but I also list another possibility which is equally good, and not as strong.

6 servings

5 small zucchini, no longer than 5 inches
¼ cup coarse or kosher salt
½ cup flour
polyunsaturated oil for frying
salt

Cut off the two ends of the zucchini, then cut the vegetable in half, lengthwise. With the cut side down, make lengthwise slices no thicker than ⅛ inch. If the zucchini are longer than 5 inches, cut in half horizontally before proceeding to slice.

Put all the long, thin strips into a colander and pour the salt over them, toss to mix well, and let stand for at least two hours on the drainboard. During this time the zucchini will give up their water, which is considerable. They will have reduced greatly in bulk and be quite limp. Rinse them very well under running cold water, turning them over with your hands so that all the zucchini are rinsed free of the salt. Wrap in a towel and press out as much water as possible.

Dump the limp zucchini into a deep bowl and sprinkle on ½ the flour. Toss all together very well, then sprinkle on the rest of the flour and toss again.

Meanwhile, heat the oil in a deep skillet or deep fryer. Oil should be at least ¼ inch in depth. Heat to almost smoking. Taking handfuls of zucchini at a time, shake the excess flour off, and toss them into the hot oil. They will fry to a deep gold in a matter of seconds. Remove with a skimmer and drain on paper towels, and proceed with the rest of the zucchini.

The zucchini can be completely cooked in this one operation by leaving them in a few seconds longer, but I prefer to do them just to the light golden stage ahead of time, then replunge them in even hotter oil just before serving. They come out much crisper with the second frying which takes only a split second. Drain again on paper towels, sprinkle with salt, and serve at once.

ARMENIAN YOGHURT DIP

CHOLESTEROL RATING 1
CALORIES PER SERVING 20

1 cup plain low-fat yoghurt
1 garlic clove

Discard the center sprout from the garlic clove and grate the garlic directly into the yoghurt. Grate the garlic very, very fine; it should be almost a liquid. Mix well with the yoghurt and let stand for at least 3 hours before using. (Armenians consider this proportion of garlic to yoghurt minimal.)

ORIENTAL YOGHURT DIP

CHOLESTEROL RATING 1
CALORIES PER SERVING 20

1 cup plain low-fat yoghurt
¼ teaspoon curry
¼ teaspoon cumin
1 teaspoon lemon juice
salt and pepper

Blend all ingredients together and let stand for at least 1 hour. The proportions can be altered to suit your taste.

DESSERTS

White Strawberries

EVERYONE'S MENTAL PICTURE OF A DESSERT IS A MULTICOLORED CONCOCTION weighed down with whipped cream. Few people over sixteen still crave such fantasies, but they are constantly confronted with them when dining out.

At dessert time, all too many cooks go into high gear with cream, butter, and egg yolks. They feel that the choice is either rich, creamy desserts or giving in and serving plain fresh fruit. Though fruit is always enjoyable, it should not have to be the inevitable conclusion of every sensible meal.

Fruits, of course, are important in these recipes. But they are used in ways that transform the raw materials into fanciful desserts. A *Poire au Vin Rouge* (Pear Poached in Red Wine), for example, starts out life as a simple fruit, but at the end of the recipe it's a ruby-colored jewel of a dessert.

Whipped desserts are included to bring the glamorous look of soufflés to the table. Three sherbet recipes are given, each demonstrating a different principle that can be adapted into a colorful array of flavors. The cookie tray does not have to be neglected either. It can be filled with varieties from small meringues to morsels of golden sesame seeds. Even cakes—without their usual butter and eggs—are included because there always are occasions for them.

No, the low-cholesterol diner does not have to sit out the dessert course. He should enjoy it.

The wines that come with dessert add immeasurably to that enjoyment. Champagne, of course, is always festive and correct, but certainly not necessary. French Vin Mousseux, which is a white wine prepared in the champagne process, can be great fun. Sweet Vouvray or very fruity Rhine wines are an excellent change. French sweet Sauternes or Barsac wines are especially appropriate. Dessert Sauternes should not be confused with the American version of Sauternes which is a dry white wine. A change of wine for the dessert course is not necessary, one could always continue with the wine served during the meal.

Fruits

BANANES FLAMBÉES

Bananas in Flaming Sauce

CHOLESTEROL RATING 1
CALORIES PER SERVING 315

Flaming desserts always create a spectacular effect. Too often the whole show is in the burning alcohol and not in the taste that follows. Here you have the best of both, since the sauce is carefully prepared ahead and becomes a flavorful vehicle for the fiery presentation.

8 servings

8 firm ripe bananas (not overripe)
½ cup flour
polyunsaturated oil for frying bananas
2 cups fresh or canned fruit juice (pineapple, orange, apricot, or a mixture)
½ cup sugar
½ cup polyunsaturated margarine
¼ teaspoon freshly grated nutmeg
½ cup rum
⅓ cup brandy
⅓ cup rum
2 tablespoons sugar

Peel the bananas and roll them in the flour until they are coated evenly; shake off the excess. Pour the oil into a skillet to about ¼-inch depth and heat well. When the oil is hot, add the bananas and fry them quickly on both sides so they brown evenly. Quick frying is important so they don't become overcooked and mushy.

Add more oil as needed. Drain the bananas on paper towels, remove to a dish, and put aside. This can be done hours before needed.

Make a sauce for the bananas, either directly in a chafing dish or in a large flameproof pie plate in which they will be served, or make the sauce in a small pot and transfer it to the dish later. Combine the fruit juice, sugar, margarine, and nutmeg. Bring to a boil and let simmer for about 15 minutes or until the liquid thickens a little. This, too, can be prepared well in advance.

When ready to serve, pour the fruit sauce into the serving dish and put it on heat. If you are using the pie plate, put an asbestos pad between it and the fire. Heat the sauce until it bubbles, then add the ½ cup rum. Put the bananas into the sauce and cook them for about 3 minutes, turning once or twice. Meanwhile, in a small pot, heat the ⅓ cup brandy and ⅓ cup rum until very hot, but not boiling. If the liquors are not hot enough they will not ignite, so make sure they are really hot. The sauce must also be hot for proper flaming.

At the very last minute, sprinkle the two tablespoons of sugar over the bananas, pour on the hot liquors and ignite with a match. While the flames dance, turn the bananas over and over with a long fork and spoon. When the flames die down, serve the bananas on individual dishes, spooning sauce over them liberally.

(As your fancy pleases, you can add thinly sliced nuts and seasonal fruits to the sauce. It's a nice touch, if not overdone.)

BANANES FARCIES

Stuffed Bananas

CHOLESTEROL RATING 1
CALORIES PER SERVING 314

Most people would just bake a banana plain. Not the French. First they stuff them, then bake to puff the filling, and finally they present them at the table aflame with rum. A showstopper every time.

4 servings

4 bananas
3 tablespoons powdered sugar
½ cup rum
¼ teaspoon cinnamon
1 teaspoon vanilla
2 egg whites
¾ cup rum for flaming
¾ cup grilled almonds for garnish (page 227)

Rinse and wipe the unpeeled bananas, then slit each one the entire length of the curved inside. Carefully remove the banana pulp with a teaspoon and place in a bowl. Put the banana skins in a plastic bag and refrigerate until needed for stuffing; this will keep them from turning dark brown.

Mash the banana pulp with a potato masher, and once it has been fairly well broken up, continue mashing with a fork while adding the sugar. When the pulp is quite smooth, add the rum, cinnamon, and vanilla. Cover and put in a cool spot for 2 to 3 hours, stirring from time to time. Beat the egg whites until they are very firm and delicately fold them into the banana mixture.

Spread each banana skin to make a wide opening and fill them with the mixture. Reclose the slits a little. Place the stuffed bananas on a lightly greased baking dish that will hold the 4 of them snugly. If the dish is too large, the bananas may fall over during the baking. Place in preheated 350° oven and bake for 10 to 12 minutes, or until the filling has puffed nicely and turned a light brown.

Just before the bananas are finished, heat ¾ cup of rum. Remove the bananas from the oven and sprinkle them with the grilled almonds. To flame the bananas, pour the heated rum over them and ignite it with a match. The dish can be lighted in the kitchen and brought aflame to the dining room, or set afire before the guests; in either case, serve at once.

FRUIT KEBABS

CHOLESTEROL RATING 1
CALORIES PER SERVING 120

Variety can be the spice of this unusual dessert. As the seasons change, different fruits should be substituted. However, if fruits as fragile as peaches are used, they should be firm so as not to distintegrate under the high heat. Pears, apricots, even seedless grapes, can be placed on the skewers.

6 servings

MARINADE

¼ cup honey
¼ cup dark rum
juice of ½ lemon
¼ teaspoon nutmeg
¼ teaspoon ground ginger

FRUITS

½ grapefruit
1 tart apple, unpeeled, quartered, then cut into 12 pieces
2 bananas, cut into 12 pieces
½ cup pineapple chunks (12 pieces)
1 orange, in sections
6 maraschino cherries

In a shallow dish mix the honey, rum, lemon juice, nutmeg, and ginger. Remove sections from the grapefruit half and put them aside. Squeeze the juice from the grapefruit shell into the above marinade. Put the grapefruit sections in the marinade. Then proceed to cut the fruit, adding each one to the marinade just as soon as it is cut. Spoon over some of the marinade immediately to prevent discoloration. Oranges or canned pineapple present no discoloration problem. When all the fruit is in the dish, baste well, cover, and let stand for at least 1 hour. Baste and turn occasionally.

String fruit on six 6-inch skewers. Begin with apple, the peel side going on first, facing the skewer end. Finish with the cherry. Put the completed skewers on a baking dish and baste liberally with the marinade. Place under broiler, about 6 inches away from flame. Baste several times during broiling. Kebabs should be finished in about 10 minutes. For the last 2 to 3 minutes of broiling time, bring the baking dish to within 3 inches of the flame to give a nice brown to parts of the fruit. Serve at once, spooning sauce over each kebab.

COMPOTE D'ORANGES

Sliced Orange Compote

CHOLESTEROL RATING 1
CALORIES PER SERVING 235

In many restaurants in France the dessert cart will include bowls of poached fresh fruit. This orange dessert is often included, usually made of whole poached oranges. Even though they do look very pretty, I find whole oranges much more difficult to eat than slices. Also, when the oranges are presliced, guests can help themselves to just a little bit if they're not hungry. If you have the patience to slice even more of the rind than the recipe calls for, do so; the more the better. In the cooking, the rind turns soft and sweet; it is mighty good to eat and is a natural decoration.

6 servings

6 good quality seedless oranges
2 cups water
1 cup sugar
¼ teaspoon salt
good pinch nutmeg, freshly grated
½ cup Grand Marnier or other orange liqueur

Carefully remove the rind from 3 oranges, cutting it in long strips and making sure none of the white part of the peel is included. A potato peeler works fine for this. Cut the rind into very, very thin julienne strips. Meanwhile, bring water, sugar, salt, and freshly grated nutmeg to a boil. Add the orange strips and simmer, partially covered, for 15 minutes.

During the simmering, remove the white part of the peel from the 3 oranges above, and completely peel the remaining three oranges. Cut the oranges across in even ¼-inch slices. Place the slices in a deep bowl that can withstand boiling syrup. When the orange-rind syrup is ready, pour it immediately over the orange slices. Add ½ cup orange liqueur at once (use more liqueur if your taste is for a strong alcohol flavor). Cover closely at once, let cool completely, then refrigerate for at least 3 hours.

By pouring the boiling syrup over the oranges, you actually poach the oranges slightly, and the alcohol steams off so only the liqueur flavor remains.

This compote should be served well chilled. Transfer the slices to a serving bowl with a lot of the rind heaped on top. Pass with cookies, such as almond tuiles, page 223.

PÊCHES POCHÉES À LA MIDI

Baked Peaches

CHOLESTEROL RATING 1
CALORIES PER SERVING 170

Peaches reach the height of their goodness during the summer months. It is also the season of cold main dishes for dinner. How nice it is to finish off the meal with a hot dessert as a change of pace. The syrup from baked peaches should not be thrown away. It can be frozen and reused for the same dish, or will provide the syrup base for *Bananes Flambées,* page 195.

6 servings

¾ cup sugar
½ cup water
¼ teaspoon cinnamon
½ teaspoon nutmeg
2 tablespoons polyunsaturated margarine
6 large ripe peaches
2 tablespoons Grand Marnier or other orange liqueur
¾ cup strawberry sauce (optional)

Preheat oven to 350°. Put sugar, water, cinnamon and nutmeg together in a small heavy pot and boil rapidly on high heat for 10 minutes. When finished, remove pot from fire and add the margarine.

Meanwhile, plunge the peaches into boiling water for a few seconds, then remove their skins. Place peaches in a baking dish that has a cover (lacking a cover use aluminum foil). Just before pouring the hot syrup over the peaches, add the orange liqueur to it. Pour the syrup on the peaches and cover immediately. Place in oven for about 20 minutes, or until the peaches are soft when tested with a sharp knife. Baste several times during the baking.

Serve hot. If you like, you can pass a cold strawberry purée sauce with this dish.

PÊCHES EN PICHET

Peaches in a Pitcher

CHOLESTEROL RATING 1
CALORIES PER PEACH 50

A friend who lives in southern France often shocks her more conservative friends with her treatment of two exceptional local products —peaches and wine. She slips peeled peaches into a clear glass pitcher and pours chilled dry white wine over them. During the meal, the wine is served from the pitcher and at dessert time a long-handled spoon is used to retrieve the delectable wine-soaked peaches. In a warm land where peaches are delicious and bountiful and white wine is often a little coarse, this merging of the two regional products is an inspired thought. It is worth copying anywhere.

6 servings

6 good quality, ripe peaches
2 bottles dry white wine, not best quality

Plunge the peaches into boiling water for ½ minute and lift out with a skimmer. As soon as you can handle them, slip off the skins. If the peaches are really ripe the skins will almost slide off. Immediately put the peaches in a wide-mouthed glass pitcher. If one pitcher is not large enough to hold all the wine, use two. Pour the chilled wine over the peaches right away to prevent discoloration.

Put the pitcher in the refrigerator for at least 2 hours, so the peach flavor will perfume the wine and also to thoroughly chill the pitcher, which will then keep the wine cool throughout the meal. Pour wine from pitcher during the meal and serve the wine-soaked peaches for dessert. Pass plain cookies, such as lemon pecan wafers, page 221.

POIRES AU VIN ROUGE

Pears Poached in Red Wine

CHOLESTEROL RATING 1
CALORIES PER SERVING 340

Thanks to the good quality pears available in the United States, this is one delicious French recipe that does not lose a thing when made here. It is easy to prepare and is best if done the day before so the pears become an even darker red. The prettiest way to present them is to keep the fruit whole, standing upright in a large serving dish with a good deal of the syrup around the pears. The syrup is spooned over each serving.

8 servings

1 quart red wine
2¼ cups sugar
1 small lemon, thinly sliced
½ teaspoon cinnamon
8 pears of good quality, Anjou or Bartlett

In a covered enameled or tin-lined copper pot, boil the red wine, sugar, lemon, and cinnamon. Once brought to a boil, simmer for about 20 minutes, still covered.

Meanwhile carefully peel the pears (a potato peeler works fine). Leave the stem intact, but remove a slice from the bottom, so the pears will stand up solidly in the serving dish.

As soon as each pear is peeled, rub it with a cut lemon, and drop it in a bowl of clear cold water; this is to prevent discoloration. If you have selected normal-size pears, leave them whole; if oversized, cut them in half and remove stems. If you want to speed up the cooking, or prefer a sliced compote, then cut the fruit into thick sections and remove seeds.

When the wine syrup is ready, place the pears in the boiling liquid, cover, and cook slowly until they can be easily pierced with a knife, but are still slightly firm. Remember, the pears will continue to soften while cooling in the hot syrup. A whole pear should take 30 to 35 minutes, depending on the ripeness and size of the pear; halves or slices will take much less time.

During the cooking process, turn the pears quite often so they will be evenly colored by the wine syrup. Use two wooden spoons for turning in order not to bruise the fruit. When the pears are done, place them in a serving dish that will also hold the sauce. Boil down the wine syrup to ½ its volume, strain it, and pour over the pears. Chill well.

PRUNES IN PORT WINE

CHOLESTEROL RATING 1
CALORIES PER SERVING 275

As good as "port and prunes" sounds to the ear, it is even better on the tongue. Americans have the idea that prunes are strictly a breakfast item. The French know better. They, however, liberally lace plump prunes with plenty of sweet port wine. It is a beautiful combination (and toast could never follow it).

6 servings

30 large prunes
½ to ¾ bottle sweet port wine
1 small lemon
½ teaspoon cinnamon
pinch ground cloves
¾ cup water
1 cup toasted slivered almonds

Choose large, good quality prunes, counting on 5 per person for an average portion. Rinse the prunes and place them in a deep bowl. Cover with port wine. Place a cover on the bowl and let soak overnight, or at least 3 hours.

Put the prunes and port in an enameled or tin-lined pot. Add the grated rind and juice of the lemon, the cinnamon, ground cloves, and water. Bring to a slow simmer and cook for about 20 minutes, depending on the quality of the prunes. Do not overcook or they will turn mushy. Chill well. At serving time, place in a large glass bowl, sprinkle with the toasted almonds, and pass a small bowl of the almonds as well.

FRAISES CARDINALE

Strawberries in Raspberry Sauce

CHOLESTEROL RATING 1
CALORIES PER SERVING 150

Fresh strawberries with raspberry sauce sounds like gilding the lily, but if the lily ends up as a far more beautiful creation, who can complain? In this very French dessert there is a delightful flavor play between the sweet of the strawberries and the slight tartness of the raspberries. Père Bise, that extraordinary restaurant on Lake Annecy in eastern France, even envelops tiny wild strawberries *(fraises des bois)* in a raspberry sauce. Other restaurants are known to add whipped cream as well. That really is gilding the lily.

6 servings

3 pints fresh strawberries
2 tablespoons sugar
grated rind of 1 orange
1 cup fresh orange juice
1 tablespoon Grand Marnier, or other orange liqueur

1 pint fresh raspberries, or 1 10-ounce package frozen berries
1 teaspoon Grand Marnier, or other orange liqueur
1 teaspoon lemon juice
For fresh raspberries only: ½ cup sugar

Carefully rinse and hull the strawberries and put them in a shallow bowl. Sprinkle over them the sugar, grated orange rind, orange juice, and Grand Marnier. Mix gently with a wooden spoon or rubber spatula, cover, and refrigerate for 2 hours. Turn them a few times during this marinating period.

If you are using fresh raspberries, clean and rinse them carefully. Put the raspberries (fresh or frozen) in the blender. Add the Grand Marnier and lemon juice. Sugar is added only to fresh berries. Blend until you have a purée of the fruit, the seeds remaining in the sauce. Chill.

About 15 minutes before serving, remove the strawberries from the orange marinade with a skimmer. Save the orange liquid for other dessert sauces. Place the berries in a deep serving bowl, pour about half the raspberry sauce over them, and turn them carefully. Pass the rest of the sauce separately.

Whips

APRICOT WHIP

CHOLESTEROL RATING 1
CALORIES PER SERVING 187

Here is more proof that delicious desserts don't have to be full of eggs, cream, and butter. The use of dried instead of canned apricots brings a strong fresh flavor to this apricot whip. That fresh flavor is intensified by the addition of orange juice and liqueur. This dessert is prettiest served in a soufflé dish.

6 servings

½ pound dried apricots
1 pint boiling water
1½ tablespoons gelatin
¼ cup cold water
½ cup sugar
½ cup orange juice
1 tablespoon orange liqueur
3 egg whites

Rinse the apricots and place in a saucepan; pour boiling water over them. Cover and let stand for 2 hours. Put the covered pan over moderate heat and cook gently until the fruit is tender (about 30 minutes). Cool slightly, then pass the fruit and liquid through a food mill. The mill is preferable to a blender because it is certain to remove any tough pieces of skin that may remain.

Return the apricot purée to the pot and put on very slow heat. Soak the gelatin in the cold water and, once it is softened, add the gelatin to the purée. Then add sugar and orange juice to the purée and stir until the sugar and gelatin dissolve. Add the liqueur. Keep the mixture on very low heat while you beat egg whites until they are very stiff. Mix ¼ of the egg whites into the apricot mixture. Then add the mixture to the rest of the egg whites and fold gently. Pour into a serving dish and chill until firm.

CITRON EN NEIGE

Lemon Snow

CHOLESTEROL RATING 1
CALORIES PER SERVING 162

Gossamer Lemon could be another appropriate name for this featherlight dessert. There is so little solid matter holding it together that it actually quivers when brought into the dining room. I like to use a soufflé dish as a mold, and add, just before serving, a few green and yellow candy decorations. The final touch of color alleviates the pure white of the froth. And if disaster should occur when unmolding, simply heap the "Snow" into individual dessert dishes and top with a touch of green.

Although Lemon Snow is delicately delicious just as is, at times you may like to pass a sauce with it. Then the Green Mint Sauce (page 229) is a good visual and taste counterpoint.

6 servings

1 cup sugar
1½ cups water
1½ tablespoons gelatin
½ cup water
1 teaspoon grated lemon rind
1 cup lemon juice
6 egg whites
green and yellow candies for decoration (optional)

Put the sugar and 1½ cups of water together in a pot, stir over heat until the sugar dissolves and boil for 2 minutes. Meanwhile, soften the gelatin in ½ cup water and add this to the hot syrup, stirring to completely dissolve the gelatin. Add the grated lemon rind and lemon juice. Cool, then refrigerate, stirring occasionally, until the syrup becomes thick and just begins to jell. This will take about 1½ hours. (The setting can be hastened by stirring the lemon syrup in a bowl set inside a deeper bowl of ice.)

Whip egg whites until they are very stiff. Place the bowl with the egg whites inside a deeper bowl that contains ice and water. Slowly and delicately fold the thickened lemon syrup into the egg whites. Leave this mixture over the ice and fold lightly from time to time to hasten the setting of the Snow. (By causing the Snow to set quickly over ice, there is less chance of the egg whites breaking down and collapsing.)

Lightly oil a 6-cup soufflé dish or whatever mold you select. Carefully pour the Lemon Snow into the mold and refrigerate until set, which should take about 3 hours since so little gelatin is used. This dessert can be prepared the day before.

At serving time, run a hot knife around the dish, invert onto a chilled serving platter, and place a hot towel over the inverted soufflé dish for a few seconds. Holding the two dishes together, give a sharp shake which should loosen the Lemon Snow; if not, repeat with the hot towel and shake again. Decorate with green and yellow candies. Pass with optional Green Mint Sauce.

PALAIS DE GLACE

Ice Palace, an Egg White and Caramel Mold

CHOLESTEROL RATING 1
CALORIES PER SERVING 205

I imagine the name for this delicious dessert comes from the enchanting skating pavilion tucked behind the Champs-Elysées in Paris. The Parisian *palais* has a glass-domed roof imitated in this dessert by the thin layer of caramel that automatically forms on top of the mold. The tangy flavor of the caramel plays against the smooth creamy sauce, and the two make a particularly mellow combination. Although *Palais de Glace* is quick and easy to make, it looks impressive as it comes to the table and is a sheer delight to eat.

6 servings

1 tablespoon gelatin
¼ cup cold water
½ cup sugar
3 tablespoons cold water
6 egg whites
pinch of salt
4 tablespoons sugar
2 teaspoons vanilla
few drops polyunsaturated oil

Creamy Dessert Sauce (page 229)

In a very small pot soften the gelatin in ¼ cup of water for 3 minutes. Then put the pot on slow heat that gradually brings the mixture to the boiling point and completely dissolves the gelatin. At the same time, in another pot pour 3 tablespoons of water over ½ cup sugar, but do not stir. Put this sugar-and-water on a high flame to caramelize and brown. Hold the handle and shake the pot with a rotating motion a few times during the cooking. The gelatin and caramel should both be on the stove before you begin to beat the egg whites.

Add the pinch of salt to the egg whites and begin beating them with an electric beater. When the whites are quite firm, add the 4 tablespoons of sugar and continue beating until the whites are very firm. Raise the heat under the gelatin and, just as it begins to boil, pour it onto the egg whites and beat it in thoroughly, still using the electric beater. By this time the caramel should be quite dark and thick and ready to be poured into the egg white mixture while you continue beating. Pour the caramel in quickly, because it will harden as it cools. Add vanilla and beat at high speed for 1 minute more. Scoop the mixture into a lightly oiled 6-cup bowl. An ordinary mixing bowl will do nicely since its round bottom will produce the desired domed effect when unmolded. Smooth the top of the caramel mixture and refrigerate for at least 3 hours, or overnight.

To unmold, run a hot flexible knife around the dessert, first reaching halfway down the sides of the bowl, then a second time reaching all the way to the bottom. Dip the bottom of the bowl in hot water for a few seconds, then place the serving dish over the bowl and invert. The serving dish should be a little shallow so it can hold some sauce.

Pour some of the Creamy Dessert Sauce around the bottom of the dessert and pass the rest in a sauceboat. Serve with plain cookies like Drop Cookies (page 222).

COLD SOUFFLÉ WITH FRUIT JELLY, HOT SAUCE

CHOLESTEROL RATING 1
CALORIES PER SERVING 261

French chefs have a constant supply of leftover egg whites in the kitchen. This comes from their automatic use of egg yolks to thicken and enrich all those luscious sauces.

We can thank the thrifty nature of the French for this exceptional cold soufflé. What started out as a way to use up all those whites evolved into a superb finale to a meal.

How could they make something special of a dessert that, in other hands, is just a plain old molded whip? For one thing, by starting off with jelly, which allows a tremendous range of flavors. Secondly, and most importantly, by adding boiling hot jelly to the beaten egg whites. It doesn't take much to cook egg whites, and boiling jelly is just enough to do it. Thus the unfinished, raw flavor of ordinary whip is overcome. Egg whites also turn shiny smooth with that bit of heat.

A word about the fruit jelly. It cannot be a preserve, no matter how good. Seeds and pulp would ruin the recipe. The only other absolute necessity is a good strong arm for beating the egg whites by hand. In a pinch an electric beater can be used, but the volume won't be quite so impressive.

8 servings

2 tablespoons gelatin
1 tablespoon white liqueur (Cointreau, Kirsch, Framboise, etc.)
2 teaspoons water
1 pound fruit jelly—not preserves—(apricot, raspberry, currant, prune, etc.)
6 egg whites
pinch of salt

HOT SAUCE

½ pound fruit jelly, same flavor as in soufflé
¼ cup water
2 tablespoons white liqueur, same as in soufflé

Soften the gelatin with the white liqueur and the 2 teaspoons of water. Meanwhile, slowly heat the fruit jelly: it should be boiling when you finish beating the egg whites. While the jelly is heating it will begin to liquefy. Once it is really hot, add the softened gelatin. Meanwhile, beat the egg whites to which you have added the pinch of salt. They should be beaten until really very firm—about 5 or 6 minutes of strong beating. Keep an eye on the jelly, if it looks too thick (you must be able to pour it) add a tablespoon or two of water. Prune jelly especially might need some dilution.

Once the jelly is boiling strongly it is to be poured slowly over the egg whites while the beating continues. It is best if you can have someone help at this point—to pour the jelly while you continue beating the whites. The heat of the jelly will poach the egg whites a bit, giving them a better flavor and a glossier appearance. Once all the jelly has been incorporated into the whites, continue beating for 1 more minute.

Place a moistened round of waxed paper in the bottom of a 2-quart charlotte mold. Pour the soufflé mixture in the mold, then tap the mold firmly to settle the soufflé well into the container. Smooth the top of the soufflé and place in the refrigerator for at least 2 hours. At serving time loosen the soufflé from the sides of the mold by sliding a knife all around. Place the serving platter over the top of the mold, reverse, and give a sharp shake to unmold the soufflé. Remove paper.

In a small pot heat the fruit jelly for the sauce with the water and liqueur. Bring to the boiling point, then pour a little over the top of the soufflé, and pass the rest in a sauceboat.

Sherbets

ORANGE SHERBET

CHOLESTEROL RATING 1
CALORIES PER SERVING 125

If you need some sherbet in a hurry but find you are out of fresh fruit, that ever-ready can of frozen orange juice in the freezer can save the day.

4 to 5 servings

¼ cup sugar
1 cup water
½ teaspoon gelatin
1 6-ounce can undiluted frozen orange juice
½ teaspoon orange liqueur
1 egg white

Dissolve the sugar in the water slowly over a moderate flame and bring the mixture almost to the boiling point. Meanwhile soften the gelatin in a little extra cold water. Then add this to the sugar syrup just as soon as it is removed from the heat. Stir until the gelatin is completely dissolved. Cool the mixture. Then add the undiluted orange juice and orange liqueur. Stir well.

Pour the mixture into an electric ice cream mixer or in an ice cube tray. Freeze for about 1 hour with the freezer set at its coldest point. Remove it from the freezer and scoop the orange mixture into a bowl. Whisk the egg white until it is rather stiff, but still moist. Break up the frozen mixture with a fork until it is mushy, then fold in the beaten egg white. Scoop the sherbet back into the freezing tray and return to the freezer until firm, about 2 hours. Then, reset freezer to normal position. If you are using an ice cream freezer, add the lightly beaten egg white to the mixture at the beginning, before it goes into the freezer.

PEAR SHERBET

CHOLESTEROL RATING 1
CALORIES PER SERVING 218

This is a superb dessert that is surprising for the purity of its flavor. Eating it is like biting into the coolest, freshest pear possible. Flavor like this cannot be bought prepackaged.

8 servings

1¼ cups sugar
1¼ cups water
3 pounds good quality eating pears
½ lemon
3 tablespoons lemon juice
1 egg white

In a flat pan boil the sugar and water together for 10 minutes covered; this will make a light syrup. Meanwhile, peel, core, and quarter the pears and drop them immediately into a bowl of cold water in which you have squeezed the ½ lemon. The lemon will prevent the pears from turning brown.

Remove the pears from the cold water and drop them into the bubbling syrup and cover. Simmer slowly until they are soft and a sharp knife will pierce their pulp easily. This should take 15 to 20 minutes. Turn the pears once during the cooking and baste a few times. Let them cool in the syrup.

Drain the fruit, reserving the syrup. Pass the pears through a food mill. A food mill is better than a blender since it will screen out any thick fibers that may have remained. There should be about 1 quart of purée. Add lemon juice and egg white (very lightly beaten) and mix well. Taste; if you would like a sweeter flavor, add some of the syrup. Put the purée in an ice cream freezer, or in an ice cube tray. Once the sherbet is hard, remove and beat it until it becomes very fluffy. Then refreeze in a serving mold.

STRAWBERRY GRANITA

CHOLESTEROL RATING 1
CALORIES PER SERVING 120

For some reason or other, the myth exists in the United States that French ice cream is great. Not true at all. The honor belongs to the Italians, who make a *gelato* like none other. But as good as their ice cream is, even more typical of Italian fare is *granita,* the wonderfully fresh, flavored ice. It is so much better after a *pasta* meal than anything thick and rich. Here is a *granita* you can whip up in a flash, and at any time of the year. Even though it is based on frozen strawberries, the taste says "fresh" thanks to the helpful addition of orange flavoring.

6 servings

grated peel and juice of 1 orange
2 teaspoons orange liqueur
2 10-ounce packages frozen strawberries

Put six sherbet dishes in the refrigerator to chill. In the blender place ½ the quantity of grated orange peel, orange juice, and liqueur. Cut 1 package of frozen strawberries into large-sized chunks and add to the blender a few chunks at a time while blending at high speed in between additions. Keep mixing with a wooden spoon. When all has been puréed, spoon immediately into three of the chilled dishes and place in the freezer.

Repeat the process with the remaining ½ of orange peel, juice, liqueur, and strawberries. Freeze for at least 2 hours. If the granita is frozen for more than 6 hours, remove it from the freezer 10 minutes before serving time.

Baked Desserts

APPLE CRISP

CHOLESTEROL RATING 1
CALORIES PER SERVING 285

Apple crisp is strictly an American dish, but it is so good that it ought to be part of international cuisine. It fits well into the low-cholesterol diet if one simply substitutes polyunsaturated margarine for the butter usually used in the topping. To make up in a way for the missing butter flavor, a bit of orange flavor has been added to the filling. It enhances the dessert immeasurably.

8 servings

2 pounds tart cooking apples
½ cup dark brown sugar
½ teaspoon cinnamon
½ teaspoon nutmeg
1 tablespoon lemon juice
grated rind of one orange
2 tablespoons orange juice
1 cup flour
¼ teaspoon salt
½ cup dark brown sugar
6 tablespoons very cold polyunsaturated margarine

Peel, core, and slice apples (not too thin) into a large bowl. Sprinkle ½ cup of the brown sugar over the apples. Add the cinnamon and nutmeg and toss well. Sprinkle on the lemon juice, orange rind, and orange juice and toss again. Then pack apple slices firmly into a deep-dish pie pan and press lightly on top.

In a small bowl mix together the flour, salt, and the other ½ cup of brown sugar. Cut in the margarine in small pieces, and toss the mixture quite thoroughly. Sprinkle the mixture over the apples and press down firmly with the palms of your hands. Bake in 375° oven for about 45 minutes, or until apples are soft. Serve warm.

PEACH CRISP

CHOLESTEROL RATING 1
CALORIES PER SERVING 275

Though this recipe resembles Apple Crisp, there are small but important differences in the two recipes. The peaches are much sweeter to begin with, so less sugar is used in the filling. Peaches also give off much more juice than apples, so a thicker topping is required to absorb the extra liquid. But whether Peach Crisp resembles something else or not, you will find it a great success on its own.

8 servings

2 pounds firm ripe peaches
¼ cup light brown sugar
½ teaspoon nutmeg
½ teaspoon cinnamon
1 tablespoon lemon juice
grated rind of 1 orange
1 tablespoon orange liqueur
¼ cup fine bread crumbs
1½ cups flour
¼ teaspoon salt
½ cup dark brown sugar
5 tablespoons very cold polyunsaturated margarine

Plunge the peaches into boiling water for a few seconds, then remove skins. Cut peaches into thick slices and put in a mixing bowl. Sprinkle the light brown sugar, nutmeg, and cinnamon, over the peach slices and toss well. Sprinkle on the lemon juice, orange rind, and orange liqueur and toss again. Let stand for 10 minutes.

Meanwhile, in a small bowl mix together the flour, bread crumbs, salt, and dark brown sugar. Cut the cold margarine into the flour mixture in small pieces and toss quite thoroughly. Put the peaches in a deep-dish pie pan and press down gently with your hands. Pour any juice the peaches have rendered over them. Sprinkle the flour mixture over the peaches and smooth nicely with the back of a spoon. Bake in a 375° oven for 45 to 50 minutes, or until the top has turned a nice golden color. Serve warm.

PIECRUST

CHOLESTEROL RATING 1
CALORIES PER SINGLE SHELL 1,140

I have tried every possible piecrust recipe calling for polyunsaturated oil products. Most of the results were unsatisfactory. Then I decided to revive an old French trick (often forgotten today) of adding a bit of liquid oil to a pastry made primarily with a solid fat. The resulting lightness was just what I was looking for. The combination of the two different fats (margarine and oil) is what does it. They react to heat differently, and the resulting interaction brings about just the right degree of leavening. The texture is also much finer than in pastries made with liquid polyunsaturated oil or margarine alone. More flour than is used in other pastries is required for use with polyunsaturated products because of their very low melting point. To achieve a nice golden color, brush a little of the liquid oil over the surface and edge of the piecrust just before putting the pie in the oven.

ONE DOUBLE PIECRUST
OR TWO SINGLE PIE SHELLS

3 cups sifted all purpose flour
1 teaspoon salt
¼ pound very well chilled polyunsaturated margarine
1 tablespoon polyunsaturated liquid oil
¾ cup ice water

Measure the sifted flour and resift with the salt into a deep bowl. Cut margarine into small pieces directly into the flour. Work flour and margarine with a pastry blender until the margarine has been cut very fine, about the size of small peas. Add the oil and work a few strokes more.

Sprinkle on about ½ of the ice water and stir with a fork. Sprinkle on about ½ of the remaining water and with your fingers work the water into the dough lightly until it forms a smooth ball and your hands come away clean. If the dough feels a little dry, sprinkle on a few drops more water. Use just the amount of water necessary, and no more, or the pastry will be tough.

Chill dough for at least half an hour before using. Roll, place in pie pan, prick well with a fork, and, if you are preparing a pie shell, place parchment or wax paper on the pastry and fill with dried beans to prevent it from buckling and changing shape. A smaller pie plate or soufflé dish can also be used as a weight on the paper. Bake at 350° for 15 to 20 minutes or until it is golden brown.

TARTE AUX FRAISES

Glazed Strawberry Pie

CHOLESTEROL RATING 1
CALORIES PER SERVING 320

Typical French fruit tarts usually have a rich cream filling under the fruit topping. This makes a nice contrast, but not nearly as healthy a one as results from a filling made of the fruit itself. In this recipe the strawberry filling has a consistency similar to custard, and the uncooked berries under the filling provide a difference in textures. I always find it a soul-wrenching experience to mash beautiful fresh berries, but the resulting flavor is more than enough reward for such cruelty.

8 servings

1 baked 9-inch pie shell (page 216)
6 cups fresh strawberries
5 tablespoons cornstarch
1 cup sugar
2 tablespoons lemon juice
2 cups Whipped Topping (page 227)

Bake a 9-inch pie shell and cool. Meanwhile, wash, hull, and dry the strawberries. Reserve 2 cups of the largest and best looking berries. Put the remaining 4 cups of berries in a heavy pot and mash them. Add cornstarch, sugar, and lemon juice to the mashed berries. Stir well and put pot on a low to moderate flame, stirring constantly until the mixture becomes thick and clear. When cooked, it will change from a starchy look to almost a clear jelly appearance. Cool, then chill.

At serving time, cut the reserved 2 cups of berries in half, lengthwise, and place in the bottom of the pie shell, cut side down. You can keep aside a few whole berries to decorate the top, if you wish. Spoon the chilled glaze over the berries and smooth the top nicely.

Spread Whipped Topping over the top of the pie, but leave a large circle in the center exposed. The contrast between the red berries and the white topping is most attractive. Decorate with the reserved whole berries, if desired, by placing them in the center.

MERINGUES

CHOLESTEROL RATING 1
CALORIES PER MERINGUE 48

Meringue puffs can be stubborn and refuse to stay puffed. Here is a slightly different way to treat them that assures perfect results every time. That assurance comes from the precooking of the egg whites and sugar, much as in a fondant. You will find these puffs stay deliciously crisp for weeks.

about 25 puffs

2 egg whites
1½ cups sugar
¼ teaspoon cream of tartar
⅓ cup cold water
1 teaspoon vanilla

Preheat oven to 275°. Line a baking sheet with parchment paper, or use an unlined Teflon cookie sheet. You can use one of two methods for the cooking, either use the top of a double boiler, or else an ordinary pot placed on an asbestos pad over a low flame. In either case, combine all ingredients except the vanilla in a pot and mix well for a good minute or two with an electric beater at low speed.

Place the pot on heat and continue beating at medium speed (with long bursts of fast speed) for about 10 minutes or until the mixture is quite firm and holds its shape. Remove from heat, add vanilla, and continue beating at high speed for another minute. Place nicely rounded tablespoons of the batter on the prepared cookie sheet, allowing about ¾ inch between the puffs. Bake for about 1 hour, or until the puffs have just faintly browned and are dry and crisp to the touch.

SESAME SEED COOKIES

CHOLESTEROL RATING 1
CALORIES PER COOKIE 32

These cookies look so pretty that everyone just assumes they will be delicious. And they are. That is, they are if freshly grated nutmeg is used. The canned, pregrated variety won't do the trick. One also counts on the natural nutty flavor of the sesame seeds to make up for the elimination of butter. It does. Instead of buying small jars of sesame seeds at the supermarket, it is much more economical to buy bulk packages at health food shops.

During the rolling and dipping of the cookies, a quick hand is needed. If the rolled dough is allowed to sit in the water too long it will get soggy. I find that working with 3 cookies at a time is most efficient. It is also advisable not to pour all the sesame seeds into the dish at once. They get wet when the cookies are rolled in them, and tend to clump together. It is much better to keep adding seeds from time to time, assuring a constant supply of dry seeds.

about 6 dozen cookies

¼ pound polyunsaturated margarine
½ cup sugar
1 egg white
½ teaspoon vanilla
¼ teaspoon freshly grated nutmeg
2 cups flour
pinch of salt
1¼ teaspoons baking powder
¾ to 1 cup sesame seeds
¾ cup ice water

Cream the margarine and sugar together very well, until the mixture is light and fluffy. Add the egg white, vanilla, and nutmeg. Mix well. Sift the flour, salt, and baking powder together and gradually work this into the margarine-sugar mixture. When the flour has been worked in, knead for a few minutes until you have a nice smooth ball. If you find the dough too stiff, add a few drops of water. Chill for at least ½ hour.

Prepare a small bowl containing the ice water. Put some of the sesame seeds in a shallow saucer. Have two forks ready. With a teaspoon, take a small piece of the dough and roll it into a small smooth ball. Hold this ball on a fork and dip it into the water for a few seconds, lift out, and hold a second to let excess water drip off. Immediately drop the cookie into the saucer of sesame seeds. With second fork, roll the dough ball around in the seeds. Then transfer the ball to an oiled cookie sheet, lightly pressing in the seeds as you do. (By keeping one fork for the water only, and the other for the seeds only, you don't end up with a messy mixture of the two.)

Bake in a 325° oven for 20 to 25 minutes, or until the seeds have turned a nice golden color. Do not wait for them to turn dark.

VIENNESE CRESCENTS

CHOLESTEROL RATING 1
CALORIES PER COOKIE 46

The secret here is the freshly chopped almonds. If you try using packaged almond powder or bits, you will end up with no flavor at all. Remember, the flavor of fresh butter has already been sacrificed, and with so few ingredients, each one counts. But to guarantee the success of these delicious bits, do as all the great Viennese pastry chefs do: bury a vanilla bean in a jar of powdered sugar, keep it handy on the shelf and the subtle vanilla flavor will always be ready to work its magic when powdered sugar is called for.

about 90 cookies

½ pound polyunsaturated margarine
½ cup sugar
2 teaspoons vanilla
2¼ cups sifted flour
1 cup freshly chopped almonds
vanilla-flavored powdered sugar

Using a wooden spoon, work the margarine and sugar together until the mixture is very light and fluffy; add vanilla, and beat more. Resift the flour and work into the creamed mixture. This is a scant measure of flour, but it gives tastier results; if you find it too hard to work with, increase the quantity to 2½ cups. Chop fresh almonds until very fine (use either one of the Swiss plunger-choppers or a blender; but just grate coarsely, not too powdery). Work almonds into the dough with the spoon, then knead for a few minutes until it is thoroughly blended and smooth. Chill for at least ½ hour.

Take 1 teaspoon of the chilled dough and work it into a long shape with your fingers, then fold into a crescent on an ungreased baking sheet. Repeat with the rest of the dough.

Bake in a 325° oven for about 15 minutes or until the cookies have turned a sandy color. Do not overbake. Immediately after removing the cookies from the oven, sprinkle them very generously with vanilla-flavored powdered sugar. (Leftover dough freezes perfectly, but first be sure you have made enough of these delicious morsels. They go fast.)

BLACK WALNUT CRESCENTS

CHOLESTEROL RATING 1
CALORIES PER COOKIE 45

A local farmers' market offers fresh black walnuts in the late fall, and I couldn't help but try baking them in the purest form possible. The preceding delicately flavored Viennese Crescents were the starting point. With just a few minor adjustments the cookie changed character and became a robust morsel.

about 90 cookies

- *½ pound polyunsaturated margarine*
- *½ cup sugar*
- *1 teaspoon vanilla*
- *2 tablespoons maple syrup*
- *2¼ cups sifted flour*
- *1 cup freshly ground black walnuts (blender works fine)*
- *vanilla-flavored powdered sugar for sprinkling after baking*

Follow preceding directions for Viennese Crescents, add maple syrup along with the reduced amount of vanilla. Bake a few minutes longer, 18 to 20 minutes, until the cookies are a deep tan color.

LEMON PECAN WAFERS

CHOLESTEROL RATING 1
CALORIES PER COOKIE 42

The tang of fresh lemon can always be counted on to deliver a flavor punch. Combine it with fresh pecan nuts and you have as rich and tasty a cookie as ever filled the cookie jar. This is another dough that freezes perfectly, so you can always have some on hand for quick baking.

6 dozen 1½-inch wafers

½ cup polyunsaturated margarine
1 cup sugar
1 egg white
1 tablespoon grated lemon rind
2 tablespoons lemon juice
1½ cups sifted flour
1 teaspoon baking powder
⅛ teaspoon salt
1 cup finely chopped pecans (or walnuts)

Cream the margarine and sugar until they are very light and fluffy. Then beat in the egg white, lemon rind, and lemon juice. Sift in the flour, baking powder, and salt and mix thoroughly. Stir in the chopped nuts. With your hands, shape the dough into two rolls, about 1½ inches in diameter. Wrap them in waxed paper and chill thoroughly, at least for 1 hour. Slice dough in thin rounds, place the cookies on a greased cookie sheet, and bake for 12 to 15 minutes in a 350° oven.

DROP COOKIES

CHOLESTEROL RATING 1
CALORIES PER COOKIE 43

These simple-to-make cookies can be the base for any number of interesting variations. The recipe given here is for plain vanilla cookies, but they are equally good flavored with almond extract, lemon rind and lemon extract, or, on the exotic side, orange rind and Grand Marnier. Drop cookies are most often served with fruit desserts. Store in an airtight container.

approximately 40 1½-inch cookies

½ cup polyunsaturated margarine
½ cup sifted granulated sugar
2 teaspoons vanilla
4 egg whites, lightly beaten
1 cup sifted flour

Cream the margarine and sugar together until very smooth. Add the vanilla (or any flavoring desired), lightly beaten egg whites, and finally sift in the flour, a little at a time to prevent lumps from forming, and stir it into the creamed mixture.

Onto a well-oiled cookie sheet drop teaspoons of the batter about 3 inches apart. With the back of the spoon flatten the cookies a little; they will spread farther during the baking. Bake in 350° oven for 8 to 10 minutes, or until the edges have browned. Remove immediately from baking sheet.

TUILES AUX AMANDES

Curved Almond Cookies

CHOLESTEROL RATING 1
CALORIES PER COOKIE 60

Tuiles derive their name from the curved clay roof tiles seen especially in the south of France, and they are among the most popular cookies in that country. The whole trick to getting the pretty curved shape is to mold the cookies while they are still piping hot, right out of the oven. They are lifted from the baking sheet with a spatula and placed on a rolling pin, bottle, or any long round utensil. As they cool they crisp into the shape of the mold. Speed is essential, so do not bake more than one tray at a time. Store the *tuiles* in an airtight container. If they do get soft, they can be crisped with a fast return to a hot oven.

approximately 30 2-to-2½-inch cookies

2 egg whites
½ cup sifted sugar
5 tablespoons flour
¼ cup melted polyunsaturated margarine, cooled
1 teaspoon vanilla
1 cup slivered almonds

Using a wire whisk, beat the egg whites and sugar together until the whites are soft and foamy. Little by little add the flour, melted margarine, and vanilla. Gently fold in slivered almonds. Onto a well-oiled baking sheet, drop heaping teaspoonfuls of the batter about 3 inches apart. With the back of the spoon, flatten each cookie a little. When the baking sheet is filled, lift it a few inches from the tabletop and bring down sharply on the table. This will smooth out the cookies into thin even circles. Place in a 400° oven for about 5 minutes, or until they turn a delicate golden color and the edges are a light brown.

Have a rolling pin or bottle ready before removing the cookies from the oven. Working rapidly before the cookies cool, remove them with a spatula and place them immediately on the rolling pin or bottle. You should be able to fit 5 or 6 on the rolling pin. Using the palm of your hand, give a quick and gentle squeeze to each cookie so it will take the curved shape better. If the cookies cool and harden before you finish the shaping, return the cookie sheet to the oven for a few seconds to soften them with the heat. The first shaped cookies will be hard by the time you reach the end of the rolling pin, so they can be removed to make room for others.

BUTTERSCOTCH CAKE

CHOLESTEROL RATING 2
CALORIES PER SERVING 318

Every cookbook needs at least one cake recipe, and here is your low-cholesterol cake. But this is not just a token recipe. This cake happens to turn out rich tasting and deliciously moist. No one would ever guess how it achieves its lusciousness, and I leave it up to you whether or not to tell your guests that the secret is . . . mayonnaise.

No eggs or shortening are used; the mayonnaise does the job of both, and more, since it also prevents the cake from drying out. You can experiment with many other flavors, but not chocolate. Some possibilities are fresh lemon, melted raspberry or mint jelly, but the butterscotch version pleases everyone.

The packaged pudding that the recipe calls for usually contains a minimal amount of hydrogenated vegetable oil. But since this is dispersed over 12 portions, it divides down into a negligible amount per person. If you make praline, or can find it in a fancy food shop, use it instead and be perfectly pure.

I like the cake without icing, just with a sprinkling of powdered sugar, but it can be frosted with Sea Foam Icing (page 230) or served with Whipped Topping (page 227).

12 servings

1 tablespoon polyunsaturated margarine
2 cups all purpose flour
¾ cup sugar
3¾-ounce package instant butterscotch pudding
1½ teaspoons baking powder
1 teaspoon baking soda
1 cup mayonnaise
1 cup water
1 teaspoon vanilla
½ teaspoon almond extract
1 tablespoon powdered sugar

Select a 9-inch round or square cake pan, approximately 2 inches deep. Grease the bottom with ½ the margarine. Cut a waxed-paper liner to fit the pan, put it in, and grease the waxed paper with the rest of the margarine.

Sift together into a bowl the flour, sugar, butterscotch pudding, baking powder, and baking soda. Working slowly to keep the batter smooth, stir in the mayonnaise, water, and flavorings. Mix thoroughly until there are no lumps at all. Pour the batter into the greased cake pan and smooth the top. Tap the pan a few times on the countertop to settle the batter well into the pan.

Put the cake in a 350° oven for 40 to 45 minutes or until a toothpick plunged into the center comes out clean. Cool before removing from the pan and then pull off the waxed paper. Sprinkle with powdered sugar or ice as desired.

GÂTEAU AUX CERISES

Almond Cake with Cherries

CHOLESTEROL RATING 1
CALORIES PER SERVING 465

This is another cake to make when the occasion arises, a pretty one that has an "occasion" air about it. The red cherries peeking throughout the cake make it particularly appropriate at holiday time.

10 servings

8 ounces glacé cherries
2¼ cups all purpose flour
1 teaspoon salt
2 teaspoons baking powder
¾ cup polyunsaturated margarine
6 tablespoons sugar
½ cup polyunsaturated oil
4 ounces ground almonds
1 teaspoon vanilla
1 tablespoon Kirsch
polyunsaturated margarine for greasing cake pan
powdered sugar

Put the cherries in a small strainer and rinse them under very warm water to remove the sugar coating. Dry them on a paper towel, cut them in half, and put in a small bowl.

Sift together the flour, salt, and baking powder. Take two tablespoons of the sifted flour and add to the cherries. Toss the cherries and flour together to coat them very well and set aside.

In a deep mixing bowl, cream together the margarine and sugar, then gradually add the oil. Add the sifted flour, a little at a time, then the ground almonds. Beat well until the batter is quite smooth. Add the vanilla and Kirsch and mix again. Finally, fold the cherries and their flour into the batter.

Grease a 9-inch cake pan with margarine, line the pan with waxed paper, and grease the paper. Spoon the batter into the cake pan and put in a 350° oven for 1 hour. Reduce the heat to 325° and bake for another 45 minutes or until the cake springs back when pushed in the center. With the cherries, almonds, and oil in the batter, this cake requires a long, slow baking.

When the cake is finished, remove it from the oven and allow it to cool in the pan for 30 minutes before removing it to a cake dish. Sprinkle with powdered sugar.

Sauces and Toppings

GRILLED SUGARED ALMONDS

CHOLESTEROL RATING 1
CALORIES PER RECIPE 917

These almonds are handy to have around to add a finishing touch to many desserts. They can be kept in a tightly covered jar in a cool, dry place.

1 cup grilled almonds

1 cup sliced almonds
few drops water
1½ tablespoons granulated sugar

Spread the almonds on a cookie sheet, sprinkle on the sugar and mix well. A spatula is handy for this. Wet your fingertips and shake the water off on the almonds. The water helps to caramelize the sugar a little when baking. Place the almonds under a hot broiler for about 3 minutes, turning them often with the spatula. Do not take your eyes off them for a second; they can burn in a wink.

WHIPPED TOPPING

CHOLESTEROL RATING 1
CALORIES PER CUP 75

No denying it, a large bowl of sweet, fluffy whipped cream is a luscious sight. Even food companies that cater to diet-conscious people know it and have put nondairy whipped toppings on the market. Beware. Most of them are loaded with cholesterol-rich coconut oil and a list of chemicals so long it almost runs off the box. But one can still have a whipped topping that is without cholesterol, better tasting than the commercial product, that looks just as good and costs much less. Skimmed-milk powder, ice water, and just a touch of gelatin are all that's necessary.

Most recipes for whipped skimmed-milk topping instruct you to run to the table with it before it disintegrates back into liquid. With this one you can make the topping hours ahead and put the running shoes away. In fact, some setting time is necessary, since a very small quantity of gelatin is used—just enough to hold the froth in suspension, but not enough to really jell. There are two very important points to the success of this recipe: first—ice water, not just cold water. I like to put it in the freezer until crystals begin to form. Second—electric beater, not a blender, which goes too fast and does not incorporate enough air into the mixture.

7 to 8 cups topping

1 teaspoon gelatin
¾ cup liquid skimmed milk
1 cup ice water
1 cup skimmed-milk powder
2½ tablespoons granulated sugar
1½ teaspoons vanilla
few drops lemon juice

Chill the bowl and beater thoroughly. Meanwhile, moisten the gelatin in ¼ cup of the skimmed milk. Heat in a small pan the remaining ½ cup skimmed milk, add the softened gelatin and stir until it is completely dissolved. Set aside to cool and thicken. The consistency should be about that of a thin custard.

Pour the ice water into the chilled bowl and add about ¼ cup of the skimmed milk powder. Begin beating at low speed, then beat for ½ minute at high speed. Return speed to low and continue adding the rest of the powder slowly. Increase speed to medium while adding the sugar, vanilla, and lemon juice. Turn to high speed, add the gelatin-milk mixture, and continue beating. Long beating, 7 to 10 minutes in all, is essential to incorporate as much air as possible into the topping. Scoop it into a serving bowl and refrigerate for at least 2 hours.

GREEN MINT SAUCE

CHOLESTEROL RATING 1
CALORIES PER TWO-TABLESPOON SERVING 90

This is a very pretty and taste-awakening sauce. It is preferable to start with real mint jelly, and not mint-flavored apple jelly. The bit of cognac is added to cut the sweetness of the Crème de Menthe, but can be omitted. The yoghurt brings a mildness to the sauce which otherwise might overpower the dessert it accompanies.

2½ cups sauce

1 cup mint jelly
1 tablespoon cognac
¾ cups green Crème de Menthe
½ to ¾ cup plain low-fat yoghurt

Put all ingredients except the yoghurt in a blender and blend until smooth. Add ½ cup of yoghurt, taste for degree of sharpness desired. If you would like a slightly milder sauce add the remaining ¼ cup of yoghurt. Chill.

CREAMY DESSERT SAUCE

CHOLESTEROL RATING 1
CALORIES PER TWO-TABLESPOON SERVING 33

1 13-ounce can evaporated skimmed mlik
¼ cup sugar
2 tablespoons potato starch or cornstarch (not flour)
⅓ cup skimmed milk
1 teaspoon vanilla
2 teaspoons fruit liqueur (Grand Marnier or Kirsch)
1½ teaspoons cognac

Pour the evaporated skimmed milk into a small pot, add the sugar, and put on a slow fire. Mix the potato starch or cornstarch with the skimmed milk until you have a thin, smooth paste and slowly add to the hot milk while mixing with a wire whisk. Keep whisking until the sauce thickens, then add the vanilla, liqueur, and cognac. Simmer for 1 minute more. Chill.

SEA-FOAM ICING

CHOLESTEROL RATING 1
CALORIES PER RECIPE 1,663

I don't think anyone finds the taste of uncooked icings really pleasant. The usual powdered sugar mixed with egg white always feel granular and raw on the tongue. Cooked icing is easy to make and well worth the bit of time and effort. Although the recipe as given here calls for dark brown sugar to give a strong hint of caramel flavor, other variations are possible. Use white sugar for a plain vanilla frosting, or brown sugar with strong coffee added for a mocha flavor. Grated orange rind and orange liqueur are interesting added to the vanilla frosting.

Icing for the tops of 2 9-inch layers,
or the top and sides of a single layer

2 cups dark brown sugar
⅔ cup water
1 egg white
pinch salt
pinch cream of tartar
1 teaspoon vanilla

Combine the sugar and water in a small pot and stir until the sugar is dissolved. Put on heat and boil, without stirring, to the soft ball stage (238°). Meanwhile, add the salt and cream of tartar to the egg white and beat until frothy. When the syrup is ready, pour it into the egg white in a steady stream while continuing to beat constantly. An electric beater is almost a necessity for this. Add the vanilla and continue beating over a pot with boiling water. The water should not touch the egg white bowl. Continue beating over the water until the icing holds its shape. Spread over the cake at once.

9

SAUCES, SPREADS, BATTERS

White Treacle Mustard

THIS FINAL CHAPTER IS MOSTLY ABOUT RECIPES TO PUT ON OTHER RECIPES —to complete them and make them better. The sauces and spreads that follow do not have to be made strictly according to instructions. They leave a wide field for your own taste and imagination.

The mixing of salad dressing is a popular hobby, so the two dressings suggested here should be used only as a starting point for your own additions. The basic hot margarine dressing merely hints at the variations that can be played on the theme. For the same reason, only one mayonnaise dressing is given. But a good mayonnaise recipe is included, and the list of sauces that can be derived from that one base is almost limitless. Among the sauces are Tartar, Remoulade (mustard), Fresh Herb, Thousand Island (without the hard-cooked egg yolk), Curry and on-and-on as the spirit moves you. Even chutney can be mixed with mayonnaise for an unusual combination.

The Basic Brown Sauce is at the bottom of many great dishes in French cuisine. Every time an addition is made to the basic sauce, the name is changed, but underneath they are all the same.

The thick tomato *coulis* hardly needs any suggestions. It is such an exceptional sauce that ideas for use seem to drift out of its aroma. Three prepared sauces offer three strikingly different tastes—horse-radish, anchovy, and mustard-dill. With these at hand, almost any dish in need of cold sauce will meet its match. And for a tasty wrapping for other things, the frying batter will take care of anything from fish to fowl to vegetables.

A few suggestions for snacks for the cocktail hour is our way of saying that now that we've come to the end of *Haute Cuisine for Your Heart's Delight* we'd like to toast you, and your good health.

Sauces

SAUCE BRUNE

Basic Brown Sauce

CHOLESTEROL RATING 1
CALORIES PER CUP 370

Great French cooking is based on great French sauces, which fall into two basic categories—the white and the brown. The white sauces, of course, get their unctuous velvetiness through butter, egg yolks, and heavy cream. Happily, the goodness in brown sauces is derived from meat, vegetables, and stock.

With a good basic brown sauce waiting in the refrigerator (or freezer), you are prepared to make a dazzling array of other sauces by adding red wine, Madeira or port, tomato, truffles, mushrooms, curry, fresh herbs, or even mustard. Possibilities are plentiful, but none will amount to anything if the basic brown sauce is not good. Although long, slow cooking is called for, it takes very little real time away from you.

1 quart of sauce

¼ pound polyunsaturated margarine
¼ cup diced lean boiled ham (optional)
1 onion, sliced thin
2 carrots, sliced thin
1 celery stalk, sliced thin
4 to 6 sliced mushrooms (optional)
4 tablespoons flour
6 cups hot beef stock or bouillon
3 tablespoons tomato paste
¼ teaspoon thyme
herb bouquet (4 parsley sprigs tied around 1 bay leaf)
salt and pepper

Melt the margarine in a heavy saucepan and add the optional ham (it gives extra flavor), onion, carrots, celery, and optional mushrooms. Cook slowly in the uncovered pan, stirring often until the vegetables begin to brown at the edges. This should take 10 to 15 minutes. Sprinkle in the flour and, using a wooden spoon, blend it thoroughly with the vegetables. Continue cooking slowly, stirring almost constantly, until the flour turns a dark brown. This browning should be achieved over a slow fire rather than high heat, because if the flour is browned too quickly it will have a burnt flavor.

Take the pan from the heat and blend in the beef stock slowly. The better the stock, the better the sauce, and a homemade stock is best of all. Use a wire whisk for this blending to assure a smooth mixture free of lumps. Return the pan to the fire. Add the tomato paste, thyme, and herb bouquet. Sprinkle on salt and pepper lightly; the stock has been seasoned already. Simmer slowly, partially covered, for 2 to 3 hours, skimming off any fat or foam that rises to the top.

Strain the sauce through a fine sieve, pushing out all the juices from the vegetables. Taste for seasoning and correct if necessary. Put the sauce in the refrigerator and when it is thoroughly chilled remove the fat that rises and congeals on the surface. The sauce is now ready for any additional flavorings and seasonings.

COULIS DE TOMATES À LA PROVENÇALE

Thick Provençal Tomato Sauce

CHOLESTEROL RATING 1
CALORIES PER CUP 205

The busy housewife may well ask, "With the enormous variety of canned, frozen, dried, and dehydrated sauces available to me, should I waste my time making a tomato sauce, of all things?" My answer is Yes, because in none of those cans or packages can you get the strong, heady flavor of Provence, which comes from more than merely adding garlic. I can't recommend this sauce too highly. There is another bonus, too: since the juice is squeezed out of the tomatoes first, the family can have the unheard-of treat of drinking uncanned fresh tomato juice.

This *coulis* goes well with any pasta or rice, with boiled chicken, veal, or beef; also on hamburgers or with meat loaf. It's really too fine a sauce to put on pizza. Obviously the sauce should be made when tomatoes are at their peak in flavor; it would be a shame to put out all the work and time if the product is inferior to begin with. The recipe can be easily halved, but since it is so tasty and versatile, and also freezes perfectly, this larger quantity is suggested.

Approximately 5 to 6 cups of sauce

6 pounds fresh tomatoes
⅓ cup polyunsaturated oil
1 cup finely diced onions
⅓ cup flour
½ teaspoon sugar
5 cloves mashed garlic
3 1-inch pieces orange peel (no white)
1 large herb bouquet (6 parsley sprigs tied around 2 bay leaves)
½ teaspoon fennel seeds
½ teaspoon dried basil
¼ teaspoon coriander
1 teaspoon salt
½ teaspoon pepper
½ teaspoon celery salt
pinch saffron
2 to 4 tablespoons tomato paste

Plunge tomatoes into boiling water for a few seconds and remove skins, then cut in half and gently squeeze out the seeds and juice. Coarsely chop the remaining pulp. There should be 7 to 8 cups of tomato pulp. Heat the oil in a heavy pot, add onions, and cook slowly for about 15 minutes with cover on. Do not allow onions to brown; they should just be transparent. Remove lid and stir in flour, cook together 2 to 3 minutes, still not allowing the mixture to brown. Add the tomato pulp, all the seasonings and herbs, cover pot, and simmer slowly for 15 minutes.

Add 2 tablespoons tomato paste and simmer very slowly, partially covered, for 1 to 1½ hours; stir occasionally, making certain to scrape the bottom of the pot so the mixture does not stick or scorch as it thickens. As you stir, press the tomato pulp against the sides of the pot to make the sauce smoother. If there is any risk of scorching, add a little tomato juice or water. Cook until the sauce is very thick and will stand up in a mass on a tablespoon. Remove herb bouquet and orange peel; if color seems a little pale, or you would like to intensify the tomato flavor, add the other two tablespoons of tomato paste. Taste for seasoning and add more salt and pepper if necessary.

HORSERADISH SAUCE

CHOLESTEROL RATING 1
CALORIES PER ONE-TABLESPOON SERVING 48

This is an excellent sauce to serve with hot corned beef, boiled beef, leg of lamb, cold meats, and even fish. It is best to make it at least 2 hours before serving so that all flavors will blend thoroughly.

1¼ cups sauce

½ cup mayonnaise (see page 240)
½ cup plain low-fat yoghurt
2 tablespoons grated horseradish
1 teaspoon hot prepared mustard
½ teaspoon vinegar
salt and pepper

Mix all the ingredients with a wire whisk until they are thoroughly blended, and then chill. If the sauce is to accompany hot food, remove it from the refrigerator about 1 hour before serving.

MUSTARD-DILL SAUCE

CHOLESTEROL RATING 1
CALORIES PER ONE-TABLESPOON SERVING 22

Couldn't be easier, couldn't be zippier, and couldn't be more different. Although it is especially designed to go with cold fish, you'll find that this sauce makes an equally snappy combination with lamb, hot or cold.

1¼ cups sauce

1 cup fresh dill, approximately 1 bunch
4 tablespoons hot prepared mustard, English type
4 tablespoons mild prepared mustard
¼ cup vinegar
4 or 5 tablespoons sugar

Pick the feathery tops off fresh dill branches and press down a little when measuring the cupful. Put all ingredients in a blender and purée until they are well blended and the dill is finely chopped. Do not overblend; the dill pieces should not disappear. The amount of sugar you put in depends on how hot the hot mustard is—if very hot, put in the extra tablespoon.

The sauce will not be the same if made with dried dill. But if fresh dill is not available to you, experiment with the quantity of dried dill necessary. Much will depend upon its strength and freshness. Begin with 2 tablespoons and add more gradually as needed.

ANCHOVY SAUCE

CHOLESTEROL RATING 2
CALORIES PER ONE-TABLESPOON SERVING 85

You can count on this lively anchovy sauce to save many an otherwise bland dish. Mix with a little bit of leftover rice and vegetables and you're on your way to a memorable main-course salad. It can also even lift poached frozen-fish filets to illusions of taste grandeur. Best of all, it beautifully complements that very Italian fried cheese sandwich *Mozzarella in Carròzza,* page 155.

¾ cup sauce

½ cup mayonnaise (see page 240)
2 teaspoons lemon juice
2 teaspoons capers
2 teaspoons evaporated skimmed milk
1 tablespoon brandy
6 anchovy filets, chopped
1 teaspoon oil from anchovy filets
1 teaspoon minced parsley

Put all ingredients except the minced parsley into the blender and blend until smooth. Scrape the sauce into a bowl and fold in the parsley.

If you lack a blender, pound the capers and anchovy filets together until smooth, then gradually blend in the other ingredients.

Salad Dressings

MAYONNAISE

CHOLESTEROL RATING 2
CALORIES PER ONE-TABLESPOON SERVING 110

Mayonnaise figures prominently in a number of recipes in this book even though it contains egg yolk. In making mayonnaise, one egg yolk is forced to absorb almost a cup of beneficial polyunsaturated oil, greatly diluting the effect of the yolk. Furthermore, mayonnaise is used in such a small quantity per serving that the actual ingestion of the yolk is negligible. For these reasons, doctors and heart associations allow mayonnaise on low-cholesterol diets.

Store-bought mayonnaise can be used for any recipe in this book, but the results will not be quite the same as with homemade mayonnaise. Making mayonnaise is also one way of not wasting all the leftover egg yolks always found in kitchens that follow low-cholesterol diets.

about 1½ cups mayonnaise

2 egg yolks
½ teaspoon prepared mustard
1 teaspoon lemon juice
½ teaspoon salt
1¼ to 1½ cups polyunsaturated oil
additional lemon juice, vinegar, white pepper, Tabasco sauce (optional)

It is easy to make mayonnaise as long as the following few rules are observed:

1. All ingredients must be at room temperature.

2. The eggs yolks must first be beaten with the seasonings to "poach" the yolks slightly.

3. Oil must be added very slowly at first, a few drops at a time.

4. Egg yolks can absorb only so much oil, do not exceed this amount or the sauce will turn thin.

Put the egg yolks in a warmed bowl, add the mustard, lemon juice, and salt. With a wire whisk or electric beater, beat the yolks until they turn thick and look almost opaque. This should take about 1 minute. Then, while continuing to beat, begin adding the oil, a few drops at a time at the beginning, waiting until the yolks have absorbed the oil before adding any more. The amount of oil added each time can be increased after about ½ cup has been beaten in. Keep adding the oil until a maximum of 1½ cups has been absorbed by the yolks. Taste and add more lemon juice, vinegar, salt, pepper, or a few drops of Tabasco sauce as desired. Scrape the mayonnaise into a bowl, cover tightly and refrigerate until needed.

CORRECTING TURNED MAYONNAISE: If the sauce curdles, warm a clean bowl, add an egg yolk, 1 teaspoon of prepared mustard, and beat well. Add about 1 tablespoon of the turned sauce and beat until it has been absorbed by the yolk, then slowly add the rest of the turned mayonnaise.

BLENDER MAYONNAISE

CHOLESTEROL RATING 2
CALORIES PER ONE-TABLESPOON SERVING 103

about 1¼ cups sauce

1 whole egg
¼ teaspoon dry mustard
1 teaspoon salt
1 tablespoon lemon juice or vinegar
1 cup polyunsaturated oil

Put the egg in the blender with the mustard and salt and blend at high speed for about ½ minute. Add lemon juice and blend a few seconds more. Slowly add the oil in a thin stream while the blender continues to turn. When the sauce is thick, taste and correct if necessary.

MAYONNAISE DRESSING

CHOLESTEROL RATING 2
CALORIES PER ONE-TABLESPOON SERVING 111

Count on this sauce to dress up any cold vegetable or combination thereof. Add a few extra drops of lemon juice and take it to the table with cold fish, too.

1 cup of dressing

1 cup of mayonnaise, preferably homemade
1 teaspoon mild prepared mustard
1 tablespoon lemon juice
½ teaspoon curry powder
salt and pepper
1 tablespoon minced parsley

With a wire whisk beat all the ingredients together except the parsley, which is folded in at the end.

HOT VEGETABLE DRESSING

CHOLESTEROL RATING 1
CALORIES PER ONE-TABLESPOON SERVING 80

This hot melted margarine sauce will dress up plain boiled vegetables very successfully. On the other hand, when served with deliciously mild vegetables like asparagus or artichokes, it heightens their flavor without overpowering it.

1¼ cups dressing

1 cup polyunsaturated margarine
1 tablespoon dry white wine
1 tablespoon lemon juice
1 teaspoon Worcestershire sauce
¼ teaspoon soy sauce
salt and pepper

Combine all ingredients in a small pot, heat slowly and allow the sauce to take on a light brown color; bring to the boiling point just before serving.

HERBED FRENCH DRESSING I

CHOLESTEROL RATING 1
CALORIES PER ONE-TABLESPOON SERVING 67

This dressing can make even iceberg lettuce taste like something. It should also be kept handy for marinating leftover cooked vegetables. Then they can be mixed with cooked rice and a bit of mayonnaise for a luncheon dish that doesn't taste or look like leftovers.

1¼ cups of dressing

⅔ cup polyunsaturated oil
2 tablespoons vinegar
2 tablespoons lemon juice
2 teaspoons prepared mustard
1 tablespoon finely chopped shallot
1 teaspoon oregano
2 tablespoons parsley
salt and pepper

Put all ingredients in a covered jar and shake vigorously to blend them together.

HERBED FRENCH DRESSING II

CHOLESTEROL RATING 1
CALORIES PER ONE-TABLESPOON SERVING 67

This is a milder dressing than the preceding one with more emphasis on (preferably) fresh herbs. The two versions can be used almost interchangeably, depending on your pleasure.

1¼ cups of dressing

⅔ cup polyunsaturated oil
1 tablespoon vinegar
3 tablespoons lemon juice
½ teaspoon minced tarragon
½ teaspoon minced chives
½ teaspoon minced fresh basil or ¼ teaspoon ground basil
1 teaspoon minced parsley

Put all ingredients in a covered jar and shake vigorously to blend them together.

Batters

PÂTE À FRIRE

Frying batter, with beer

CHOLESTEROL RATING 1
CALORIES PER RECIPE 628

The leavening quality of the beer makes this a particularly light batter. The flavor of the beer, however, hardly comes through at all: it is not at all pronounced, there is just a hint of something special. This batter is especially good for frying fresh fish fingers and just about any vegetable you can think of.

about 2 cups batter

1 cup flour
½ teaspoon salt
½ cup beer, room temperature
½ cup warm water
1 tablespoon polyunsaturated oil
1 egg white

Sift flour and salt, slowly stir in the beer and warm water, and add the oil. Mix well and let rest in warm place at least 3 hours. (This batter needs a long "working" period because the yeast in the beer is rather light. You will notice tiny bubbles on the surface when it is "working.") Beat the egg white until stiff and fold carefully into the batter; allow to rest another 10 minutes. Carefully dip in morsels to be fried, letting excess batter drip off, then place in hot frying oil, and fry quickly. Drain on paper towels.

CROUSTADES

Fried Pastry Rounds

CHOLESTEROL RATING 1
CALORIES PER SERVING 275

You'll be delighted at the way these pastry rounds dramatize what might otherwise be an ordinary dish. They are a light and crisp base for sautéed foods. They also remain crisp, unlike toast, which gets soggy almost as soon as any food is put on it. Best of all, they are a snap to make since no dough has to be made. Instead the recipe calls for the prepared biscuit dough that comes in cardboard tubes and is found in the refrigerated cases at most stores.

These pastry rounds are included in the recipe for *Croustades de Champignons* (Mushrooms on Pastry Shells), page 42, but would serve equally well with Mushrooms in Creamy Sour Sauce, page 41, *Gratin d'Endives au Jambon* (Gratin of Endive and Ham), page 60, *Poivrons aux Oignons* (Green Peppers and Onions), page 179. They will turn any of these recipes into an enjoyable first course.

A pizza specialty in Naples consists of frying the pizza dough rather than baking it and achieves a less heavy bread base. These *croustades* are amazingly similar to the Neapolitan pastry, making pizza-assembling easy.

The fried rounds can be kept in the refrigerator for days, or in the freezer indefinitely. After a little reheating in the oven they are as good as new.

6 pastry rounds

1 4-ounce tube buttermilk baking powder biscuits
flour for rolling biscuits
polyunsaturated oil for frying

Pull the dough apart into 6 sections. Roll each biscuit out on a floured board, rolling it as thin as you can. It should extend to over 6 inches in diameter. Cut into 5- or 6-inch circles with a large pastry cutter.

While preparing the dough, heat the oil in a large frying pan until it is quite hot, almost smoking. There should be about 1 inch of oil in the pan. Fry the rounds one or two at a time, depending on the size of the pan. They fry very quickly because they are so thin, needing just a matter of seconds on each side. They will puff slightly. Drain them on paper towels. The rounds can be reheated later in a 350° oven for a few minutes.

For the Cocktail Hour

TOASTED ALMONDS

CHOLESTEROL RATING 1
CALORIES PER SERVING 85

At some of the best bars in Europe delicious toasted almonds are served for nibbling with cocktails. The reason the almonds are exceptional is that they are freshly toasted. The preparation is very simple and requires almost no time and effort. For best results, however, do not buy preskinned almonds; they will not be as fresh tasting as those with skins.

Serves 8 to 10

2 cups almonds with skins
few drops polyunsaturated oil
1 teaspoon salt

Preheat oven to 350°. Meanwhile, put almonds in a deep bowl and pour enough boiling water in to cover them by at least 2 inches. Let steep for 2 to 3 minutes, then drain. As soon as you can handle them, slip the skins off. If they don't pop off easily, repeat process with boiling water, but let steep for only 1 minute this time. Using a paper towel, spread a few drops of oil all over a cookie sheet and wipe off any excess oil with the towel. Spread almonds on sheet in a single layer and place in oven for 15 minutes or until they turn an even sand color. With a spatula turn the nuts from time to time, at least 4 to 5 times during the toasting. Sprinkle salt evenly over the almonds, return to oven and turn off heat. Let the nuts continue to toast for another 3 to 5 minutes, turning them 2 or 3 times. The almonds should now be a deep tan color, but not brown. If the nuts are overroasted they will lose their delicate flavor. Store in tightly covered jar.

HUMMUS

Chick Pea Purée

CHOLESTEROL RATING 1
CALORIES PER SERVING 93

Aren't you a bit bored with that ubiquitous cocktail dip—sour cream mixed with dried onion soup, or minced clams, or what have you? Your friends probably are, too, and would welcome a change. Hummus (or Hummous) can be a welcome change, and one with a lot of character. It comes from the Middle East, where it is served with aperitifs or as a first course at dinner. It is rather thick, more like a paste really, and is especially good with flat Arab or Syrian bread, available now in most supermarkets. Put the hummus in a bowl and serve it with warmed bread cut in wedges. Toast does nicely, too, and for real weight watchers, celery sticks make a good dipping vehicle.

Dried chick peas can be used, but it is much simpler to buy precooked ones in a can. If the regular bean section of your market doesn't have them, look among the Italian products, because chick peas are an all-important ingredient in minestrone. The other unusual ingredient in the recipe is tahini (or tahina). This is ground hulled sesame seeds and is a very thick, opaque product available in health food shops. It keeps well and has a nutty flavor that can enhance many other dishes.

When served as a first course, ⅓ to ½ cup of the mixture is spread on a plate, a small depression made in the center and a little olive oil poured in—no more than a teaspoon. Finally, sprinkle with chopped parsley or paprika, or both, and pass the same flat bread.

2 cups of purée, enough for 12 aperitif or 5 to 6 first-course servings

1 1-pound 4-ounce can of chick peas
juice of 2 lemons
3 tablespoons tahini
1 or 2 garlic cloves, chopped
1 tablespoon polyunsaturated oil
½ teaspoon ground cumin seed
large pinch cayenne pepper
½ teaspoon salt
½ cup chopped parsley
for decoration: paprika and a few whole parsley leaves

Drain chick peas, reserving the liquid. Put in a blender the lemon juice, tahini, garlic, oil, and 3 tablespoons of the reserved chick-pea liquid. Blend until well mixed, then add ½ the quantity of chick peas and blend thoroughly. Add the rest of the peas and continue blending until it becomes a thick purée. You will have to scrape down the sides of the blender a few times. If you find the mixture too thick, add more of the reserved liquid, but no more than a tablespoon at a time. Scoop into a bowl and add the cumin seed, cayenne pepper, salt, and parsley.

Hummus is best if made at least a day before so the flavors can mellow. Keep in a cool place. At serving time spoon the mixture into a bowl and sprinkle with paprika. Top with a few parsley leaves.

Hummus can be made without a blender by using a food mill. First purée the chick peas, then add the remaining ingredients.

TAPÈNADE

Provençal Olive Purée

CHOLESTEROL RATING 3
CALORIES PER SERVING 110

Outside of Provence one rarely comes across this zesty hors-d'oeuvres spread. The unusual name is derived from the old Provençal word for capers *(tapène),* an important ingredient in the recipe. A special note must be made of the kind of olives used. They should be the oil-cured variety that often have a slightly shriveled appearance. The pungent quality of the recipe starts with these olives, but of course they have a drawback: they are almost never prepitted, so count on some extra time when starting out. You can use the large, smooth, pitted California olives and end up with something quite good and mild, but entirely different. Anyone who has had the real thing in Provence would sneer at it, but the California olives are easier to work with.

Traditionally the mass of ingredients is pounded together in a mortar. Not necessary today: a blender will do it, reluctantly, but it will do it with a bit of help from you by mixing the purée often. In France, tapènade is usually served as a spicy accompaniment to the late-afternoon glass of cold white wine. Here it can star at the cocktail hour. Heap into a small bowl and surround it with toast or crackers. Since it freezes perfectly and is also used as an important ingredient in another dish elsewhere in this book, you could easily double the recipe once you're making it.

Olives are used sparingly in this book because they should appear in moderate amounts in a low-cholesterol diet. But when you feel like eating olives, I think this is the way you should have them.

2 cups of purée, 20 aperitif servings

1½ cups pitted oil-cured black olives
⅓ cup polyunsaturated oil (Optional: ¼ cup extra)
2 tablespoons lemon juice
2 tablespoons cognac
1 3¼-ounce can tuna fish, in oil
1 3¼-ounce bottle capers, drained
1 ounce anchovy filets in oil
1 garlic clove, chopped
1½ tablespoons English mustard powder
½ teaspoon freshly ground black pepper
large pinch each, cloves, ginger, nutmeg

Pit the olives. In the blender put ⅓ cup oil, the lemon juice, cognac, and ½ the quantity of the olives, tuna, capers, anchovy filets, plus all the garlic, mustard, pepper, cloves, ginger, and nutmeg. Blend on low speed until you have a smooth mass. Continue blending, while slowly adding the remaining ingredients, a little at a time. When it's quite smooth, give it a few seconds at high speed.

You may find that your blender labors a bit under the amount of heavy bulk. If so, from time to time help it by mixing up the purée with a wooden spoon or rubber spatula. If you are really unhappy about the strain on the blender, you can add another ¼ cup of oil, but only if really necessary. When all finished, put in a tightly covered container in the refrigerator. It keeps well and is better still if made at least a day ahead so that all the flavors will blend together.

INDEX

E

F

G

H

I

K

L

M

N

O

P

T

V

W

Y

Z